Major John André

BY ROBERT McCONNELL HATCH

Thrust for Canada
The American Attempt on Quebec in 1775–1776

Major John André
A Gallant in Spy's Clothing

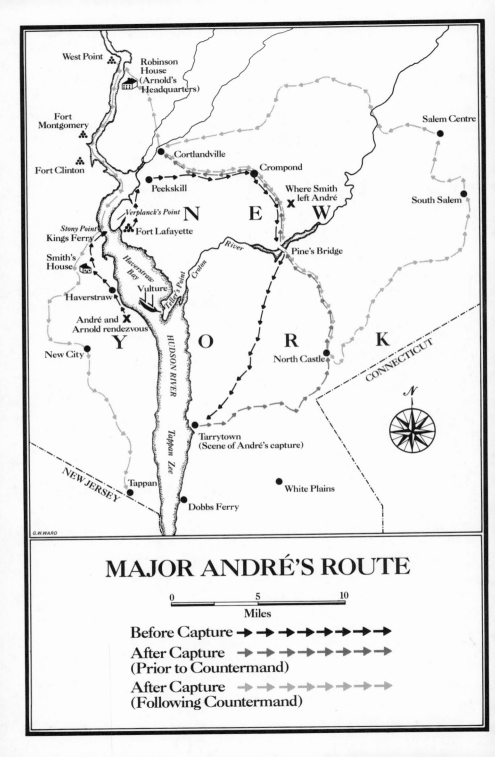

MAJOR ANDRÉ'S ROUTE

0   5   10
Miles

Before Capture ➤ ➤ ➤ ➤ ➤ ➤ ➤ ➤

After Capture ➤ ➤ ➤ ➤ ➤ ➤ ➤ ➤
(Prior to Countermand)

After Capture ➤ ➤ ➤ ➤ ➤ ➤ ➤ ➤
(Following Countermand)

Major
John André

A Gallant in Spy's Clothing

ROBERT McCONNELL HATCH

Illustrated with Photographs and a Map

Boston

HOUGHTON MIFFLIN COMPANY

1986

Library of Congress Cataloging in Publication Data

Hatch, Robert McConnell.
Major John André : a gallant in spy's clothing.

Bibliography: p.
Includes index.
1. André, John, 1751–1780. 2. Spies — United States —
Biography. 3. United States — History — Revolution,
1775–1783 — Secret service. I. Title.
E280.A5H24   1986   973.3'86'0924 [B]   85-19681
ISBN 0-395-35324-6

Printed in the United States of America

S 10 9 8 7 6 5 4 3 2 1

FOR HELEN

Contents

Illustrations

Major John André

Countermand —
A Different Drumbeat

It HAD BEEN ANOTHER UNEASY DAY for the dragoon
patrol, and the men were exhausted by long vigilance as they
toiled northward in the early shadows. They had been riding
across the so-called Neutral Ground that lay between the Continental Army's outposts on the Hudson River and the British
lines above New York. Only once or twice during the long
day had they glimpsed another human being, but they knew
that a few of the inhabitants must still be there, watching the
road from behind barred doors and shuttered windows. Even
though the passing patrol belonged to the Second Continental
Light Dragoons, the doors stayed shut and the houses silent.

Westchester had once been a rich and lovely land, but now
the riders passed a repetitious landscape of weed-choked cornfields, abandoned orchards, gardens gone to thicket, all because of the Cowboys and Skinners. The young major at the
van of the small troop reined in every now and then to make
a slow inspection of the landscape, trying to discern what
might be a hiding place. Much of his time these days was
spent in tracking down Cowboys and Skinners, and he took
his duties seriously.

The Cowboys called themselves partisans of the Crown,
and some of the time they rustled beef cattle for the British

Army. The Skinners called themselves patriots, but this did not stop them from robbing anyone they came upon. Occasionally the two camps got together and traded plunder. It was what the major called "the dirty traffic," and he had been trying to persuade the governor to come into the Neutral Ground with enough force to put a stop to it. A few isolated Continental patrols were hardly enough.

Major Benjamin Tallmadge was just twenty-six, but he was already a seasoned cavalryman. He had served with the Dragoons for four long years. A pen-and-ink sketch of him by John Trumbull shows him in uniform, wearing his horsehair-crested dragoon helmet. The artist caught a hint of superiority and disdain in his subject, depicting him as a man of breeding, the eyes assured and forthright, the curled lip faintly supercilious. The son of a minister, Tallmadge was a graduate of Yale and had become a favorite of General Washington, who valued men of good family and superior education. For the past two years, he had been Washington's deputy in the Army's secret service.

It was sundown when the cavalry patrol dismounted at North Castle, the cluster of rude farm buildings that served as headquarters. Tallmadge reported immediately to his superior officer, Lieutenant Colonel John Jameson. He found him sitting at a table, pondering over a peculiar incident that had occurred that morning just north of Tarrytown. As Jameson related it, three American irregulars had been hiding near the Tarrytown bridge, waiting for whoever might happen along. After some little time, a solitary horseman had appeared and they had challenged him. It was then that the contradictions began.

The horseman, sizing up the three young men in civilian clothes, must have decided that they were Cowboys. He had said that he hoped they "belonged to the lower party," meaning that favoring the Crown. One of the men had lied, declaring that this was so. Whereupon, the rider had brought out his watch with its attached seals and a military ring and announced that he was a British officer on important business and must not be detained. The three took the watch and ordered him to dismount. Realizing that he had made a bad guess, he tried to right matters. He was pleased, he said, to find that they were men of the upper party, as he was himself. To prove it, he produced a pass from General Benedict Arnold.

The men were more interested in money than in passes, so they searched their prisoner. They found very little money but they did locate some mysterious papers hidden in his boots. The prisoner quickly made an offer: if one of them would take a note to the British post at Kingsbridge he would receive a reward of a hundred guineas.

The three eyed their prisoner suspiciously. They decided that the offer was a trick — going to Kingsbridge would only bring a British patrol down upon them. The safest thing would be to take the stranger to North Castle and let the officer in charge decide what to do.

Jameson pointed to a heap of tightly folded papers on his desk. On top was the pass signed by General Arnold, a safe-conduct stating that he had given one John Anderson "permission to pass the guards to the White Plains or below if he chooses, he being on public business by my direction."

The name John Anderson was familiar to both officers. They recalled that Colonel Elisha Sheldon, Jameson's immediate superior at North Castle, had recently received a letter from Arnold saying that an unnamed "business associate" of his would be coming through the lines from New York.

That slight mystery deepened when Sheldon received another letter, this time from a certain John Anderson, whom he did not know. Anderson said he would be coming through the lines on business "of so private a nature that the public on neither side can be injured by it." He added that he would "endeavour to obtain permission to go out with a flag from Dobbs Ferry on Monday next, the 11th, at twelve o'clock."

Then came an enigmatic flourish: "I trust I shall not be detained but, should any old grudge be a cause of it, I should rather risk that than neglect the business in question, or assume a mysterious character to carry on an innocent affair and, as friends have advised, get to your posts by stealth." All of this was in explanation of Anderson's appointment with a "Mr. G——." Colonel Sheldon was thoroughly confused. He sent the letter to General Arnold.

Arnold had cleared up some of the mystery. "Mr. G——" stood for "Gustavus," he said, a pseudonym he himself had adopted for security reasons. Anderson, he repeated, was on approved business.

Sheldon had been called away, and Jameson, as second in command, must deal with Anderson and the compromising papers. He made two grave mistakes. He failed to await the arrival of Washington's deputized intelligence chief before making a disposition of the prisoner. And he sent the prisoner, in the custody of Lieutenant Solomon Allen and four militiamen, to Arnold's headquarters at the Robinson house, opposite West Point. Furthermore, he handed Allen a letter addressed to Arnold notifying the West Point commander that papers "of a very dangerous tendency" had been found on John Anderson.

Jameson did manage one wise decision. He would send the papers themselves to Washington, who was returning from Hartford after conferring with Rochambeau. In a letter to the commander-in-chief, Jameson explained that Anderson had been carrying a pass signed by Arnold, that he had tried to bribe his captors, and that he was now en route, under guard, to Arnold's headquarters. Jameson then added a self-serving sentence to his letter: "He [Arnold] is very desirous of the papers and everything being sent to him, but as I think they are of a very dangerous tendency, thought it proper your Excellency should see them." This implied that Arnold had already learned of the captured papers and had asked to see them, but that Jameson had refused. Nothing of the kind had taken place.

As soon as Tallmadge began to read the papers, which still bore the crease marks of John Anderson's feet, he suspected treason in high places. There was a report on the strength of the West Point garrison, a listing of the ordnance, a detailed pinpointing of weak spots in the defenses. There were the minutes of a recent council of war dealing with strategy. And they were all, as Tallmadge instantly recognized, in the bold handwriting of Benedict Arnold.

Tallmadge pointed out the inconsistency in Jameson's handling of the matter. The colonel bridled, and we cannot be sure as to what was said next. Tallmadge would testify, however, that he proposed a drastic course of action, "a measure which I wished to adopt, offering to take the whole responsibility upon myself, and which he deemed too perilous to permit."

Throughout his long life, and even in his *Memoir*, Tallmadge refused to reveal the precise nature of his suggestion. But it is not hard to guess what he had in mind. He proposed to arrest Benedict Arnold, his commanding general, and hold him prisoner until Washington arrived.

To Jameson, such a suggestion bordered on outright mutiny. He dismissed it — curtly, no doubt — but he agreed to modify his orders. At Tallmadge's urging, he issued a countermand directing Lieutenant Allen to take Anderson, not to the Robinson house, but to a Captain Jeronimus Hoogland at South Salem, where a detachment of dragoons was stationed. He would not budge, however, when Tallmadge urged that he hold up the letter alerting Arnold to Anderson's capture. "Strange as it may seem," Tallmadge comments in his *Memoir*, "Lieut. Col. Jameson would persist in his purpose of letting his letter go on to Gen. Arnold."

When the countermand reached Solomon Allen he made an about face with his little troop and returned to North Castle.

"As soon as I saw John Anderson," Tallmadge says, "and especially after I saw him walk (as he did almost constantly) across the floor, I became impressed with the belief that he had been bred to arms. I communicated my suspicion to Lt. Col. Jameson and requested him to notice the gait, especially when he turned on his heel to retrace his course across the room." Otherwise, he saw a slim young man, boyish-looking, with an olive complexion that was neither British nor Yankee. His speech was that of a gentleman, his bearing correct and manly, and he had an elegance of manner that seemed at odds with his weathered beaver hat and ill-fitting, claret-colored coat with tarnished gold lace. He looked travel-worn and fatigued.

Adding a dragoon guard to their retinue, Tallmadge and Lieutenant Allen escorted the prisoner to South Salem, where they were met by Lieutenant Joshua King, post commander in the absence of Captain Hoogland. King decided at first glance that this was no ordinary spy. To be sure, the coat was threadbare, the beaver hat commonplace, and the prisoner badly in need of a shave. But King noted the expensive boots, the nankeen vest and breeches, and decided that this must be "a reduced gentleman." When a barber removed the ribbon binding the prisoner's queue, King noticed that a profusion of costly powder shook loose.

John Anderson was confined in the bedroom of Dr. Isaac Bronson, the surgeon's mate. He paced the floor continuously and, during the afternoon, asked if he might walk in the adjoining yard. King gave permission, but he posted a strong guard and remained steadfastly at the prisoner's side. After a while, Anderson began to speak. "He observed that he must make a confidant of somebody," King relates, "and he knew not a more proper person than myself, as I had appeared to befriend a stranger in distress." At first Anderson talked about the British Army. Then he made the admission that his name was not John Anderson. He asked if he might communicate with General Washington.

King took his charge back to Dr. Bronson's bedroom and gave him pen and paper. While King looked over his shoulder, the prisoner wrote a letter to the commander-in-chief. One sentence more than any other caught King's attention: "The person in your possession is Major John André, Adjutant General to the British Army."

I

"Sustain Me, Hope!"

W HILE STILL A LAD, John André was turning out pencil
sketches and caricatures that were the delight of his three
doting sisters and younger brother. One of his efforts depicts
the burial of brother William's pet dog. It shows the five young
Andrés forming a tenderly supportive cluster, while a cherubic
child, probably a Swiss cousin, romps heedlessly in the fore-
ground.* At one side a gravedigger stands ready, but an un-
seemly grin sets him apart from the rest and accents the closeness
of the grieving Andrés.

As members of London's colony of exiled Huguenots, the
Andrés were a tightly knit family, conscious of their French
origins. John André's forebears, subjected with fellow Huguenots to the stern measures imposed on French Protestants
by a hostile government, had migrated from Nîmes in southern
France to Genoa and Geneva, where they prospered as merchants and inclined to big families. His paternal grandparents,
Jean and Louise Vazeille André, produced ten children, three
of whom migrated to London — David, John Lewis, and
Anthony, John André's father. All three became importers.
Anthony identified with the Levantine trade and opened a

---

*Thought to be the son of John André's aunt Marie, who lived in Geneva.

counting house in Warnford Court, hard by bustling Throckmorton Street. Occupying rooms above his place of business, he soon gained so firm a foothold in his adopted country that he could afford to take on both a wife and family.

On May 18, 1749, a year after his naturalization as a British citizen, Anthony André exchanged vows with Marie Louise Girardot at Quidenham parish church in Norfolk. Daughter of Paul and Marie Foissin Girardot of Paris, she, too, was a Huguenot. Portraits of the pair, done in middle life, show Anthony every inch the solid, eminently proper, merchant in brocaded coat and ruffled shirt, and Marie the fastidious matron, elegantly coiffured and attired. John André was the first of their five children, followed by three girls, Mary Hannah, Anne Marguerite, and Louisa Catherine, and by William, nearly ten years younger than his brother. According to the register of the Church of St. Martin Orgars, a Huguenot parish, John André was born on May 2, 1750.

The Andrés started their married life in the rooms over the counting house, while Anthony developed his importing business and invested a share of the profits in Grenada real estate. Presently they were in a position to exchange their meager quarters for a house in Clapton, a London suburb where, according to John André, "ruminating herds" and "bounding flocks" still gave an aura of rusticity to the countryside.

At first, John André was schooled by a private tutor, the Reverend Thomas Newcomb, who wrote poetry for his own edification and who is said to have had one or two of his more distinguished couplets incorporated in Pope's *Dunciad*. When André sat at his feet, Newcomb was a tottery, gout-ridden old man, who may have encouraged in his charge a fondness for light verse. Subsequently, André is thought to have attended St. Paul's School in London, but we soon find him, as a teenager, enrolled in the Academy at Geneva, Switzerland.*

---

*Founded as a seminary, the Academy gradually enlarged its scope until it became the University of Geneva in 1873.

Although John André majored in mathematics and military drawing, his schedule included art lessons, flute lessons, and instructions in ballroom dancing. Nor did he lack for a busy social life. Some of the Andrés had settled in Geneva, and through them he made friends and acquaintances outside the Academy. One of these was Pierre-Eugène Du Simitière, an aspiring artist several years his senior. The two would meet again, long afterward, in America. "Our tastes for the arts were similar," Du Simitière says, "and we both learned to draw under the same master, 'tho at different periods of time." A miniature of John André, on ivory and bordered with pearls, probably dates from his Geneva days. It shows a solemn youth with powdered hair, a small mouth, small chin, and brooding dark eyes.

When André was seventeen his father ordered him home. Dancing, sketching, and playing the flute might befit a carefree student, but it was time for Anthony André's older son to fill his niche in the family business. When he had mastered bookkeeping he could take on weightier responsibilities. An enviable career should be his, as merchant and importer. It never occurred to Anthony that his son might not take kindly to trade or to his father's associates and the prosaic life of a London merchant.

Anthony's place of business faced on a hushed courtyard walled off from London's clamorous inner city. Here John André labored, perched on a tall stool and bent over the great ledgers that chronicled profits, losses, and the ebb and flow of the family business. His back pained him when he straightened up. His legs, wrapped around the stool, ached when he unwound them. Each day seemed an eternity, given over to tallying columns of dry figures with a scratchy quill pen. His thoughts reverted continually to his Geneva days — to the military drawing in which he had excelled to his brief introduction to military science. These fanned enthusiasms that trade failed to kindle.

André would often quit the counting house for the London

streets. The city was home to more than two thirds of a million people, including immigrants from most of Europe, Jewish refugees from Germany and Poland, blacks from the West Indies. Carts, wagons, and sedan chairs shoved through the teeming streets. Peddlers hawked their wares — lace and lavender, foodstuffs, buttons and needles, brooms and baskets. On his way from Clapton, André passed the Royal Exchange and the Bank of England, bulwarks of Britain's primacy in world trade, as well as the unprepossessing shops of hosiers, haberdashers, wigmakers, and apothecaries. He could see goldsmiths at their benches, tailors deftly guiding their needles to turn out masterpieces of apparel, printers at their presses on Fleet Street and Paternoster Row.

Taverns with names like the Mitre, the Turk's Head, and the Horn on the Hoop catered to citizens of every stripe. Some hosted political societies and gentlemen's clubs. Some were the haunts of thieves, bawds, and disturbers of the peace. And every neighborhood had its coffee house, where friends and colleagues might fraternize, do business, read the newspapers. Each had its clientele — merchants and bankers at one, doctors, lawyers, and men of the cloth at yet another. Some featured a political preference, be it Whig or Tory. John André accompanied his father to coffee houses patronized by merchants and importers, near the Royal Exchange.

When he was on his own, André might visit a coffee house frequented by actors and playwrights, for he was to be a lifelong theater buff. The stage in André's time was having a resurgence that would leave its mark. David Garrick was at his peak, performing Shakespeare and Sheridan at Covent Garden and at the Theatre Royal in Drury Lane, and there were lesser luminaries whose names shone in their own day. André was captivated by everything about the theater — acting and directing, writing and scene painting. He might have devoted his life to the stage had it been more permissible for a young man of his social station.

We may be sure, too, that André often visited London's

pleasure gardens, which offered an abundance of entertainment on spring and summer evenings. Here he and the lady of his choice might stroll through formal gardens and watch the play of fountains. He might guide her across rustic bridges and down sylvan pathways. After a candle-lit supper, the two might watch a display of fireworks or dance away the hours until closing time.

There was a darker side of London life that John André saw on his rambles through town. Strumpets and beggars roamed the streets. Drunkenness was everywhere in evidence. Men were hanged for crimes as petty as draining someone's fish pond or setting fire to a cornfield. Vast crowds assembled to watch public hangings, and a visit to the women's prison to see inmates flogged was deemed a respectable pastime. On London's waterfront, André's blood was stirred by the sight of tall ships putting out to sea, for he yearned to visit exotic ports of call. But Thameside swarmed with footpads and bawds, with drunken sailors and ragged, thieving children. For the poor, life was consistently brutal and could be short. Indeed, hunger claimed many lives. Dr. Johnson was told that about twenty Londoners starved to death every week.

Emotions that seethed below the surface could explode in fearsome strikes and riots. André was eighteen when John Wilkes stood for Parliament in an election that shook the city. Expelled from Commons for criticizing an address by the king, he was a favorite of the lowly and the deprived. On the night of the election, mobs stormed through the streets shouting, "Wilkes and liberty!" Magistrates who sought to quell the disturbance were cursed and stoned. For two dangerous nights the riots raged, testifying to a bottled-up anger among the poor. And that same year stevedores and sailors went on strike, threatening the livelihood of merchants like Anthony André. Coalheavers boarded colliers to evict terrified crews. Gangs of irate seamen strode menacingly through the city. And there were riots to protest low wages and the cost of food. Theater

riots, prompted by the high price of tickets, became so commonplace that the stages at both Covent Garden and Drury
Lane had to be fenced off with spikes.

André sketched some of what he observed, but he confined
himself to familiar subjects. He drew a caricature of a man in
a cocked hat and surcoat, wrapped in his own thoughts and
smiling absently — perhaps a family member or a Clapton
neighbor. Two drawings of a church congregation, some of
its members sound asleep, others conversing openly during a
long-winded sermon, may derive from his own woolgathering
in the family pew. His work shows talent, but a career in art
was as inappropriate for a well-bred young gentleman as that
of actor. He was predestined, by every circumstance, for a
life in trade.

In the spring of 1769 a family crisis brought matters to a
head. Anthony André expired at fifty-two after a short illness,
leaving £25,000 to be divided equally among his five children
when they came of age. John, nearly nineteen now, must
address himself purposefully to the family business.

John André, with his mother and two older sisters, vacationed
that summer in Buxton, a Derbyshire health spa. Favored by
the infirm and ailing, Buxton was not all that a vacationing
family might choose, but for André it promised respite from
Warnford Court. Its curative waters had been recognized even
in Roman times. Indeed, miracles had been attributed to St.
Anne's well, its most celebrated resource. Yet it had never
caught up with fashionable Bath and was described by one
visitor as "a poor, stony little town" with ancient facilities and
springs that should be sampled gingerly. Its waters were enclosed in a structure that could accommodate no more than
twenty people at a time. Visitors were advised that the springs
might impart an "inebriating giddiness" and were cautioned
not to imbibe rashly.

The Andrés had rooms at Old Hall, a musty edifice with a

couplet scratched on one of its windowpanes by Mary Queen of Scots. Wherever they went, in the hotel's hallways and sitting rooms or on the village streets, they encountered the ailing and the infirm, some on canes, others carried to and fro in chairs. Invalids in every stage of decrepitude could be seen clustered at St. Anne's Well or queued up at the baths, waiting to anoint their failing eyes, deaf ears, or creaky joints. On all sides the Andrés were reminded of human misery. Yet in this unlikely setting John André met Anna Seward, a poet, and her steadfast companion, Honora Sneyd.

Anna was the elder daughter of the Reverend Thomas Seward, canon residentiary at Lichfield Cathedral and a poet of local repute. Hers was an imposing presence, auburn hair swept back regally from a bold forehead, expressive brown eyes registering the play of strong enthusiasms. A few years older than André, she cut a formidable and copious figure as she sallied from her hotel in plumed hat and pelisse.

Anna had been a precocious child, reading Shakespeare at three, quoting Milton by the yard at nine. By the time she was twelve, she was a poet in her own right. Her verses caught the eye of Dr. Erasmus Darwin, Lichfield's foremost physician and himself a poet,* who admired her output and told the canon that his own literary efforts were no match for those of his gifted daughter. Seward took less than kindly to the remark. Nor, as Anna matured, did he relish the prospect of having an unmarried poetess on his hands. Anna was ordered to forsake the pen for needle and shuttle, whereupon she transferred her energies to Honora Sneyd.

Honora had been taken into the Seward household when her father, a family friend, was left a widower with a large, unwieldy brood. Anna made the child her own responsibility, schooling her in good manners, in the finer things of life, and, more especially, in the writings of English poets. Anna was

---

*Charles Darwin's grandfather.

assisted at first by her sister Sarah. When Sarah died young, Anna took full charge of her malleable ward, whom she describes as "the sun of my youthful horizon." "The charms of her society," she writes, "when her advancing youth gave equality to our connections, made Lichfield an Edenic scene for me from the year 1766 to 1771." When the nineteen-year-old André laid eyes on Honora she was seventeen and an indisputable beauty.

Whereas Anna intimidated John André, Honora conquered him on sight. Her blue eyes made something inside him melt; her light brown hair and fresh complexion left him spellbound. There were things about Anna that he found hard to take — her flamboyance, her managerial ways, her possessive attachment to Honora — but if he would win Honora he must have Anna on his side. He set about charming both ladies.

By every rule, Honora should have succumbed just as precipitately to John André. He was lithe and graceful, with olive skin and coal black hair. He possessed both wit and imagination. There were few things he could not do to please a girl, whether extolling her in verse, sketching her pretty likeness, serenading her with his flute, or sweeping her masterfully across a ballroom floor. Yet he found Honora hard to reach. She would encourage him with her smiles, beckon to him with her bewitching eyes, but only up to a point. Always she kept a distance between them. As the days passed, André thought he was gaining ground. His heart leaped when Anna asked the Andrés to be her guests at Lichfield — an invitation he made sure was accepted. Perhaps the extra days in Lichfield would work a change in Honora, removing the subtly defined barrier. Before leaving Buxton, he painted her picture — a miniature on ivory that failed to catch her magic but that would sustain him, for all its ineptness, when he got back to London. He kept the original and made a copy for Anna.

Our travelers rattled toward Anna's house in the same stagecoach. When they caught sight of Lichfield Honora pointed out the towers of the cathedral rising above trees and rooftops. "Never shall I forget the joy that danc'd in Honora's eyes when she first showed them to me from Needwood Forest on our return from Buxton to Lichfield," André says. "I remember she called them the Ladies of the Valley — their lightness and elegance deserved the title. Oh, how I loved them from that instant!"

Daniel Defoe describes Lichfield as made up of two disparate communities, the town and the cathedral close. The town embraced the shops and marketplace and was home to tradesmen, artisans, and others of lowly station. But the close "is the fairest," Defoe writes, "has the best buildings in it, and among the rest, the cathedral church, one of the finest and most beautiful in England." In the seventh century, St. Chad had made Lichfield his see, opting for "a little hovel or cell in the churchyard instead of a bishop's palace." The author of *Robinson Crusoe* writes approvingly of this but is less admiring of the mansion erected for subsequent bishops and, during Canon Seward's tenure, the domicile of the canon residentiary. "But the bishops since that time," Defoe comments, "have, I suppose, thought better of it and make shift with a very fine palace in the close, and the residentiaries live in proportion to it."

Defoe credits Lichfield with being "a place of good conversation and good company above all the towns in this county or the next." This was surely true of the Seward household, where erudite talk and readings from the poets attracted literary folk from miles around. According to one visitor, "the bishop's palace at Lichfield, where Mr. Seward, a canon of the cathedral, resided, was the resort of every person in that neighborhood who had any taste for letters. Every stranger who came well recommended to Lichfield brought letters to the palace." Some who came had literary aspirations akin to those of Canon Seward, who is said to have been a magnanimous listener, "good-natured and indulgent to the foibles of others." Although men of the cloth were especially in evidence, the Andrés may have been more impressed by two lay members of the circle. Dr. Erasmus Darwin was one. Stoop-shouldered, ample of girth, and afflicted with a stammer, he wrote verse in his spare time and had fathered several scientific inventions. He was by all odds the most brilliant and most versatile citizen in Lichfield. John Saville, the lay choral director at the cathedral, was another regular at Anna's gatherings. Although a married man, he had long nursed a secret passion for the poetess. Subsequently it would blossom into a platonic love affair that would occasion much small talk in the cathedral close.

It was Anna who shone most brightly in her charmed circle. Sometimes she would receive André and Honora in her dressing room, called "the dear blue region" by Honora because of its blue walls and the delft tiles framing the fireplace. Here she would read from her favorite poets while André sat as close to Honora as he dared and may have tenderly clasped her hand. On more formal occasions, Anna would hold court downstairs, where guests would be subjected to what André describes as "the sensible observation, the tasteful criticism, or the elegant song." Restoration drama might be discussed, or the works of Milton, or the writings of John Locke, but readings from Anna's poetry tended to predominate. A sample of her output is this tribute to John André himself, with its reference to the miniature of Honora he had painted, none too successfully, at Buxton:

> Young Genius led thee to his varied fane,
> Bade thee ask all his gifts, nor ask in vain;
> Hence novel thoughts, in ev'ry lustre drest
> Of pointed wit, that diamond of the breast;
> Hence music warbled in thy sprightly lay;
> And hence thy pencil, with his colours warm,
> Caught ev'ry grace, and copies ev'ry charm,

Whose transient glories beam on Beauty's cheek,
And bid the glowing ivory breathe and speak.

Not surprisingly, Anna and her coterie grated on Samuel
Johnson, who was born in Lichfield and turned up at rare
intervals. He had gone to school under Anna's grandfather,
who, he said, never "*taught* a boy in his life" — only "whipped
and they learned." He declared that the very sight of Anna
made him tremble. She, in turn, sensed the veiled hostility
in Johnson's "coaxing regard." Although her posturings must
have infuriated the good doctor, what most disturbed him was
the "aristocratic prejudice" on the part of Anna and her friends
toward a fellow citizen of humbler origin.

Unlike Dr. Johnson, John André was admiring of all that
took place in the bishop's palace — the nightly gatherings
with their display of wit and erudition, Anna's readings of her
own literary efforts, his moments at Honora's side in "the dear
blue region." Soon he was "Cher Jean" to everyone, delight-
ing his new friends with his charm and wit, his flute playing,
his flair for sketching and for light verse. Even Honora seemed
to thaw. Toward the end of the visit he mustered up his
courage and declared himself. Might he have her hand in
marriage?

Honora's response was favorable, although perhaps more
tepid than André would have liked. Anna, the first to be told,
went into raptures. But the senior Sewards, John André's
mother, and, more especially, Honora's father took the glad
news coolly. Honora was very young, they pointed out, probably too young to know her own mind. She tired easily and
complained of an ache in her side. And then there was the
crucial matter of Cher Jean's finances, a point stressed by
Honora's father. Although he would inherit £5,000 from his
father's estate, he had yet to show that he could support a
bride in a manner befitting a gentlewoman in less than robust
health. The two must not be impulsive. They might see each

other at judicious intervals, but they must not dream of holy wedlock until Cher Jean had proved his capacities as a budding merchant and an adornment to the world of trade.

It was Anna who came to the rescue of the crestfallen pair, reminding them that true love thrives on adversity. Cher Jean must address himself to the family business. He must save his money, acquire the outlook and mien of a budding merchant. He must take his father's place at Warnford Court, at the coffee houses near the Royal Exchange, at the family seat in Clapton. If he would have Honora, there could be no further talk of a preference for the military.

Of course Anna was right. Cher Jean could not dispute her logic. Honora was his very life, and passing up a possible military career was a small sacrifice for so dazzling a prize. But to be separated from his intended, even for brief intervals, would be a heavy load. He implored both Anna and Honora to write him frequently. Anna was happy to oblige. But he was disappointed in Honora. The ache in her side made writing burdensome, she said. Anna would do the writing for her, but she promised to add postscripts to Anna's letters.

For over a year Anna and Cher Jean exchanged letters. A few of his have survived. In some he addresses her as "Nancy," a family nickname. More often he calls her "Julia," a name agreed upon between them. Long afterward she would publish three of his letters, not as he wrote them but as she wished them to be, edited and tidied up.

The first letter to Anna still survives as André wrote it, differing in several particulars from her edited version. Written, as he says, by "a poor novice of nineteen," it voices concern for the ailing Honora and makes no secret of his dependence on Anna's letters.

> I cannot think of any pleasure while I know she suffers [he writes]. Nay, I suffer most cruelly for her myself. . . . The

least bit of a letter will always be receiv'd with the greatest joy. . . . Therefore write, tho' it were only to give us the comfort of having a piece of paper that has recently been under your fair hand. [He pleads for a postscript from Honora] tho' it were only to tell me that she is my sincere friend who will neither give me love nor comfort. [She is the focus of his fondest dreams.] There is something pleasing in the ramblings of the mind [he confesses]. My castles in the air are of the noblest structure. Materials are never wanting, their only fault is being without foundation.

Honora was still holding him at arm's length, still playing hard to catch. He embellished the letter with three doodles, showing a postman on horseback, some writing materials, a hand guiding a quill pen.

In his second letter André returns to his "castles in the air," all owing their existence to the inaccessible Honora:

From the midst of books, papers, bills and other implements of gain, let me lift up my drowsy head awhile to converse with dear Julia. And first, as I know she has a fervent wish to see me a quill-driver, I must tell her that I begin, as people are wont to do, to look upon my future profession with great partiality. I no longer see it in so disadvantageous a light. Instead of figuring a merchant as a middle-aged man, with a bob wig, a rough beard, in snuff colour'd clothes, grasping a guinea in his red hand, I conceive a comely young man, with a tolerable pig-tail, wielding a pen with all the noble fierceness of the Duke of Marlborough brandishing a truncheon upon a signpost . . . while in perspective, his gorgeous vessels, "launch'd on the bosom of the silver Thames", are wafting to distant lands the produce of this commercial nation.

Thus all the mercantile glories crowd on my fancy emblason'd in the most refulgent colouring of an ardent imagination. Borne on her soaring pinions, I wing my flight to the time when heaven shall have crowned my labours with success and opulence. I see sumptuous palaces rising to receive me. I see orphans and widows, and painters and fiddlers and poets, and

builders, protected and encourag'd; and when the fabrick is
pretty nearly finished by my shattered pericranium, I cast my
eyes around and find John André by a small coal fire in a gloomy
counting-house in Warnford Court . . . in all probability never
to be much more than he is at present. But oh, my dear Honora!
It is for thy sake only I wish for wealth.

Cher Jean had never been enamored of Clapton. But now,
under Honora's spell, even Clapton glows.

> This morning I return'd to town [he writes]. It has been the
> finest day imaginable. A solemn mildness was diffus'd through-
> out the blue horizon. Its light was clear and distinct rather
> than dazzling. The serene beams of the autumnal sun, gilded
> hills, variegated woods, glittering spires, ruminating herds,
> bounding flocks — all combin'd to enchant the eyes, expand
> the heart, and chase all sorrow but despair! In the midst of
> such a scene, no lesser grief can prevent our sympathy with
> nature. A calmness, a benevolent disposition seizes us with
> sweet, insinuating power. The very brute creation seem sen-
> sible of these beauties.

A lamb's head, sketched in a margin, adorns the letter.
André pictures Anna and Honora seated by the hearth in
"the dear blue region." He identifies with the fire tools and
with the Biblical characters featured on the delft tiles framing
the fireplace. "E'er it be very long," he writes, "your blazing
hearth will burn again for me. Pray keep me a place — let
the poker, tongs or shovel represent me. But you have Dutch
tiles, which are infinitely better, so let Moses, or Aaron, or
Balaam's ass be my representative."
The last of the three letters speaks of a visit to Lichfield
in late October.

> With what delight my eager eyes drank their first view of the
> dear spires! [he exclaims]. What rapture did I not feel on
> entering your gates, in flying up the hall steps, in rushing into
> the dining-room, in meeting the gladden'd eyes of our dear

Julia and her enchanting friend! That instant convinc'd me of the truth of Rousseau's observation "that there are *moments worth ages.*" Shall not those moments return? Ah, Julia! The cold hand of absence is heavy upon the heart of your poor *Cher Jean.* . . . Sustain me, Hope! Nothing on my part shall be wanting which may induce thee to *fulfill* thy blossoming promises.

Although he had not made peace with the marketplace, André assures Anna that life with Honora would more than atone for it.

I have now completely subdued my aversion to the profession of a merchant, and hope in time to acquire an inclination for it [he writes]. Yet God forbid I should ever love what I am to make the object of my attention! That vile trash, which I care not for but only as it may be the future means of procuring the blessing of my soul! Thus all my mercantile calculations go to the tune of *dear Honora.* When an impertinent consciousness whispers in my ear that I am not of the right stuff for a merchant, I draw Honora's picture from my bosom, and the sight of that dear talisman so inspirits my industry that no toil appears oppressive.

John André returned to Lichfield at Christmas to find two rivals for Honora's hand. Thomas Day* and Richard Lovell Edgeworth** had come to the cathedral town to observe some of Erasmus Darwin's scientific experiments and to learn what they could from the inventive doctor. In the meantime Day, a notably solemn young man, was engaged in an experiment of his own. He had adopted two female juveniles, aged eleven and twelve, and was in the process of trying to mould them

---

*Thomas Day would win fame as the author of *Sandford and Merton,* a book for young readers exhorting honest toil and moral rectitude through the adventures of two small boys. It would be a best-selling juvenile for nearly a century after Day wrote it in the 1780s.
**Father of Maria Edgeworth, the novelist.

into such paragons of womanhood that one or the other would one day make him an ideal wife. He had taken them to France, where they had been schooled in good manners and ladylike behavior, but the two did battle with each other, cursed and swore like troopers, and not infrequently joined forces against Day himself. He had given up on one and was now devoting himself valiantly to the other. To instill poise in his remaining pupil, he took to dropping hot sealing wax on her neck without warning, or discharging a pistol within inches of her ear. But he was seeing much of Honora.

Edgeworth, older and less ingenuous than Day, was dapper, smooth-spoken, and possessed of the tidy income that Cher Jean lacked. A favorite at social gatherings and a polished dinner guest, he was seen regularly at Lichfield parties. Women, including Honora Sneyd, relished his company. Indeed, the two were often seen together, although Edgeworth had a wife and three children.

By the time of André's visit, Edgeworth had fallen hopelessly in love with Honora.

> I saw a woman that equalled the picture of perfection which existed in my imagination [he admits]. I had long suffered from the want of that cheerfulness in a wife without which marriage could not be agreeable to a man of such a temper as mine. I had borne this evil, I believe, with patience, but my not being happy at home exposed me to the danger of being too happy elsewhere. The charms and superior character of Miss Honora Sneyd made an impression on my mind such as I never felt before.

Only Anna was suspicious.

The holidays flew past, crowded with dinners, card parties, cotillions, and a costume ball. Anna, at her most scintillating, held sway at the bishop's palace. "We went every day to Lichfield," Edgeworth writes, "and most of the days to the palace, where the agreeable conversation of the whole family, and in particular the sprightliness and literary talents of Miss Seward, engaged us to pass many agreeable hours." But for André the visit proved anything but agreeable. Before it ended he knew that he had lost Honora. He may have read it in her eyes, sensed it in her tone of voice or in something unmistakable in her manner. Or perhaps her father advised him to end the engagement. However he was told, he left Lichfield abruptly.

"I never met Mr. André again," Edgeworth says, "and from all that I then saw, or have since known, I believe that Miss Honora Sneyd was never much disappointed in the conclusion of the attachment." Indeed, if we are to take Edgeworth's word for it, although André's "talents" were not lost on Honora he "did not possess the reasoning mind which she required." For whatever reason — parental opposition to the match or a seventeen-year-old's fickleness of heart — she had lost interest in Cher Jean.

Early in 1771 John André purchased a second lieutenancy in the Royal Welsh Fusiliers, forsaking the family business and abandoning all hope of winning Honora. That same year Thomas Day proposed to her and was rejected. In 1773, four months after his wife's sudden death in childbirth, Richard Lovell Edgeworth offered his hand to Honora with the happiest of results. The two were joined in holy wedlock by Anna's father, although Anna had always taken a dim view of the match.

II

Poets and the Highly Placed

IN PURCHASING HIS COMMISSION, John André had embarked on a course now open to men of relatively modest station. Once the preserve of the nobility's younger sons, the officers' corps had come to include men from the lower ranks of the aristocracy and from mercantile families like André's own. Indeed, one could point to officers of humble origin who had advanced to high rank solely on merit. Although the pay was indifferent and preferment could be a slow process, André's commission brought with it considerable social status, even in a society that tended to distrust standing armies. He hoped, moreover, to accelerate the preferment process. The colonists' quarrel with Parliament had subsided for the moment, but a strong military presence in America seemed assured. His chances of swifter promotion would escalate if his regiment saw duty overseas.

As a freshly enrolled fusilier, André had broken with the tight little world of London Huguenots to enter a domain steeped in British tradition. The Royal Welsh Fusiliers, or 23rd Foot, was an old and venerated regiment. It had won renown at the battle of Minden, where its members had turned back the French cavalry at a crucial moment. "I have seen what I never thought to be possible," declared the French commander, "a single line of infantry break through three lines of cavalry in order of battle and tumble them to ruins." John André gloried in his scarlet coat with blue facings, his gorget, and crimson sash. If he rose to high rank he would be on a footing with the ablest of the career men, the brightest of the younger sons. He would become, indisputably, British.

Every St. David's Day officers of the regiment dined together and made honorary Welshmen of new colleagues. André's induction was a proud moment that he would not forget. At the peak of festivities the regimental mascot, a goat bedecked with flowers and ridden by a drummer boy, was coaxed and goaded into the banquet hall. It was a ceremony fondly chronicled by a regimental historian:

> After the cloth is taken away, a bumper is filled round to his Royal Highness, the Prince of Wales (whose health is always drunk to first that day), the band playing the old tune "The Noble Race of Shenkin," when an handsome drum-boy, elegantly dressed, mounted on the goat richly caparisoned for the occasion, is led thrice round the table in procession by the drum major.

On one occasion the goat had dumped its rider, leaped over the heads of startled banqueters, and vanished through the doorway and out into the night. But nothing so untoward occurred at André's induction. In line with regimental custom, he stood on his chair at the proper moment, placed one foot on the table, and valiantly swallowed a raw leek. When he had managed this, he was pronounced an honorary Welshman.

André paid £450 for his commission. He also assumed the cost of his uniform, tent, mattress, fusil, and sword, all of which set him back an additional £220. But this was less than he would have paid to join the Foot Guards or a cavalry regiment. His duties as a junior officer necessitated his making sure that his men wore clean shirts, that their hair was free of lice, that their cooking arrangements were sanitary and their beds tidy, and that they reported on time at tattoo. But with his business experience he was probably given his share of more exalted duties. He may have been called upon to relieve senior officers of some of their time-consuming paper work. He may have kept the books, filled out forms and certificates, and helped with official correspondence, all of which would have distinguished him from less gifted colleagues.

In August the Fusiliers were reviewed by King George III on Blackheath Common. André and the major's son were picked to carry the regimental colors. As the king and his retinue walked slowly past, saluted in turn by the officers of each unit, André dipped his colors solemnly, almost to the ground. It was a proud moment. He would not forget Honora, but he gloried in that moment — and in what it intimated for his budding career.

André was not long with the Fusiliers. In the fall he purchased a first lieutenancy in the 7th Foot, which brought with it higher pay and ampler opportunity. Like the Welsh Fusiliers, his new regiment was time-honored and highly regarded. "Great attention must be paid to the faces, legs and shoulders of recruits," advised an officer's manual. "Fine hair is also particularly desired, it being so greatly an ornament and addition to the appearance of a soldier. . . . A good figure (at least a genteel one) is a circumstance to be also considered in the young officer." André met these standards to perfection, in his tall, mitre-shaped headgear and immaculate regimentals. Early in 1772 he was picked for advanced training at the Georgia Augusta, a military program affiliated with the University of Göttingen. Although his fluency in German had recommended him, his exemplary working habits and respectful way of handling himself were not lost on senior officers.

André crossed the Channel with young George Rodney, the son of Admiral Sir George Rodney, who was also bound for

the Georgia Augusta. In Göttingen the pair teamed up with
four other Britons to engage a local literary light, Heinrich
Christian Boie, as tutor and guardian angel. Boie was among
the Göttingen disciples of Gottlieb Friedrich Klopstock, a poet
famous for his popularization of old Teutonic myths. Others
included Ludwig Hölty, Johann Heinrich Voss, Johann Friedrich Hahn, Johann Martin Miller, the brothers zu Stolberg,
and August Bürger, who lived a few miles away. Kindred
spirits, they spent long hours in literary talk, subsisted on a
pittance, dedicated their odes and lyrics to one another, and
published very little. Hölty, a promising poet, would die young.
Bürger would turn out some enduring ballads. Voss would find
his niche as a translator of Greek and Roman classics. Through
Boie's good offices, André was admitted to the group, which
reminded him of literary evenings at the bishop's palace, of
"the dear blue region," and matchless Honora.

That same September the disciples had staged an impromptu rite that must have warmed Klopstock's romantic
heart.

> Upon a beautiful evening [Voss would remember], we were
> taking a walk to a neighboring village and were enjoying the
> beautiful nature around us. As we entered an oak grove the
> idea came into our minds to form a league of friendship under
> the beautiful trees. We adorned our hats with oak leaves, laid
> them under one of the trees, took one another by the hand,
> danced around the tree, called on the moon and stars to witness
> the founding of the league, and promised one another an ev-
> erlasting friendship.

The event gave birth to the Göttingen Hain, a name derived
from the oak grove where the disciples had danced together.
At subsequent gatherings, a vacant chair, festooned with flowers, was set aside in Klopstock's honor. Patriotism, comrade-
ship, and manly virtue were extolled. André seems to have
taken to such doings and to have attended several gatherings

of the Hain. But with no Honora present they may have had a hollow ring.

During the fall André was ordered to rejoin his regiment, which had been assigned to Canada. He left Göttingen on November 1, after a sendoff that would find its way into the writings of Johann Voss. Young Rodney had arranged a farewell dinner for his fellow countryman. No members of the Hain were invited, for André, in the press of leave-taking, had failed to tell them of his departure. Nevertheless, when Boie and Voss got wind of it they gathered up Hahn and Hölty and proposed that each write a farewell poem in their friend's honor. "We first made merry," Voss says, "and then each of us went by himself into a separate alley and composed by the light of the moon." Boie was chosen to present their offerings to André, whom he located at Rodney's party. He was warmly received and given an honored place at the dinner table, while a servant was dispatched to summon Voss. "Never in my life have I felt prouder than when the Englishmen all came to meet me and embrace me," Voss says. "André, in particular, pressed me to his heart and said, 'You are a noble fellow — you love your fatherland!'"

After downing champagne until midnight, the celebrants streamed outside to wend their way through some of Göttingen's darkened streets. Joined by other members of the Hain and by random citizens, they staged what was known as a *landesvater*, a serenade in song borrowed from one of the local literary societies. "Then we held a 'landesvater', the first for me," Voss writes. "In half an hour I had counts and barons and my Boie for brothers." The frolicking stretched into the small hours, but when André left Göttingen that same morning both Voss and Boie were on hand to see him off. "He took leave of us with tears," Voss remembers, "and I was obliged to promise that I would accept a position in England if he could get one for me."

Having reported to his superiors, André returned to Germany for further study. This time he saw little of Göttingen but managed to visit Voss on at least one occasion, when he dashed off a poem for his admiring friend. It makes no reference to the Hain but may owe much to Honora:

> The boat was trimm'd, the tilt outspread,
> The main shone silver bright,
> And on the fatal moment sped
> That tore her from my sight.

> And did a thought of me then rise
> And help to urge a tear?
> And in those drops that grac'd thine eyes
> Had A—— too a share?

> Ah! well thou mightst have deign'd to lose
> One piteous drop for me,
> Full oft the bitter tribute flows,
> Beloved main, to thee!

> And now the boatmen ply'd the oar,
> And swift they floated on;
> The lessening vessel fled the shore,
> For me she's ever gone.

André was mostly at Gotha, where he made the acquaintance of Georg Christoph Lichtenberg, a popular satirist. Although Lichtenberg held no brief for the Göttingen Hain, he thought well of André, ranking him with Sir Francis Clerke as one of the two "most distinguished Englishmen whom we have had here during the last sixteen years."* He describes André as "a man of nearly womanlike modesty and gentleness."

At about this time André painted a self-portrait on ivory. It shows him in uniform, a trifle insolent, obviously pleased with

---

*Clerke would one day become Burgoyne's aide-de-camp and lose his life at Saratoga.

his proud calling, his face still unlined and boyish. He is every inch the assured young officer, very much at home in his regimentals. There is no hint here of his heartbreak at losing Honora and his sad, hurried departure from Lichfield.

André was no longer restricting himself to self-portraits, however, or to the familiar, lowly subjects that inform his earlier efforts. Lichtenberg tells us that he painted, "for his own pleasure," likenesses of the Duke and Duchess of Gotha — an indication of the exalted circles he now frequented. His urbanity and wit had won him admirers and friends among the German nobility. He was a favorite at the court of Saxe-Gotha, where he was lionized by the duke and duchess, and at Strasbourg, where he caught the fancy of a Mlle. de Welling, maid-in-waiting to a German princess. Years later he would speak of her as "a sort of flame." It was his associations with the highly placed, not with the Göttingen Hain, that he would enthuse over when he got home.

André had relatives in Offenbach, including Johann André, a composer of songs and light opera. Before leaving Germany he paid a visit to the city and introduced himself to his gifted kinsman. If he brought along his flute, the two may have played duets far into the night. But his months in Germany were at an end. Late in 1773 he returned home to be told that Honora had become Mrs. Richard Lovell Edgeworth. "Ah, how deeply was I a fellow sufferer with Major André on this marriage!" exclaimed Anna Seward in later years. No doubt André was a fellow sufferer, although less acutely now. The news came as no surprise.

André's regiment had been sent to Quebec City. Still on leave, he would journey to Canada by way of the American colonies — possibly, it has been said, to ferret out information at the behest of senior officers. This is no more than a guess, for there is no evidence to substantiate it. But as one who had lived abroad and traveled extensively, he was a well-qualified observer.

In midsummer 1774, after a round of farewells, André sailed for Philadelphia aboard the packet *St. George*. Among his fellow passengers was a youth named Samuel Smith, whose father was a prominent Baltimore merchant and who was himself an outspoken critic of king and Parliament.* He and André spent long hours debating the colonists' alleged grievances, which threatened to bring about armed conflict if they were allowed to fester. Nothing Smith said could persuade André that the so-called grievances had not been trumped up by a few mischievous agitators.

The *St. George* docked in early September. Delegates to the First Continental Congress had arrived in Philadelphia. They were crowding inns and boarding houses and could be seen conversing in small clusters on street corners. There was a great uneasiness throughout the city.

André immediately sought out the officers of the Royal Irish, the regiment on police duty in Philadelphia. They had much to tell him. Congress threatened to meet in secret, and only last fall the tea ship *Polly* had been seized by a Philadelphia mob. Flags had been lowered to half-mast when word reached the city that the port of Boston had been closed. Officers and men in the Royal Irish had been ordered not to retaliate, but all of them itched to even the score. André was jolted by what he heard.

Philadelphia was unlike any other city John André had ever seen. It was laid out like a chessboard, with broad avenues joined at right angles by evenly spaced side streets. There were few narrow alleys and crooked roadways to remind him of downtown London. Its citizens, he quickly learned, were as inhospitable to the British military as its streets were geo-

---

*He would subsequently enroll in the Continental Army and serve with distinction in Smallwood's regiment.

metrically arranged. A few seemed fairly respectful as he passed, but others hardly acknowledged his gaze and still others returned it with open hatred.

André was appalled by the intransigence of Congress. The Stamp Act had been repealed. The Townshend Acts had been rescinded, less than three years after their enactment. The tax on tea seemed a trifling matter and no excuse for outrages like the *Polly* incident in Philadelphia and the so-called tea party in Boston. Moreover, many Americans were friendly to the Crown. Even in Congress a majority of delegates was said to favor reconciliation. But a hard core of radicals took charge of proceedings and rode herd on moderates. Congress met, not at the State House as moderates urged, but at the Carpenters' Hall behind closed doors. Delegates talked bitterly of taxation without representation. They had boycotted trade with Britain, made a bid for Canadian support, and appealed to the British public over the heads of king and Parliament. The day after Congress convened, word came that Boston had been shelled. Church bells tolled, crowds thronged the streets, and intemperate talk filled the coffee houses. But there was no truth in the rumor.

André remained only a short time before continuing to Boston, which resembled an armed camp. The port was shut down, the courts were all but suspended. There was a greater show of anger than in Philadelphia. British officers told André that their troops could contain an outbreak, but Sir Hugh Percy and others who should know were not so sure. "Our affairs are in the most critical situation imaginable," Sir Hugh had written home. "Nothing less than the total loss or conquest of the Colonies must be the end of it. Either is indeed disagreeable, but one or the other is now absolutely necessary."

Nor was New York any more encouraging, although it had kept a lower profile than its neighbor to the north. When André stopped there after visiting Boston he was told that self-styled "Sons of Liberty" had hanged the king's magistrates in effigy

and that a "Committee of Correspondence" had assumed un-
authorized powers and was hounding the king's supporters.
Even supposedly loyal merchants refused to provide shipping
for British troops and supplies. Moderate voices were still
heard — there were more of them than in Boston — but their
influence was waning. One citizen told him that New York's
congressional delegation had been "converted into fixed re-
publicans."

André was glad to quit the colonies. If he was indeed collecting information for senior officers, he must submit an
alarming report. He went by boat to Albany, whose even-
tempered Dutch citizens seemed more tractable than their
New England neighbors. Continuing on foot to Lake George,
he walked beside a crowded coach and amused himself by
taking pot shots at unwary squirrels and songbirds. At Lake
George he boarded a bateau, to sail past bleak mountain ranges
and miles of empty shoreline to the waterway linking Lake
George with Lake Champlain. At Fort Ticonderoga he took
note of the breached walls, the dilapidated barracks, the under-
strength garrison with many of its members unfit for service.
Nor was he reassured when he passed the spectral battlements
at Crown Point. Erected only a few years previously, they had
been gutted by fire and were manned by a token garrison.

In a letter to his sister Louisa, André describes Indian hunting parties encountered on the lakes and a night spent wrapped
in bearskins in the log hut of some German settlers. His bateau
entered Canada by way of the Richelieu River and tied up at
St. John's, a dreary military post southeast of Montreal. The
place looked neglected and undermanned, with sod redoubts
and antiquated barracks. It would afford scant protection against
an attack from the south. He traveled overland to Montreal,
where he booked passage on a Quebec-bound schooner. "We
had scarce any provision on board," he wrote Louisa, "and
were cluster'd up, by way of keeping out of the cold, with a
black woman, an Indian squaw in a blanket, an Indian boy

and the sailors, round a stove in a dungeon-like part of the vessel."

André had no sooner debarked at Quebec than he was invited to a ball given by the governor, General Guy Carleton. It was a splendorous event, setting the tone for what would be a busy and festive winter.

My acquaintances thicken [he wrote his sister Mary], and I begin to sort them and select those whom I choose to be connected with. [He described nocturnal sleigh rides with Canadian friends, who] every now and then make parties into the country in which I, with my equipage, join in the string and drive out a lady. We dine, dance rondes, toss pancakes, make a noise and return, sometimes overturn, and sometimes are frostbit.

André reveled in the Quebec winter. The snow lay so deep that roads were marked by long lines of fresh-cut fir trees.

We are to see nature wear this twelfth-cake-like appearance a couple of months longer [he wrote Mary in early March]. I own I am not tired of it. The spirit of society which reigns here during this season, and the dresses we wear, banish the idea of cold, and the brightness of the weather cheers one's spirits. Imagine a heaven of the purest blue and an earth of the purest white, and over the country trace out roads above enclosures, through rivers, etc. planted on either side with branches of fir to mark them, and numberless carioles, sleighs, etc., driven about, and you will have some notion of the appearance of the country.

André was fascinated with the Indians he saw. In his letter to Mary he described a tribal dance he had attended:

You would have been mightily delighted to have seen the gentlemen, almost as lightly clad as your grandpa Adam, smeared over with vermilion, blue, black, etc., from head to foot, throw themselves into the most horrid contortions and represent with the wildest yellings and howlings the history of a warlike expedition from their first going out to the scalping and mutilating their enemy. The undress of the ladies is a blanket tolerably impregnated with bear's grease and vermilion, which they wear capuchin fashion. Their finery is a man's shirt copiously besprinkled with vermilion, fine bead necklaces, earrings, etc., a little sort of winding blue kilt or petticoat coming down to the knees, and blue cloth leggings (a sort of trousers), with shoes worked with porcupine quills, black, red, yellow, etc.

André made a sketch of an Indian dance that includes French Canadians and British regulars as well as braves in breechcloths. The Indians exert themselves with an abandon that escapes the self-conscious whites. A brave perched on a table beats time on a tom-tom, another brandishes a gourd rattle. Whites and red men dance singly or in pairs, while an urchin, ignored by his elders, bawls lustily. In the background an old woman, in her nightclothes and clutching a candle, upbraids the celebrants.

In writing to Mary, André mentioned forthcoming maneuvers that would require him to rough it, Indian style, in the Canadian bush:

> We are to go 30 miles out of town, and the amusements of the day are to be hunting upon snowshoes, or large rackets tied to one's feet. In short, we are to take humanity a peg lower and in proportion as our beds are bad we are to fatigue ourselves the more. Such, dear Mary, is the life of Quebec. Today silken dalliance clothes our limbs and we wreathe the bow and wind the dance. Tomorrow we hut in a style little above the brute creation.

André anticipated a long stay in Canada. "We shall probably, if we do not go to Boston, move to Montreal next spring," he wrote the family, "and the year after to the back posts of the 5 lakes." But a calamity on Lake Champlain would change all this. He would be assigned, not to interior Canada, but to St. John's on the Richelieu, the neglected outpost he had passed on his way north.

III

Chronicler for a Diehard Garrison

JOHN ANDRÉ WAS STILL AT QUEBEC when one Moses Hazen, a citizen of St. John's, galloped into town to tell a shocking story. American rebels had captured Fort Ticonderoga, raided St. John's, and made off with the king's sloop. Later that same day, word reached the city that the rebels had returned to St. John's but had been driven off by British regulars.

Hazen's story shook the city. The attack on Fort Ticonderoga had been led by Ethan Allen, an upstart from the New Hampshire Grants. His next in command had been Benedict Arnold, another New England troublemaker. At the head of fewer than a hundred men, they had caught the garrison off guard and seized the fort without firing a shot. Next day they had occupied Crown Point. Arnold had led the first raid on St. John's, seizing the king's sloop with her cargo of military stores. But the second raid, under Ethan Allen, had been beaten back. Three or four men who were slow of foot had been left behind and captured in the course of Allen's humiliating retreat.

General Carleton met the crisis by calling out the militia and declaring martial law. He assigned most of his British regulars, including 474 men from the 7th and 26th regiments and thirty-eight artillerists, to St. John's and reinforced them with ninety French Canadian volunteers, twenty Royal Highland Emigrants recruited among Canada's Scottish settlers, and a contingent of Caughnawaga Indians. Major Charles Preston of the 26th was put in command of the garrison. At his side were Captain Edward Williams of the Royal Artillery, Lieutenant William Hunter of the Royal Navy, François Marie Picoté de Belestre of the French volunteers, Captains Samuel Mackay and David Monin of the Royal Highland Emigrants, and François Verneuil de Lorimier, a seasoned bushfighter, at the head of the Caughnawagas. A few miles downriver, the old stone fort at Chambly was declared a supply depot under Major Joseph Stopford of the 7th Foot and a garrison of some eighty men.

Captain John Marr, Carleton's engineer, hurried to St. John's to renovate the run-down fort. All summer he rode herd on work crews to the whine of saws and thud of axes, linking the two redoubts with a palisade, installing additional artillery, constructing a broad moat to shield the post from land attack. While Marr strengthened the fortifications, Lieutenant Hunter laid the keels for a schooner and two row galleys. By autumn, St. John's had become formidable enough to discourage a frontal attack and to slow, if not halt, an army advancing from the south.

Late in August, Lorimier and an Indian war party traded shots with the enemy near Lake Champlain. Two tribesmen were wounded before Lorimier could beat a retreat. When he returned next morning to inspect the site, he found the body of an American officer identified from papers on his person as Captain Remember Baker of the Green Mountain Boys. The Indians removed Baker's head and carried it exultantly to St. John's, where André may have seen it.

Baker was the first casualty in an American thrust for Canada. At first Congress had deplored the taking of Fort Ticonderoga and had decreed that captured artillery be returned to the mother country as soon as "the restoration of the former harmony between Great Britain and these colonies, so ardently wished for by the latter, shall render it prudent and consistent with the overruling law of self-preservation." Irked by such pussyfooting, Ethan Allen called for an all-out attack on Montreal, a conquest of Canada. "We should have little to fear from the Indians," he said, "and would easily make a conquest of that place and set up a standard of liberty in the extensive Province of Quebeck." Benedict Arnold offered to lead an invading army of two thousand men.

Allen and Arnold spoke for most of their countrymen. Only a year previously, Parliament had enacted the Quebec Bill, intended to regularize the government of the province and win the support of its French citizens. The measure had restored French civil law and given Roman Catholics the free exercise of their religion. It had increased the size of the province to include the Great Lakes, the lands north of the Ohio, the upper Mississippi, and the hinterland between the Great Lakes and Hudson Bay territory — all of it designated as the domain of the Canadian fur trade and closed to homesteaders.

The Quebec Bill was a landmark in the struggle for religious freedom, enabling non-English people to become part of Britain's empire without restrictions on their Church. But in the American colonies it was misunderstood, misrepresented, and bitterly resented. Homesteaders accused Parliament of trying to halt the opening of the West and confine the colonies to a narrow strip along the eastern seaboard. No decree of Parliament, they declared, could bar them from lands that they considered theirs by right.

In Protestant New England, the Quebec Bill was deemed "popish" by clergy and laity alike. Alexander Hamilton, a New Yorker, spoke for them when he foresaw dire consequences to "the protestant cause."

> Does not your blood run cold [he exclaimed] to think an
> English Parliament should pass an act for the establishment
> of arbitrary power and popery in such an extensive country?
> If they had had any regard to the freedom and happiness of
> mankind, they would never have done it. If they had been
> friends to the protestant cause, they would never have pro-
> vided such a nursery for its great enemy.

Of even greater concern to Americans was the threat of a
British army descending from a base in Canada to bisect the
colonies. Within weeks, Congress reversed itself and ruled
that the guns seized at Fort Ticonderoga should go to the
Continental Army. Delegates spoke of grabbing the initiative
and invading Canada.

> Whether we should march into Canada with an army sufficient
> to break the power of Governor Carleton, to overawe the In-
> dians, and to protect the French, has been the great question
> [John Adams wrote]. It seems to be the general conclusion
> that it is best to go, if we can be assured that the Canadians
> will be pleased with it and join.

Congress had been courting the French Canadians. In an
Address to the Inhabitants of the Province of Quebec, delegates had denounced "such low-minded infirmities" as religious prejudice and had likened the colonies to the Swiss
cantons, where Catholics and Protestants lived side by side
"in the utmost concord and peace." Now, in a second appeal,
they warned the Canadians that they would soon be pressed
into military service by "an avaricious governor and rapacious
council." Canadian clergy and the land-owning noblesse, the
seigneurs, who favored the Quebec Bill, paid no heed, but
many *habitants* — the small farmers and tenants who formed
the bulk of the population — listened to the appeal and took
it to heart.

On June 27, Congress ordered Major General Philip Schuyler of Albany to assemble and equip an army for a forthcoming

advance on Montreal. Brigadier General Richard Montgomery was named second in command. The campaign would involve a two-pronged invasion by widely separated armies. Schuyler and Montgomery would enter Canada by way of Lake Champlain and the Richelieu. The companion army would thread through the Maine woods to Quebec and would be led by Benedict Arnold.

Philip Schuyler sprang from patrician antecedents who had influenced much of New York's early history. Cautious by nature and in fragile health, he was less field commander than administrator and was ill-suited to the rough-and-tumble of a bruising campaign. Montgomery, an Ulsterman by birth, had served with Wolfe and Amherst in the French and Indian War. On the eve of the Revolution he had sold his commission and taken passage to New York, where he had married into the prestigious Livingston family. He had become a staunch champion of the rebel cause, serving in the provincial legislature. With his outstanding military credentials, he was snatched up by Congress as one of its first brigadiers.

Schuyler was short of both men and supplies. Returns came to only 1350 men late in June. He spent all summer recruiting an army, supplying it, giving it a semblance of discipline and a sense of esprit de corps. Late in August, he set forth, crossing into Canada by way of the Richelieu and establishing headquarters at Ile aux Noix, a mosquito-ridden island upstream from St. John's. From there he issued a last appeal to the French Canadians. He had come to rescue them from "enslavement," he said, "to protect them in the full enjoyment of their temporal and spiritual privileges."

John André was among the regulars assigned to St. John's, where he found himself more inconvenienced by the clouds of mosquitoes hovering around the fort than by the random shots aimed at Preston's scouting parties.

We begin to have some notion of the forces of our enemy, and I am happy to say they do not appear in a very formidable light [he wrote a friend in Quebec]. They are encamped on the Ile aux Noix about 15 miles from St. Johns, from whence they gain the east side of the Sorel River* and infest the woods opposite St. Johns, firing from the bushes on our battoes, which are constantly moving up and down the river to watch their motions. . . . We have daily expeditions into the woods. I had this duty yesterday and, tho' I am not peculiarly keen after the pleasure of being shot at, had almost as lief have met the Yankys as been bak'd in the sun for the mosquitoes' dinner.

The fort was overcrowded, meagerly supplied, short on sanitation. Accommodations were primitive even by army standards. Sleeping facilities were rude and in short supply, and eighty dependents, wives and children of British regulars, had to be quartered in log huts outside the fort. But, unlike others, André had no complaints and was singled out by Major Preston to keep an official journal for the garrison.** In its pages we can follow the series of events that began when a rebel detachment came ashore within striking distance of the fort, only to be driven back by Lorimier's Indians after a brisk exchange. The Indians, however, were not pleased with what had happened. Heavily outnumbered and losing several in their command, they had received no reinforcements from the garrison. If this was an indication of the white man's support, they said, they would quit the king's service. André was shocked by their vehemence.

Soon afterward Montgomery came downstream with eight hundred men. Detaching part of his command to protect his left flank, he advanced about a mile into the woods when the snap of twigs and rattle of dry leaves to the left of his column

*The Richelieu.
**Although the journal speaks for Preston as post commander, professional handwriting analysis shows that it was John André who wrote it.

sounded suspiciously like Lorimier's Indians. Several of his men broke ranks and fled. Others followed. Then the entire column fell apart. Only when the troops reached their bateaux did they realize that the footsteps had been those of their own flanking party.

By now General Schuyler was desperately ill with a high fever. In frail health at the start of the campaign, he had become bedridden and unable even to put pen to paper. He relinquished the command to Montgomery and left in a bateau for Fort Ticonderoga. After he had regained some measure of strength, he would devote himself to supplying the expedition.

On September 17, Montgomery set forth with his entire army. "We expected a battle as much as we expected to get there," says Captain John Fassett of the Green Mountain Boys. "The whole army soon came up [to] where we stayed that night, and it was very cold and they flung bombs among us and we had a very tedious night of it indeed." André gives the garrison's version: "The vessels were at anchor and men were landing from the boats. The gondolas advanc'd a little and fired several shots at the guard boats and at the forts, whilst we sent them some howitz shells from one of the pieces of artillery which Captn. Williams had fixed so as to serve as a mortar." Wives and children were brought inside the fort and supplied with beds. But few blankets were to be had. A consignment on its way from Montreal never reached the fort — "a loss of great importance," André reminds us, "in a climate where the nights of September and October are as cold as those of the two succeeding months in England."

Next morning a party of rebels was reported west of the fort. Captain John Strong of the 26th went to investigate with a task force of regulars and French Canadian volunteers. Presently shots broke the early quiet. When Strong returned he brought grim news. He had routed the rebels, but while his men were demolishing an enemy breastwork he had been set upon by a large detachment of rebel troops, greatly outnumbering his own command. He had managed an orderly retreat, but the enemy had occupied the road to La Prairie and had cut Preston's supply line.

Preston had instructions to keep the enemy off balance by grabbing the initiative and mounting a series of surprise attacks. Instead, he stayed on the defensive, hoping to hold off the enemy until winter slowed hostilities. Most of his Indians went home, still bitter over the garrison's failure to send them support when the enemy first attacked. There was even talk of desertion among some of the French Canadian volunteers. And Montgomery sealed off the road to Chambly and stationed Colonel Seth Warner at Longueuil, across the St. Lawrence from Montreal, with a detachment of Green Mountain Boys and 2nd New Yorkers.

One morning an American bateau, torn from its mooring in a heavy rain, was washed ashore at St. John's. Its lone occupant, a frightened teen-aged recruit, told his captors that the Americans would soon acquire a new mortar, nicknamed "Old Sow," that would lob highly destructive, thirteen-inch shells. Even Preston's regulars were now on edge. When a sentry's challenge went unanswered one stormy night, shots were fired blindly into the darkness. "In the morning a horse was found dead," André writes. "This was the enemy that our sentry had seen and challeng'd."

André still played his flute on occasion and sketched likenesses of his fellow officers. But he was dismayed by what he saw. The rebels, after all, were fellow Englishmen. They were driving a wedge through Canadian society just as they had done in their own country. Among the French, neighbors and even families were divided. *Habitants,* formerly docile, had turned on their *seigneurs* and parish priests. English Canadians, too, were at loggerheads. Some, like the Royal Highland Emigrants, were loyal to king and Parliament, but others, in both Montreal and Quebec, openly supported Montgomery. Even the Indians were divided. The western tribes were loyal, but many of the Caughnawagas, who lived near Montreal, sided with the Americans. To André's way of thinking, this was an uncalled-for war, a clash of brothers. "Englishmen fighting against Englishmen," he laments, "French against French, and Indians of the same tribe against each other."

Preston still had the edge in firepower, but there were uneasy moments. Shots had landed in the north redoubt, even entering the staff room. Lieutenant Hunter's schooner, the *Royal Savage,* had been damaged. André refers to this as the "daily little cannonade," but no one could be sure when the enemy might score a telling hit.

One day some Indians, wreathed in smiles, came to the fort. Ethan Allen, they said, had tried to capture Montreal with a ragtag assortment of American and French Canadian troops. He had crossed the St. Lawrence by night and was awaiting reinforcements when a task force from the city descended on his command, put him to flight, and after a brief chase took him prisoner, along with most of his followers. He now lay in irons aboard a British brigantine. But the Indians also brought some alarming news. *Habitants* on the lower Richelieu were flocking in large numbers to Montgomery's banner.

Enemy artillery began to find the range. A Royal Highland Emigrant was killed, a sentry wounded. Heavier artillery had arrived from Ticonderoga, and a new battery opened fire from the east bank of the Richelieu. Early in October "Old Sow" opened up, ineffectually at first. "The witty observ'd the Sow had brought her pigs to a fine market," André says. But he overheard laughter in the rebel battery and admitted that "anything relating to the Sow was a better joke to them than to us." The joking stopped when the big mortar began to score. An officer in André's regiment was killed. A French volunteer had both legs blown off, a carpenter lost an arm. A shell toppled a chimney and reduced one of the barracks to "a pile of rubbish in which scarcely a habitable corner was to be found." As more shells found their mark, André's report turned grim and ominous:

> Our shatter'd house, together with the ruinous traverses and mud ditches, broken platforms, etc., exhibited a very ragged scene. Within doors, if that cou'd be called within doors where doors and windows were broken to pieces, the appearance was no better. Heaps of boards, earth, glass, brick and other rubbish lay promiscuously scatter'd. The rooms, by the partitions being broke, were mostly laid together, and the roof and ceiling were open on every side, especially where the shell had mark'd its path.

Food was running low. Shelter was lacking now, even for the wounded.

> Salt pork was our daily fare [André says], with sometimes a few roots, and we reduced ourselves about this time to ⅔ of the usual allowance. The men were many of them flux'd, yet enjoy'd, or rather, had better health than cou'd have been hop'd. The situation of the sick and wounded was a very cruel one. They were neither out of reach of danger, nor were they shelter'd from the inclemency of the weather, or provided with any of those things which might alleviate their sufferings. The weather grew very cold, and, as the windows of the house were all broken, as many as cou'd find room in the cellars slept there. The rest, unable either to get a place or to bear the heat and disagreeable smell arising from such numbers being crowded together, slept above in cold and danger, or walk'd about the greatest part of the night.

Some of the French volunteers deserted, singly or in small groups.

"The universal cry," André says, "was to go up with the vessels to attack the enemy and to send a party to land at the same time to spike their guns." But Hunter would not cooperate. He warped the *Royal Savage* near one of the redoubts, where American artillery found her range and sank her to the ports. When Preston made no secret of his disgust, Hunter declared huffily that, after "many years at sea," he could "rig a ship, navigate and maneuvre her" as capably as the next man. But he would not risk his remaining vessels.

There were further casualties — a fusilier, a mattross in the Royal Artillery. The rain had become "incessant," André says. "The weather began to be exceeding cold and the men to fall sick." Yet there were cheerful moments. A herd of cattle, loose in the vicinity, was driven triumphantly into the fort by Captain Monin and a troop of Royal Highland Emigrants. And "9 fat pigs came running toward the fort and were receiv'd with great cordiality."

One day rebel troops were seen threading through trees on the east bank of the Richelieu. Four days later shots were heard in the direction of Chambly. When two men showed up with a flag of truce they brought word of a most shameful defeat. Chambly had fallen to the enemy after the exchange of a few shots. Major Stopford had not only surrendered the fort to a mere handful of rebels, but he had turned over all the artillery and military stores. He requested safe passage for the enemy bateaux that would bring the wives and children of his troops to Montgomery's encampment. He and his men, now prisoners of war, would pass through on foot.

Preston was astonished at his colleague's failure to destroy the guns and ammunition, not to mention what had been scarcely a token defense of the supply depot. He may have taken comfort in the hard rain that fell. Joseph Stopford and his fellow officers, trudging upstream on foot, would get a thorough soaking.

Preston was nearly out of ammunition. "We fir'd little and only small shells," André says. On November 1 a third battery opened fire, lobbing shells into the fort at close range. Three men were killed, several wounded. "Large pieces of the wall were knock'd in," André continues. "The chimneys of the house in the small redoubt were thrown down, and the few corners where some little shelter from the weather was to be had were now no longer tenable."

That night Montgomery beat a parley. A Canadian prisoner, blindfolded and accompanied by a drummer, was led across the clearing to the gates. His name was Lacoste, he said, a hairdresser by trade. He had been captured at Longueuil, where British forces, on their way to relieve St. John's, had been turned back by Seth Warner's troops. Only a few Canadians and Indians had gotten ashore, and they had been speedily run down. Three or four Indians had been killed. Lacoste and another Canadian, Jean Baptiste Despins, had been taken prisoner.

Lacoste brought a message from General Montgomery, who suspected that some of the garrison's military stores had already been destroyed. This must cease, he warned, and the fort must be surrendered without delay. His message was curt and threatening: "Should you continue to destroy the stores and obstinately persist in a defense which cannot avail you, I will assemble the Canadians and shall deem myself innocent of the melancholy consequences which must attend it." If Preston doubted Lacoste's story, he might have one of his officers talk with Despins, now in custody aboard an American sloop.

Preston took advantage of the offer. He named André as his deputy and sent him upstream with a flag of truce. Upon reaching the enemy's encampment, André was blindfolded and led aboard the sloop where Despins was confined. Deep within the bowels of the vessel his blindfold was removed. He beheld a thoroughly cowed Canadian, shackled and under heavy guard. After a few words with the prisoner, he was convinced that Lacoste had told the truth. "There was now nothing left but to frame the best articles we cou'd for the garrison," he says.

Preston asked that his troops be permitted the honors of

war, that his British regulars be returned to England, and that an officer from each unit, in the capacity of quartermaster, be allowed to collect the men's baggage in Montreal. Montgomery granted the honors of war and pledged safe passage for the quartermasters. But he ruled that members of the garrison, British and Canadian alike, must go as prisoners of war to the colonies.

On November 3, a wet and blustery day, Preston led his men into the muddy clearing outside the fort. First came his own regiment, the 26th. It was followed by the 7th Foot, or Royal Fusiliers, John André among them. André gazed with scorn at the sloppily attired troops lined up like country yokels to witness the surrender. Such rank amateurs, he told himself, were a disgrace to any uniform. Captain Williams and the Royal Artillery followed, then Lieutenant Hunter with his pig-tailed tars, Captains Mackay and Monin with their proud-hearted Scots, and Picoté de Belestre with those who remained among the French volunteers. Last to emerge were the wives and children of British regulars, accompanied by a few ship's carpenters and artisans. As arms were grounded Montgomery announced that he would stretch the rules and allow Preston's officers to keep their swords. André was astonished. He had not expected this gesture from a man who, although he had once served with Wolfe and Amherst, was now a turncoat.

André was among the quartermasters sent to Montreal for the men's belongings. He found the city in a turmoil. Panicky citizens thronged the streets, or gathered at the waterfront seeking passage to Quebec. Carleton would describe them as "greatly frightened, both at the rebels in open arms without [the city], and at those traitors who by their art and insinuation are still more dangerous to the public safety." He had written off Montreal, ordering artillery spiked and ammunition destroyed. A vessel lay at anchor ready to hurry him to Quebec.

The quartermasters left Montreal with sixty wagonloads of baggage, including a supply of winter uniforms. They were

joined by the wives and children of some of Preston's regulars
whom an American chaplain saw as they trudged wearily into
St. John's. "Some of the regulars' wives and children this
morning came up from Montreal in a miserable plight," he
says. "Women badly clothed, children barefoot and almost
naked and covered with mud and water. My heart pitied them!"

Montgomery's soldiers eyed the wagonloads of clothing while
André and his colleagues transferred it to waiting bateaux.
Some of the enlisted men asked their officers if they might
appropriate the winter uniforms. When Montgomery forbade it, they threatened to disobey orders and seize the
clothing anyway. Anna Seward would declare that André
was "stript of everything" except Honora's picture, which
he hid in his mouth. But André himself testifies that there
was no plundering, that the rebels adhered to the surrender terms. Nor does he mention concealing Honora's picture
in his mouth — if, indeed, he had her likeness anywhere
on his person.

André was having his first good look at the rebel army. Both
officers and men impressed him as an ill-assorted, unschooled
lot, poorly disciplined and glaringly unprofessional. He gave
them no credit for taking St. John's, maintaining that the loss
was due solely to shortages of food and ammunition. "We may
thank our enemy in some sort," he writes, "for leaving us, in
such slight field works, the credit of having been only reduc'd
by famine." Nor had he changed his mind a year later, when
he spoke of the siege in a letter to his mother:

> I shall not enter into any detail of it, but be contented with
> telling you that, after two or three little skirmishes, we were
> pent up in small redoubts where we were annoyed with pitiful
> cannonadings and bombardments for seven weeks, at which
> time our provision of rusty bacon (whereof for three weeks we
> had been allowed but a scanty allowance) was entirely ex-
> hausted, our cannon likewise devoured their food, and our
> habitations were in ruins.

André had learned what war can be. He had endured cold and wet, fatigue and hunger. He had seen colleagues maimed and killed. He had known the shame of grounding arms in the presence of a despised foe. Yet he had no regrets. Although the fort had fallen, he was proud to have been part of what he deemed an honorable defeat.

A Different Drumbeat

ONE SUMMER DAY in 1775, Benjamin Tallmadge locked the schoolhouse door and left for his rented quarters on a tidy, tree-shaded street in Wethersfield, Connecticut. He stopped off at the town's general store. Other customers were there, but he paid no heed to their small talk. Going to an empty counter, he began a letter to his friend Nathan Hale, a schoolmaster like himself. Hale lived a few miles down the Connecticut River in the village of East Haddam.

> The great wheels of the State and Constitution seem to have grown old and crazy [Tallmadge wrote]. Everything bids fair for a change; every machine needs to be refitted and renewed. How soon a great, flourishing and powerful State may arise from that now stigmatized by the name of rebels, God only knows. The prospect, however, for the same seems to be great, but that we ought at present to desire it is far from being clear. We ought by all means to prepare for the worst, and then we may encounter danger with more firmness and with better prospects of success.

Hale and Tallmadge had been classmates at Yale, where they had studied Latin, Greek, and Hebrew, read the classics, reported without fail at early chapel, and complained with everyone else about the fare served them in the college commons. Upon graduating, both had become schoolmasters and been assigned to posts only a few miles apart.

After dispatching his letter to Hale, Tallmadge went to Cambridge to visit the American encampment. He was shocked to find the troops billeted in sailcloth tents, board shacks, and brush lean-tos. Miserably attired, many still in homespun, they took grudgingly to drill and showed scant respect for officers. Tallmadge located Captain John Chester, who had gone to Cambridge earlier that year with a company from Wethersfield. Chester told him that the mob gathered on Cambridge Common would never become an army until it attracted better officers. He hoped that Tallmadge would be among them.

When Tallmadge got home he wrote Nathan Hale that he had decided to enlist. But he did not urge Hale to do the same. In spite of the fact that "our holy religion, the honor of God, a glorious country and a happy constitution" were all at stake, he believed his friend's continuing as a schoolmaster served "just as good an end" as enlisting in the military. "Though we should be ready to step forth in the common cause," he said, "I could think it highly incumbent on you not to change your situation."

A whole year went by before Tallmadge would enlist, but Hale moved swiftly. Two days after Tallmadge wrote him, he was commissioned a lieutenant in the Connecticut militia.

IV

Friendly Quakers and
Worsted Stocking Knaves

Spray, torn from the lake by headwinds, pelted John André as his bateau nosed from the Richelieu into the choppy waters of Lake Champlain. He sat hunched and chilled, bundled unavailingly in a cloak. By the time he caught sight of Fort Ticonderoga he shook with cold.

Debarking at the fort, André was introduced to the commandant, Major General Philip Schuyler, who turned out to be a refreshingly civilized rebel after some of Montgomery's coarse-grained officers. Schuyler said he was returning to Albany next day. What he did not tell André was that he had been readying an inventory of the ordnance seized by Ethan Allen and his men when they captured the fort. The list included mortars, howitzers, coehorns, and assorted field pieces and was intended for Colonel Henry Knox, who was on his way from Cambridge to convey the artillery, by boat and ox cart, to Washington's army.

The next morning was glacially cold. By the time André and his boat crew had made the portage to Lake George, they had had enough of the knife-edged cold and hurriedly took refuge in a nearby inn. A sparsely furnished log building, it was already packed with travelers. The innkeeper informed André that he must share his bed with another guest, whom he introduced as Colonel Henry Knox of the Continental Artillery. Knox was a rotund, friendly looking officer of about André's age, and the two instantly hit it off. Like André, Knox had had a try at business before finding his niche in the military. He loved good books, had once operated a bookstore in Boston, and admitted to a liking for light verse. He shared André's keen interest in military science. We are told that the two conversed half the night, that Knox was impressed with André's fondness for the arts, André with Knox's familiarity with artillery and its uses. The night passed swiftly, and neither would forget the other.

André tarried nearly a month in Albany, assembling the baggage as it arrived piecemeal from Canada. He was an occasional guest at General Schuyler's table, for the urbane and hospitable Dutchman did not let the break with England prevent him from entertaining congenial prisoners of war. Schuyler still hoped for an early resolution of the conflict. He had given free rein to his thinking in a letter to his friend Jonathan Trumbull, governor of Connecticut:

> May heaven prove propitious that a speedy termination may be put to this afflicting controversy, and Britons and Americans once more regard each other with the fond tenderness of a parent and child, and jointly establish an empire on such a solid basis that no power on earth may be able to destroy it, and that it shall last until the omnipotent Being is pleased to blot out all the empires of the earth.

This was talk André relished. An evening in Schuyler's living room made the war seem more than ever a clash of brothers.

André saw much of Abraham Cuyler, the mayor of Albany and an outspoken champion of king and Parliament. Within six months of André's departure, Cuyler would stand accused of consorting with persons "unfriendly to the American cause," of making "artful and insinuating speeches" intended to "depreciate" the Continental currency, and of publicly declaring that the city would be a happier place if "twelve or fourteen" of its more prominent rebels were unceremoniously hanged. André has left us sketches of Cuyler and his wife, both looking grim and unbending.

When André was about to leave Albany he was told that his orders had been changed. Schuyler had indicated that the British officers would be interned in Connecticut, with the rank and file sent to Pennsylvania. But at the last minute the order was rescinded. All the prisoners, officers included, would go to Pennsylvania. André was to report at Lancaster, a town he had never heard of.

On his way down the Hudson, André was invited to the home of Colonel Hay of Haverstraw, who, like Schuyler, made a practice of hosting congenial prisoners of war. Among the guests gathered at Hay's table was Joshua Hett Smith, Hay's brother-in-law and a local attorney and landowner. He and André seem to have made no impression on each other. André would speedily forget Smith; nor would Smith remember André. When they met again a few years later, neither seems to have recognized the other.

Most of the prisoners crossed through northern New Jersey into Pennsylvania. Eyewitnesses tell of two large contingents that passed through Nazareth and Bethlehem, followed by their wives and children. André's more roundabout route took him through Philadelphia, where he conferred with David Franks, commissary to British prisoners and one of the city's foremost merchants. He was introduced to Franks's lively daughter Rebecca. Unlike her more circumspect father, who took care to stay scrupulously neutral, Rebecca made no effort to hide her politics. Her nimble wit and outrageous anecdotes were unsparing of the rebels. Through her offices, André made the acquaintance of another reigning belle, Peggy Shippen, whose look of blonde innocence brought out protective instincts in her many escorts. But Rebecca was more entertaining company. Before he left, André painted her picture, presenting it to her with a scrap of tender verse.

It was midwinter when André surrendered himself to the Lancaster authorities. "I will not go into or near any seaport town," he promised, "nor further than six miles' distance from the said Borough of Lancaster, without leave of the Continental Congress." Nor might he enter into a correspondence touching on the war or on the differences with Great Britain.

To André, Lancaster must have seemed a remote and forbidding outpost. Nearly seventy miles from Philadelphia, a whole world away from all that he associated with polite society, the town retained many reminders of its raw beginnings. The population included Quakers, Germans, and Scotch-Irish — the Quakers apt to be accommodating, the Germans not unfriendly, the Scotch-Irish hostile to a man. Although Major Preston and a few others had been sent to Reading, most of the officers and all the enlisted men were interned in Lancaster. The officers were lodged in downtown inns and taverns at their own expense. Since they had little ready cash and refused to draw bills of exchange that British banks might not honor, they were soon heavily in debt to uncooperative and resentful landlords.

The enlisted men were confined in dilapidated barracks dating back to the French and Indian War. Congress had forbidden the committee in charge of the prisoners to build a stockade around the buildings, hoping that this would encourage them to mix more readily with local patriots and perhaps become converts to the rebel cause. But the men remained loyal to king and country "with an extraordinary degree of firmness." They grumbled about the unappetizing food and drafty quarters and accused the committee of starving their wives and children, who were kept on paltry rations.

André's roommate, John Despard, was also a lieutenant in

the 7th Foot,* a veteran of fifteen years of soldiering. He had
enlisted as a mere lad and once, in the thick of battle, had
had the regimental standard shot from his grasp. André admired him for his many exploits, his tough professionalism.
The two quickly became inseparable and spent long hours
roaming the nearby hills together or idling on downtown streets
with fellow officers.

At liberty to go where he wished within the six-mile radius,
André became acquainted with several of the German settlers.
Although most of them favored independence and served in
the militia or on town committees, they felt only "affection
and high regard" for André according to Eberhart Michael,
one of their number. His familiarity with their homeland and
mastery of their native tongue won him demonstrations of
hospitality not extended to other prisoners.

André also got to know some of the Loyalists in town. If
he attended divine worship, he sought out St. James Church,
whose rector, the Reverend Thomas Barton, defied the threats
of strident patriots to preach loyalty to king and Parliament.
Although Barton had seen fellow Anglicans stoned, pelted
with mud, and ducked in mill ponds, he would not soften his
preaching. And André may have made himself known to Edward Shippen and Jasper Yeates, both members of the Committee of Safety and both related to Peggy Shippen. André
may have hoped they would help him locate in a private home,
for neither he nor Despard could abide their quarters in a
downtown tavern or their impatient landlord, who kept pressing them for £6.10.0 in back rent.

André's strongest ties were with the Cope family. Caleb
Cope, a plasterer by trade, was a Quaker who both took his
pacifism seriously and showed a gentle forbearance toward the

---

*Not to be confused with his brother, Edward Marcus Despard, who made an attempt
on the life of George IV and was drawn and quartered for treason.

prisoners of war. In the bosom of Cope's family André found surcease from the chilly stares and harsh mutterings of local patriots. Cope may have offered to provide lodgings for him and Despard, for André was among those who petitioned the Committee of Safety for a change of residence. Might they transfer to the homes of persons willing to take them in? Although slow in responding, the committee finally issued a list of persons who had agreed to house the prisoners on condition that they have their midday meal and supper at a common mess. Cope took in André and Despard, an act of hospitality not without consequences. One night a mob stoned his house, smashing windows and terrifying the family. But Cope would not budge. Both André and Despard remained under his roof.

John André became a favorite of all the Copes. He taught the children games, joined them at marbles, and made a protégé of twelve-year-old John Cope, the eldest son, who showed a flair for drawing. André schooled him in the rudiments of composition, explained perspective, and taught him how to sketch from life. Before long, other neighborhood lads joined the art classes. Benjamin Smith Barton, son of the Tory rector and subsequently a well-known scientist, is said to have been a pupil. Another may have been young Robert Fulton of later steamboat fame, also a native son. But John Cope was André's pride and joy. He even offered to take the lad to England for professional training, although it could mean his selling his commission. But Caleb would have none of it. He wanted John at home, where he could learn a trade and help support the family.

André was not long at the Copes'. The town fathers, at their wits' end to care for so many prisoners, asked that the officers be transferred to more remote communities, where "their opportunities of doing mischief [would] less correspond to their inclinations." Congress gave its consent, and André and Despard were among ten officers assigned to Carlisle, a frontier village forty miles west of Lancaster.

The Copes hated to see André leave. For John Cope, it was like losing an older brother. André left him one of his prized drawings. It showed a thatched English cottage beneath lush shade trees — a reminder of his own boyhood among gentler and friendlier surroundings.

One day in late March 1776, the prisoners filed out of town under a heavy guard. For all of them this was a transfer to an alien and menacing world. During a short stopover in York, André was the guest of the Reverend John Andrews, rector of St. John's Church and, like Thomas Barton, a friend to prisoners of war. But no such hospitality awaited him in Carlisle, where he had hoped to find lodgings with a family like the Copes. He was informed that no citizen would dare risk the opprobrium sure to descend on him if he opened his doors to a British officer. The prisoners must be billeted in public lodging places. André and Despard were assigned quarters in a bleak downtown tavern.

Carlisle, staked out only a few years before André saw it, straddled the wagon road to Fort Pitt and the western frontier. Residents could remember when war whoops had terrorized the countryside, when scorched clearings and blackened cellar holes had marked the warpath of rampaging Indians. Now all this was changed. The town had become a jumping-off place at the threshold to the Ohio country, to all of Kentucky, to the sparsely peopled hinterland west of the Alleghenies. Conestoga wagons rattled over the roadways carrying homesteaders whose numbers would swell to more than 25,000 before the Revolution ended. André beheld sights that would usher in a whole new age and transform a continent, but he probably attached no significance to any of it. That it had a connection with the war for independence never occurred to him.

André found Carlisle "inhabited by a stubborn, illiberal crew call'd the Scotchirish." Many of its sons had flocked to Cambridge Common, and a company of riflemen, led by Captain William Hendricks, had joined Arnold's march to Quebec. Carlisle took great pride in its riflemen, all of them schooled since boyhood in the use of their long, ungainly weapons. Attired in leather-fringed hunting shirts, leather breeches, moccasins, and wide-brimmed hats, they shouldered rifles that possessed an accuracy that no musket could match. It was said that one officer required his recruits to hit a target the size of a man's nose from a distance of a hundred yards. The British would learn to fear "these shirt-tail men with their cursed, twisted guns" and would pronounce them "the most fatal widow-and-orphan makers in the world." André watched them loping through town — a menacing lot, rude toward British prisoners.

André found no peace-loving Quakers in Carlisle, no friendly Germans with whom he could break bread and socialize. He did, however, make the acquaintance of "two or three families" willing to accord him a cautious welcome. Among them were the mother and sister of Samuel Smith, his shipboard companion on the *St. George.* With the seacoast under attack, they had left Baltimore for safer habitations. "I am highly obliged for their attention," he wrote his mother, "and the more so, as it drew great odium and much invective upon themselves."

Carlisle was a place of lonely exile for anyone as sociable as John André. He wrote Eberhart Michael that he could never start a conversation with a stranger — "generally no good results from it, nothing but uncivil and hostile answers." When he ventured outside his lodgings, people kept their distance. Few extended a greeting, and some returned his gaze with a look of glacial hatred. He and Despard had acquired fowling pieces and a pair of bird dogs. They devoted their days to the pursuit of upland game, their evenings to what books they had and to playing flute duets. He wrote Eberhart Michael that they spent their time "making music, reading books," and dreaming about their "liberation."

André exchanged several letters with Caleb Cope. In one

he asked if John might join Despard and himself in Carlisle. He said he would find him bed and board, but he could not promise a "quiet, honest family of Friends" like the Copes, for there were no such people in Carlisle.

> He will be the greatest part of the day with us, employ'd in the few things I am able to instruct him in [he wrote Caleb]. In the meanwhile I may get better acquainted with the town and provide for his board. With regard to expense, this is to be attended with none to you. A little assiduity and friendship is all I ask in my young friend in return for my good will to be of service to him in a way of improving the talents Nature hath given him. I shall give all my attention to his morals, and as I believe him well dispos'd, I trust he will acquire no bad habits here.

Caleb turned down the offer. John was only a lad, he said, and was needed at home. But he sent on a few samples of John's work. In returning them, André enclosed an assessment of his pupil's progress:

> He is greatly improv'd since I left Lancaster, and I do not doubt but if he continues his application he will make a very great progress. . . . Let him go on copying whatever good models he can meet with and never suffer himself to neglect the proportions and never think of finishing the work, or imitating the fine flowing lines of his copy, till every limb, feature, house, tree or whatever he is drawing is in its proper place. With a little practice this will be so natural to him that his eye will at first sight guide his pencil in the exact distribution of every part of the work.

By now André was thankful that John had not come. He wrote Caleb that he and Despard had "been submitted to alarms and jealousies which would have rendered his stay here very disagreeable to him, and I would not willingly see any person suffer on our account." The troubles sprang from the failure of the Canadian campaign. Captain Hendricks, pride of the region, had fallen at Quebec. His riflemen had languished all winter in a Quebec jail. During the retreat that spring, two from Carlisle, General William Thompson and Colonel William Irvine, had been taken prisoner. Carlisle seemed to be singled out for misfortune.

An American defeat known as the Cedars incident topped the list of disasters. Nearly five hundred Americans had been captured at a weakly fortified outpost west of Montreal. Rumor had it that some of the men had been butchered by Carleton's Indians. When the atrocity stories reached Carlisle, André and his fellow officers were vilified for the uniform they wore. They were suspected of espionage, were accused of encouraging their servants to act as spies and secret agents, and of turning "weak and ignorant persons" against Congress. Many citizens wanted them placed under instant house arrest.

Elsewhere, too, the war was going badly. With a British fleet off Sandy Hook, coastal communities were fearful of a thrust inland by British troops. When Congress called for the formation of a flying camp, the chairman of Carlisle's Committee of Safety pledged five companies. "The spirit of marching to the defense of our country is so prevalent in this town that we shall not have men left sufficient to mount guard," he declared. André may have paid little heed to what was brewing in Philadelphia, but he could not have missed the grim satisfaction in people's faces when word came that the Declaration of Independence had been adopted and signed.

One day a Mrs. Ramsay, who lived across the street from André and Despard, caught sight of the pair conversing with two strangers on a street corner. Sure that dark deeds were in the making, she got in touch with the Committee of Safety, which sent out a posse to overhaul the strangers. They were apprehended near the edge of town and found to have two letters in their possession, both signed by André. But, alas, the letters were in French, and no one could read them. The strangers were clapped in jail, and André and Despard were forbidden to set foot outside town. No more roaming the hills for the pair, with dog and gun. In retaliation, each smashed his fowling piece. "No damned rebel shall ever burn powder in them!" André vowed. He is described as spending the next few days staring glumly out the window, while "his two beautiful pointer dogs laid their heads at his feet."

But Mrs. Ramsay would prove a surprise to the two officers. One night a Captain Thompson, formerly apprenticed to her husband, called out his troops and ordered an advance on André's quarters. Assembling his men under the window of his intended victim, he shouted menacingly for blood. Both André and Despard had drawn their swords when Mrs. Ramsay stepped into the breach. Wagging her forefinger under Thompson's nose, she advised him to take his troops elsewhere on the double. Thompson is said to have quailed and to have ordered an immediate about-face. "You may thank my old mistress for your lives!" he shouted in André's direction. As a mark of their appreciation, the two officers sent Mrs. Ramsay a box of spermaceti candles. But she returned the offering. It was not her habit, she said, to accept favors from the enemy.

André, more than the other prisoners, seems to have grated on Carlisle's patriots. They could abide men like Despard, tough career officers who spoke and behaved in a way they could appreciate. But André, with his urbane manner and aesthetic tastes, was an alien in their midst, an affront to their rough-hewn patriotism. It was no accident that Captain Thompson had singled him out, or that a company of militia, passing through Carlisle, had fired shots through his window. What he was witnessing, he now realized, was no family quarrel, no clash of brothers. This involved another breed, men who no longer thought of themselves as Englishmen.

André still heard from Caleb Cope, who forwarded several more of John's drawings. André appraised them critically.

He must take particular care in forming the features in faces and in copying hands exactly [he commented]. He shou'd now and then copy things from life and then compare the proportions with what points he may know, or what rules he may have remember'd. With respect to his shading with India ink, the anatomical figure is tolerably well done, but he wou'd find his work smoother and softer were he to lay the shades on more gradually, not blackening the darkest at once but washing them over repeatedly, and never till the paper is quite dry.

In closing, he said he had heard talk of a possible prisoner exchange. "If this shou'd be without foundation, I should be very glad to see your son here," he said.

One morning late in November, the prisoners were assembled under close guard and marched out of town, with no hint given of their destination. When the column bore eastward, André felt a great surge of relief. They were pointed toward the British lines. Somewhere along the way he got off a last letter to Caleb Cope. There was no mention this time of taking John to England, or of an early resumption of the art lessons. "Perhaps the face of affairs may so far change that he may once again be within my reach," he said, "when it will be a very great pleasure to me to give him what assistance I can." As of now, John must develop on his own.

André would never again lay eyes on the Cope family. Long afterward Thomas Cope, John's younger brother, would speak fondly of André and of how the whole family came to love him.

He resided in my father's house on the most intimate and familiar footing [Thomas writes]. His very engaging and amiable manners, added to the goodness of his heart and the brilliant accomplishments of his mind, induced in all our family a fervent affection for his person and a high interest in his fortunes.

Thomas faults his ironhanded father for not allowing John

to join André in Carlisle. "Neither argument, solicitation nor tears availed," he says. "He would not part with his favourite child, and André, when exchanged, was compelled to leave his friend behind him." On one occasion John started for New York, where André was stationed, only to be summoned home by his father. Thomas says that "John suffered the mortification of being brought back and the bitter anguish of seeing his schemes of future greatness and happiness blighted by what he deemed a cruel interposition of parental authority." John would grow up to become the family ne'er-do-well.

> The palette and pencil were thrown aside [Thomas writes]. In contemplation of what actually was, contrasted with what he probably would have been had the early bent of his genius and inclination been properly cultivated, I cannot refrain from the indulgence of some melancholy, though perhaps useless, regrets and reflections.

At an inn near Pottstown André's party waited out a snow-storm that blocked roads and stranded travelers. The inn-keeper's niece would remember how he spent his days bent over maps on which he was working, and how when evening came he would turn merrily to his flute. She would remember, too, that he alone among the prisoners never vilified the rebels.

Crossing into New Jersey, the officers and their guards encountered small, disorganized bands of Continental troops streaming toward the Delaware. The rebels had lost Long Island and New York, had evacuated Fort Washington and Fort Lee. Washington speaks of a British officer thought to have infiltrated his ranks during the retreat. He did not know the man's identity, other than that he was a lieutenant in the 7th Foot. Was this John André? And what about the maps he was preparing at the inn near Pottstown?

The prisoners were exchanged at New Brunswick. André left immediately for New York, where he hurried off a long letter to his mother. He refers bitterly to Carlisle's "greasy committee of worsted stocking knaves [who] pestered us with resolves and ordinances meant to humiliate us and exalt themselves." Their harassment took many forms.

> Sometimes they enacted penal statutes binding us to be at home at such and such hours on pain of imprisonment, at other times broke open our letters and withheld them, or, finding us guilty of some misdemeanor, attempted to extort concessions before their tribunal. The gaol was constantly threatened, and we had examples enough to judge how well disposed they were to put their threats into execution. I was lucky enough never to see the inside of this kind of edifice but in visiting friends.

Nor were Carlisle's plain citizens any improvement on their officials:

> We were every day pelted and reviled in the streets [André writes], and have been oftentimes invited to smell a brandished hatchet and reminded of its agreeable effects on the skull, receiving at the same time promises that we would be murdered the next day. Several of us have been fired at, and we have more than once been waylaid by men determined to assassinate us, and escaped by being warn'd to take different roads. Such is the brotherly love they, in our capitulation, promised us.

André assures his mother that his troubles are now over. He is the guest of Captain Thomas Hesketh, an officer in the 7th Foot.

> My situation is so new to me [he says], that, free as I am, I scarcely dare trust my pen to its former license, but ever imagine suspicious committees may intercept my letter and make me suffer for my indiscretion. You may conclude my carcass to be very safe for this winter, and as I have some regard for myself, you may depend on it I shall do my utmost to make myself as happy and comfortable as I can.

A *Different Drumbeat*

GENERAL WILLIAM HOWE studied the young rebel who
stood before him, unflinching and erect. He looked about
twenty years old and about six feet tall. He was attired as a
Dutch schoolmaster, but papers on his person showed that he
was Nathan Hale, a captain in the Continental Army. He had
crossed Long Island Sound, made his way in disguise through
the British lines, and tried to convey secret information to the
enemy. General Howe ordered him hanged.

Hale was taken to a greenhouse near Howe's headquarters
and placed under close guard. His request for a chaplain was
ignored. So, too, was his plea for a Bible. Next morning he
was transferred to the tent of Captain John Montresor, Howe's
engineer, and allowed to write two letters, one to a member
of his family, the other to a fellow officer. Neither communication ever arrived.

Just before eleven in the morning on September 22, 1776,
Hale was taken from Montresor's tent to a tree near the artillery park. A fire had swept New York, and the air smelled
of charred wood. Witnesses to the execution included the
provost guard, a few officers and enlisted men, and a knot of
curious camp followers. Hale was pinioned and allowed to
utter his last words: "I only regret that I have but one life to

lose for my country." Then he was hanged and buried without ceremony.

Benjamin Tallmadge learned of his friend's death at an American encampment north of the city. First reports were sketchy and garbled, but as the pieces came together he understood that Nathan Hale had died well.

Imposing capital punishment for espionage was a relatively new development. Indeed, the Continental Congress had not authorized it until late in 1775. During the summer following Hale's death the British began sending out low-level civilian spies from New York, greatly to the annoyance of American commanders. Lord Stirling (an American general who laid claim to a Scottish earldom) hanged a suspected spy at his own doorstep. And one Edmund Palmer, a lieutenant in a Tory regiment, was captured by General Putnam's troops and, in spite of threats of retaliation, hanged as a spy. Espionage had become a deadly business.

V

Lessons from a Cold-blooded Chief

THE WAR seemed all but won. The rebels were "perfidious dastards," André wrote his mother, "driven from a labyrinth of citadels by much inferior numbers to their own." Howe's troops had followed the Continentals across New Jersey, establishing garrisons from the Hackensack to the Delaware.

But on Christmas night Washington struck back. Crossing the Delaware, he reoccupied Trenton without losing a man. Then he routed the enemy at Princeton, forging northward to Morristown. In a matter of days Howe had lost all of New Jersey except a toehold at New Brunswick and Perth Amboy. Yet he took the situation calmly. While serving in Parliament, he had told his constituents that he wanted no part in an American war. Now that he was involved in one, he seemed unfazed by day-to-day reverses.

When officers of the 7th Foot were ordered home to push enlistments, André switched regiments and bought a captaincy in the 26th. Eager to serve with Howe, preferably as an aide, he offered his services as an interpreter for the German mercenaries who were swelling British ranks. German dukes and princes, in need of funds to shore up the economy of their domains, had agreed to supply several thousand mercenaries at so much a head. Hessians and Brunswickers, Anspachers and Waldeckers, were pouring into New York by the shipload. Some were career men from ducal armies, others the flotsam of towns and cities, still others guileless farm boys collared by recruiting agents. Since many spoke only their native tongue, André's fluent German commended him signally to headquarters.

> I am now putting my irons in the fire [he wrote his mother].
> My wishes are to be attached as an aide-de-camp to some one
> of our commanders, for which my understanding German qual-
> ifies me (if I were equal in other respects) in preference to
> most others. I believe my name has 'ere this hour been men-
> tioned to Genl. Howe.

André joined his new regiment on Staten Island. He was billeted in the same inn as Captain John Graves Simcoe of the 40th Foot, a chunky, tart-tongued officer who had served with Gage in Boston and who had a monumental scorn for rebels. He and André soon became close friends.

Before reporting to the 26th, André submitted an account of his travels across New Jersey, together with the maps that had caught the eye of the innkeeper's niece. If it was indeed he who had made his way through Washington's ranks, his report received unusually close attention. Howe found it "exceedingly able and intelligent" and may have been even more impressed with the bundle of maps. André wrote his mother that his future boded "nothing but good."

Howe had in mind a grand strategy that should lead to peace negotiations. An army based in Rhode Island would advance on Boston, a second army would join forces with an expedition descending from Canada by way of Lake Champlain, while a third would occupy Philadelphia. A final thrust would take Virginia, South Carolina, and Georgia. But the plan must await milder weather. In the meantime, Washington was attacking outposts and supply lines in New Jersey.

> For these two months, or nearly, have we been boxed about
> in Jersey, as if we had no feelings! [exclaimed an exasperated
> redcoat]. Our cantonments have been beaten up; our foraging

parties attacked, sometimes defeated, and the forage carried off from us; all traveling between the posts hazardous and, in short, the troops harassed beyond measure by continual duty.

In the spring Howe struck back, urged on by a colleague who had come to America to thrash the rebels, not coax them toward a reconciliation. General Charles Grey had won his spurs at Minden, had campaigned on the Continent and in the West Indies, had twice been wounded in the king's service. Thin-faced and thin-lipped, he put no faith in peace talks. André was named his aide-de-camp.

As he had done for Major Preston, André kept a journal for his new chief. He describes Howe's advance into New Jersey against an elusive and exasperating foe. "They attacked the Light Infantry," he says of one engagement, "but were immediately driven back; they, however, shifted their position from one thicket to another and hung on the flanks and rear for some distance." After harassing Howe's column, they would beat a retreat to nearby hills, a tactic maddening to British regulars trained to stand their ground on Europe's open battlefields.

> Our progress in the Jerseys was from Amboy to Brunswick and thence to Hillsborough on the Millstone Creek [André wrote Major Preston]. There we remained a few days viewing Mr. Washington's advanced posts on the top of the blue mountains, but as he did not chuse to appear in the plain, and possibly as it was thought not practicable to come at him in his fastnesses, the army marched back to Brunswick and thence to Amboy, where preparations were making for conveying the troops and baggage to Staten Island.

As he was about to embark his troops, Howe had a brief skirmish with the enemy, who had left their "fastnesses" to attack the British rear. "We took three pieces of cannon and about a hundred prisoners, and did a little mischief besides with bayonets and sabres," André writes. Already he sensed

Grey's approval, and his matter-of-fact reference to "a little mischief" done with sword and bayonet should commend him even more to his new chief.

> I have the pleasure to find myself possessed of some share of the General's good will and confidence [he wrote home], and to live, I may really say, upon the most friendly footing with him. He is high in the esteem of the army, and with reason, so that improvement is not the only advantage I enjoy in this family.*

Early in June, Howe embarked his troops for a destination known only to himself and a few colleagues. His transports rode at anchor for nearly two weeks in the summer heat, packed with men and horses. On the 20th he gave orders to weigh anchor, but his flotilla, totaling 267 sail, did not clear New York Harbor until the 23rd. To nearly everyone's surprise, the ships set their course for Philadelphia. Months before, Howe had written Lord Germain proposing this strategic thrust, "the opinions of the people being changed in Pennsylvania, and their minds in general, from the late progress of the army, disposed to peace, in which sentiment they would be confirmed by our getting possession of Philadelphia." To be sure, General John Burgoyne was on his way from Canada at the head of another expedition, but Howe believed his colleague should have no trouble taking Fort Ticonderoga and forging southward to Albany. He left General Henry Clinton in New York with some seven thousand men, ready to push upstream in support of Burgoyne's army.

Before sailing, André made his will, bequeathing £700 each to his brother and three sisters, with smaller sums to his friends Walter and John Ewer, and requesting that William and his sisters pay their mother ten pounds annually throughout her life. He bequeathed his watch to Walter Ewer and deputized

---

*Grey's staff.

him to take charge of his papers in event of death. A cherished ring was bequeathed to Lieutenant Peter Boissier, another friend.

André was keeping a managerial eye on William, for he was determined that his younger brother should follow him into the military. He urged that William continue "polishing and accomplishing himself" when he finished his formal schooling. William seems to have gone along with the idea. At John André's behest, he purchased a lieutenancy in the 7th Foot.

Howe had no sooner put to sea than he ran into contrary winds and interminable calms. Whole days were lost while his ships lay motionless, turning hot as ovens. Men collapsed from heatstroke. Horses perished in their stalls. "If I could own the whole of America," declared one German recruit, "I would refuse if I had to live in these hot regions!" When Howe reached the Delaware he was too late to mount a surprise attack. "Had our passage been more successful," he wrote Clinton, "we might possibly have landed in the Delaware in time to have gotten between the Susquehanna and Mr. Washington's army, which there would not now be the slightest prospect of." Putting about, he set his course for the Chesapeake.

Smoke signals warned of Howe's coming as his fleet turned into Chesapeake Bay. A row galley got off a few harmless shots, and at Annapolis a work crew could be detected, speeding construction on a new battery. But not a shot came from shore. Howe continued to the Elk River, where he transferred his troops to flatboats and pushed upstream. Houses stood vacant, barn doors hung open. There was hardly a person to be seen. André says that the few who showed themselves were "frightened people who probably had not had time to make their escape." He was impressed by the lush vegetable gardens, teeming orchards, and fields of corn "ten to fifteen feet in height." This was indeed a land of plenty. His friend

Colonel John Bird led a foraging expedition that yielded great quantities of flour and garden produce, as well as sheep, beef cattle, and ten dozen horses to replace the many that had died at sea.

The enemy was first caught sight of near Head of Elk, where a cluster of rebel officers was seen scrutinizing the British column through spyglasses. According to Howe's German aide-de-camp, they assessed the British "as carefully as we observed them." One rebel officer, "dressed unobtrusively in a plain grey coat," was thought to be Washington himself. Soon afterward, Howe's advance guard was fired on from behind trees and thickets. "We first drew blood not far from the Elk," André reports. The rebel marksmen, who were quickly dispersed, belonged to "a corps from which great exertions were to be expected" and had steeled themselves, André was told, with "an extraordinary quantity of strong liquor."

By September 8, Howe was close to Chadd's Ford on the Brandywine, where Washington had deployed his troops. He set forth in the dark of early morning, the sky still pulsating with northern lights, as men and horses picked their way along rutted, barely distinguishable roads. A ground fog shrouded Brandywine Creek as he looped north to attack the Americans from the rear, while General Wilhelm von Knyphausen, his Hessian colleague, advanced with a smaller column on Chadd's Ford.

> The design [André explains] was that General Knyphausen, taking post at Chadd's Ford, should begin early to cannonade the enemy on the opposite side, thereby to take up his attention and make him presume an attack was then intended by the whole army, whilst the other column should be performing the detour.

The stratagem worked, as André gleefully reports. "Knyphausen's feint so perfectly answered the purpose of amusing them that they were vain enough to send expresses to Philadelphia that they had stopped the British Army." Then Howe struck from the rear. Washington's outwitted field officers managed "to drag their unwilling myrmidons to several commanding heights, rising amphitheatrically one above the other," only to be routed by the British. "Our men, jaded with a long march, loaded with knapsacks, unrefreshed by any halt, drove them from wood to wood on every side. The other part of the army under Gen. Knyphausen at the same time crossed Chadd's Ford and drove all before them." André's own regiment, kept in reserve, had had no part in the engagement, but he took pride in the showing made by other units. Washington, he wrote his mother,

> had in an involved rhapsody spirited up his men to a belief that they were to exterminate the British Army, and the resolution was formed to stand a battle. I believe they never had been wound up to such a pitch of confidence. They credited the most preposterous accounts of our weakness and dispirited state.

André gloated over their defeat.

But not all was as André would have had it. He noted that five captured field pieces and many small arms were of French manufacture — testimony to what could soon become a formal alliance. Nor did the rebels seem much shaken by their defeat. Flocking to nearby Chester, they promptly regrouped. As Washington would stress in his report of the battle, "Our troops have not lost their spirits, and I am in hopes we shall soon have an opportunity of compensating for the disaster we have sustained."

Before crossing the Schuylkill, Washington detached Anthony Wayne with fifteen hundred men to harass the British column. "Wayne came within 4 miles of us," André writes, "and adopted a plan of watching our motions and attacking our baggage or infesting our rear on the march." To put a halt to the mischief-making, Howe ordered out General Grey with two regiments of foot and a battalion of light infantry. Grey had his men remove the flints from their muskets. Not a sound must betray his approach, and he would depend solely on the bayonet. "It was represented to the men that firing discovered us to the enemy," André explains. "By not firing, we knew the foe to be wherever fire appeared, and a charge ensured their destruction."

Grey struck in the dead of night, with André at his side. In a single, terse sentence André describes what followed: "We ferreted out their piquets and advanced guards, surprised and put them to death, and, coming in upon the camp, rushed on them as they were collecting together and pursued them with a prodigious slaughter." A great number perished on the spot. Many others were overhauled and butchered as they fled. André tells us that the triumphant British refreshed themselves on some "good gin" discovered at the campsite.

André seems to have had no qualms about his part in the slaughter:

> I am extremely well and in the most happy situation with my General, who improves upon acquaintance and whom I esteem and am attached to more and more every day [he wrote his mother]. I believe I am fortunate enough to meet with his good will in return. He is much respected in the army, and this last coup has gained him much credit. I must be vain enough to tell you that he seemed satisfied with my assistance and that he thanked me in the warmest terms.

With Grey as teacher, he was no longer the gentle Cher Jean who had graced "the dear blue region" and offered his hand to Honora. Nor did it bother him that his chief was dubbed "No-Flint Grey" by outraged Americans.

On September 26, Howe's colleague, Lord Cornwallis, marched into Philadelphia at the head of British and Hessian troops. Rebecca Franks and Peggy Shippen may have been among the exultant Loyalists who cheered his entry. The prospect of British gallants paying them court all winter had both girls atingle with excitement.

André was quartered in Germantown in what he describes as "a most sumptuous house." In a letter to his mother, he admits to being "quite spoiled as a soldier." He anticipated her disapproval of the way he managed William's life.

> You will ere this have learnt the step I took with regard to William [he writes], and, altho' perhaps it may have given you a momentary dissatisfaction, I am confident you will not blame me, but perhaps be glad you have been in some measure forced into complying with a thing you must feel the expediency of. . . . I hope to see him here before winter sets in and, if in the same place, I doubt not but he will meet with great civility from Gen. Grey.

But the prospect of his mother's disapproval weighed on him.

> Beauclerc is arrived [he wrote his sister Louisa], but I have not yet seen him. I hope to hear something of William by him. I am extremely impatient to hear from England in answer to the letters which informed you of what I did with respect to him. I cannot repent the step which I think was taken at a critical time and will make him happy in the accomplishment of his wishes, yet I fear reproaches from my Mother which would be a great drawback on his satisfaction and mine.

Indeed, Marie Louise had counted on William's serving an apprenticeship in the family business and taking responsibility for the Grenada holdings. But John André would not hear of it:

> I do not dispute that his making himself familiar with pen and ink matters may be useful, but consider the lost time, the danger of his falling into bad company, the expense and the dissatisfaction it would have given him. It would likewise be a long time before he could have taken anything on himself with respect to Grenada affairs.

He himself would keep an eye on the properties. William, he assumed, was cut out for the military and must be rescued from the family counting rooms at Warnford Court.

Marie Louise had spoken of a projected vacation in France with John's sisters, but he questions the wisdom of removing them, since they are now of marriageable age, from the reach of prospective suitors.

> Your tour of France is a very good scheme [he allows], setting aside that it withdraws my sisters from all chance of prefer-ment. You can judge of those matters best *en famille*. What think you of William and I coming to see you in some retreat of that kind? *Il ne coute rien de faire des châteaux en Espagne.*

When the war was won, and this could not be far distant, a furlough in Europe would suit both William and himself.

> I am acquainted with nobody in that country [he wrote Louisa], unless you penetrate near Strasbourg, where I have a sort of flame, Mlle. de Welling, whom I recommend to your notice. She was once maid of honor to the Watch princess [a princess at whose court he had been presented with a gold watch]. Those were different times. We have no princesses here or maids of honor, unless it be of the Indian tribe, smeared with bear grease and vermillion, but these are more likely to steal watches than to give them.

On the first day of October, Washington attacked, forging into Germantown under cover of a thick, early morning fog. Six British companies holed up in Clivedon, the great stone house belonging to the Chew family. With their commanding officer, Colonel Thomas Musgrave, they would turn back charge after charge while the battle spread through fog-shrouded streets. André was at Grey's side as their troops deflected a thrust at the British center, then shifted ground to reinforce the right flank, "rushing up the streets," he writes, "scrambling thro' gardens and orchards under a pretty heavy fire." The fighting gave way to pandemonium as Washington's troops mistook friend for foe in the swirling fog. The Americans' flank was turned. Presently they were in headlong retreat, four hours after mounting their attack. André had been in the thick of battle. His mount had been struck by five shotgun pellets. "I wish I had received them myself, to make people stare with the story of 5 wounds in one day!" he exulted. But he was sobered by what he saw at Clivedon: "The house pierced with hundreds of shot, both cannon and musketry, with the dead and wounded within and without, told its story without the necessity of comment."

Washington took pride in Germantown in spite of the retreat. There were those who considered it on a par with Trenton — proof that Americans could hold their own against professional soldiers. André did not agree. He criticized Washington's strategy as too "complicated" for troops lacking in spirit, as he claimed, and plied with strong drink: "Their disposition for the attack . . . seems to have been too complicated, nor do their troops appear to have been sufficiently animated for the execution of it in every part, altho' the power of strong liquor was employed." His criticism was not unwarranted, for Washington had attempted a coordinated advance by four columns of inexperienced soldiers on a fogbound morning. But for André the war was hitting home. Among the dead was Colonel John Bird, one of his good friends.

Howe had yet to win the Delaware, where a fort on Mud Island barred the passage of British ships. André describes the methodical reduction of the fort in a letter home: "I used every morning to attend and take a peculiar delight in the clatter, nothing being so pleasant to behold as battles when one is an unconcerned spectator." And to his sister Louisa, a more detailed account:

The whole of our business has been reducing about a dozen acres of mud which had very impertinently started up in the

River Delaware and proudly assumed the name of an island. On this the Rebels had a fort which presented very uncivil batteries towards the channel thro' which ships were obliged to pass to come to Philadelphia. In this channel were sunk chevaux de frize. After a constant petard for several weeks we redoubled our noise and brought a ship or two thro' . . . to bear upon a defenseless part, and at length so battered the unfortunate fortress that the garrison set fire to the buildings and quitted it. A few days after, they also set fire to and abandoned about 15 sail of ships, floating batteries, etc., and left us masters of the navigation of the river.

Early in December, Howe advanced on Whitemarsh, where Washington was encamped, only to have a change of heart and return, without getting off a shot, to Philadelphia. André declares that the withdrawal was well advised, since to attack would have entailed undue risk. But Washington would heap scorn on his fainthearted opponent: "Gen. Howe, after making great preparations and threatening to drive us beyond the mountains, came out with his whole force last Thursday evening and, after maneuvering round us till the Monday following, decamped very hastily and marched back to Philadelphia."

André was pleased with the course the war was taking. He was much jolted when word came of General Burgoyne's surrender at Saratoga, but he considered this no more than a momentary setback. Howe had everything in his favor — a well-supplied army, every possible strategic advantage, widespread civilian support, and now Philadelphia, the rebels' seat of government and a once proud city. The rebels, on the other hand, were short of supplies, thinly dressed, with enlistments down and with Scotch-Irish recruits, "the only men they can rely on," no longer immigrating to America. André wished Sir William would crack down on those who supplied the rebel army. He had heard that the Continental Dragoons were stopping farm wagons bound for Philadelphia, that persons caught supplying the British were promptly shot. He wished Howe would do the same. If suppliers were "reduced to the agree-able alternative of choosing by whom they would be hanged, principle alone must turn the scale." Moreover, fire would be a telling weapon, applied to the homes and cornfields of rebel sympathizers. "Have we not fire as well as sword, a means yet untried?" he asks, with a pitilessness that would have pleased Charles Grey.

A Christmas snowstorm grounded both armies. André looked forward to a lively winter in Philadelphia, taking advantage of any spare time he might have to polish and revise his journal. His prospects had never been so bright. In a letter to Louisa, he speaks of his indebtedness to his chief:

> Gen. Grey shows me continually the greatest marks of friend-ship and will, I am persuaded, take the first opportunity of favouring my advancement. He gives the intercourse I have with him the most familiar and friendly turn and, I assure you, makes me as happy in his company as in that of my equals.

André was relishing his life of ease, at a safe distance from the skirmishes with enemy patrols outside the city.

> The only hardships I endure [he writes], are being obliged to sleep in my bed, to sit down to a very good dinner every day, to take a gentle ride for appetite's sake or to exercise my horses, to gossip in Philadelphia, or to consider something fashionable to make me irresistible this winter. You see what we poor soldiers go thro'. This is my present life, and it is likely to be the same the whole winter as we are immediately going into Philadelphia, where we take up our winter quarters in a very good house. I would not, however, have you imagine I am totally void of all occupation. I have always some plan to draw or event to chronicle, which makes a very agreeable pastime and lays the foundation for a journal of the campaign, which I hope during the winter to bring into some order for future perusal.

But all was not quite as André would have had it.

Our only uneasiness here is that the town of Philadelphia will be very ill supplied with provision [he concedes], and, altho' this will fall chiefly, indeed totally, on the inhabitants, it would be a very dismal circumstance and a clog to all festivity. Provisions of all kinds are exceeding dear, and flour is not to be purchased. It will perhaps be better now [that] the navigation of the river is opened, but I fear there will be much distress.

A Different Drumbeat

Washington had high standards for the Second Continental Dragoons. He wanted "none but gentlemen of spirit and of good character" for officers — men like Captain Benjamin Tallmadge, Nathan Hale's classmate. He requested that recruits be "young, light, active" and that they enlist for the duration. He wished them attired in blue coats crossed with white straps, in buff smallclothes, high leather boots, and helmets in the French style, topped with horsehair crests. The mounts should have black bridles and bearskin holster covers.

In a big barn at Wethersfield, Tallmadge taught his men how to maneuver on horseback, how to handle sword and pistol. He appealed for "likely, serviceable trotters of sufficient size," but superior mounts were hard to come by. "We have not forty horses yet," he wrote Washington, "and neither saddles nor bridles have arrived, so that little can be done towards disciplining the regiment." Early in April he was advanced to major, and soon afterward he joined Washington with what mounts he had.

The Dragoons quickly proved their worth. When Howe invaded New Jersey they harassed his slow-moving columns.

When he advanced on Philadelphia they attacked his pickets and skirmished with his cavalry. They were in the thick of battle at Germantown, and at Whitemarsh they were stationed with Morgan's riflemen. When Howe unaccountably withdrew from Whitemarsh, Tallmadge crowed: "Last night they pushed off for Philadelphia, leaving cooking kettles and blankets behind them. Thus has the mighty conqueror of America returned again to his stronghold with disgrace!"

When the army holed up at Valley Forge, Tallmadge patrolled roads and byways for miles around. He has left us an account of his duties, which kept him always on the alert:

> I had to scour the country from the Schuylkill to the Delaware River, about five or six miles, for the double purpose of watching the movements of the enemy and preventing the disaffected from carrying supplies or provisions to Philadelphia. My duties were very arduous, not being able to tarry long in a place by reason of the British Light Horse, which continually patrolled this intermediate ground. Indeed, it was unsafe to permit the Dragoons to unsaddle their horses for an hour, and very rarely did I tarry in the same place through the night.

For eighteen nights in a row he and his men slept in their clothes.

At about this time Tallmadge became involved in espionage. He was ordered to confer with a female spy — a farm girl who had gone to the city ostensibly to peddle eggs, but actually to learn what she could about the enemy — at a tavern outside Philadelphia. She returned on schedule, but as she was pouring out her story a knock at the door warned that Howe's Light Horse was in the vicinity. Tallmadge grabbed up the lass and sped off at full gallop, trading shots with his pursuers before gaining the safety of his own lines. His companion "never once complained of fear," he tells us, but he does not give her name or supply the least clue to her identity.

The Dragoons were ill equipped for winter weather. Soon after Christmas Tallmadge transferred to Trenton, where his men found themselves poorly housed and short of forage. "Congress," he fumed, "may have the full satisfaction and honor of taking the full credit of it to themselves!"

VI

Jousting Knights and Turbaned Ladies

PHILADELPHIA HAD NEVER SEEN such partying. "You have no idea of the life of continual amusement I live in," wrote Becky Franks to her friend Nancy Paca. The two had grown up together, but Nancy had moved to Maryland when she married William Paca, a delegate to the Continental Congress. Becky could hardly wait to tell her about her pretty new dress and elegant coiffure, brought to towering perfection by her hairdresser, Mr. J. Black.

> I can scarce have a moment to myself [she exulted]. I have stole this while everybody is retired to dress for dinner. I am but just come from under Mr. J. Black's hands and most elegantly, as I dressed for a ball this evening at Smith's, where we have one every Thursday.* . . . The dress is more ridiculous and pretty than anything I ever saw. Great quantity of different coloured feathers on the head at a time, besides a thousand other things. The hair dress'd very high in the shape Miss Vining's was the night we returned from Smith's — the hat we found in your mother's closet would be of a proper size.

---

*Smith's City Tavern, where weekly dances were held, was only a short distance from Becky's house.

Balls were so much more fun now. Instead of being paired all evening with the same man, as was the Yankee custom, Becky could anticipate a whole series of partners.

> I spent Tuesday evening at Sir Wm. Howe's, where we had a concert and dance [she told Nancy]. No loss for partners; even I am engaged to seven different gentlemen, for you must know 'tis a fix'd rule never to dance but two dances at a time with the same person. Oh, how I wish Mr. P. wou'd let you come in for a week or two — tell him I'll answer for your being let to return. I know you are as fond of the gay life as myself. I've been but 3 evenings alone since we mov'd to town. I begin now to be almost tired.

Becky had General Howe's permission to send Nancy a small keepsake.

> I asked his leave to send you a handkerchief to show the fashions [she explained]. He very politely gave me permission to send anything you wanted, 'tho I told him you were a delegate's lady. . . . I send some of the most fashionable ribbon and gauze.

Nancy must have been green with envy.

Howe's troops turned the city into a miniature London. Eating clubs, modeled on British prototypes and given names like the Friendly Brothers, the London Association Club, the Yorkshire Club, were formed. Cricket was played, cockfights abounded. Charles Stedman, himself a British regular, says that "gambling of every species was permitted and even sanctioned" and that one of Howe's mercenaries operated an ongoing game of pharo for both officers and men. "Too many respectable families in Britain have to lament its baneful effects," Stedman testifies. "Officers who might have rendered honourable service to their country were compelled, by what was termed a bad run of luck, to dispose of their commissions and return pennyless to their friends in Europe." In a happier vein, weekly dances at Smith's Tavern attracted the city belles and their British escorts, the girls in their most fetching silks, Howe's officers in dazzling regimentals. John André was in his element. Not since London had he known such festivities.

William André, now an officer in his brother's old regiment, was also stationed in Philadelphia, where brother John could monitor his deportment and pave his way at headquarters.

> I cannot repent the step which I think was taken at a critical time and will make him happy in the accomplishment of his wishes [John wrote their sister Louisa]. Yet I fear reproaches from my mother which would be a great drawback on his satisfaction and mine. His regiment is now here, and he has already three or 4 lieutenants under him and the prospect of many changes to bring him forward; besides this, several very eligible subjects have lately been appointed in it who will be very proper companions for him. My whole thoughts are now turned that way and I am so solicitous about him that his doing well will be essentially necessary to my happiness.

An associate of both brothers describes them as possessing the same Gallic good looks, the same lithe build and olive complexion, adding that in "address and temper" John was the most accomplished young officer he had ever met. Both brothers were welcome to the city's stuffiest drawing rooms.

In Becky Franks, John André had an influential friend and lively dinner partner. As daughter of the commissary to British prisoners, she required no introduction at headquarters, where her shafts of wit were relished by Howe and his coterie. André was often in her company, at supper parties and concerts, at the weekly dances in Smith's Tavern.

Peggy Shippen, another favorite, had blossomed into a beguiling, if pampered, seventeen-year-old. Her antecedents included an acting governor of the province, and her father, Edward Shippen, had served on the Common Council and been a judge on the vice-admiralty court. Cautious by nature, with a mind trained in jurisprudence, he was known to be neutral, although admiring of Howe and friendly with the

British. Peggy was his favorite child. André escorted her to
the theater, to balls, dinner parties, and cotillions. He even
gave her a lock of his hair. But when he sketched her likeness,
there was a hint of caricature in the drawing. The slightly
simian face, with its pert smile and mocking eyes, is dwarfed
by a ludicrously top-heavy coiffure. Contrary to legend, she
and André seem never to have been in love. Peggy had high-
ranking admirers, as when she was piped aboard the flagship
Roebuck on the captain's arm, and she had no wish to narrow
the field. Nor was André inclined to a romantic involvement.
There were other entrancing partners, one especially.

Peggy Chew, daughter of a former attorney general and
chief justice of the province, had grown up at Clivedon, the
family seat that Colonel Musgrave and his troops seized and
barricaded during the battle of Germantown. Whereas Peggy
Shippen was a spoiled and sometimes imperious blonde, Peggy
Chew was a good-natured brunette, with lively brown eyes
and a zest for partying. André was her frequent companion,
guiding her through minuets, escorting her to dinner parties,
whiling away long afternoons at Clivedon. Sometimes he extolled her in verse. When she impulsively climbed a fruit tree
in her father's orchard, he compared her seductiveness to that
of the legendary apple on the tree of knowledge:

> The Hebrews write and those who can
> Believe an apple tempted man
> To touch the tree exempt;
> Tho' tasted at a vast expense,
> 'Twas too delicious to the sense
> Not mortally to tempt.

> But had the tree of knowledge bloomed,
> Its branches by much fruit perfumed,
> As here enchants my view —
> What mortal Adam's taste could blame,
> Who would not die to eat the same,
> When gods might wish a Chew?

When André returned one of Peggy's ribbons picked up after a dance, he enclosed this playful ditty:

So this sad vestige, only emblem left
To soothe the mind of latest joy bereft,
Serves but to show how pleasures pass away
Like morning dew, before Apollo's ray.
If I mistake not, 'tis the accomplished Chew
To whom this ornamental bow is due,
Its taste like hers, so neat, so void of art,
Just as her mind and gentle as her heart.
I haste to send it, to resume its place
For beauty should sorrow o'er a bow's disgrace.

Peggy saved the poems. And after André left Philadelphia, she spoke of him many times. Grace Galloway, a family friend, tells of how Peggy and her sister Nancy, a year after the British had evacuated the city, devotedly kept a birthday pact they had made with André and his friends:

Nancy and Peggy Chew drank tea with me. All their discourse was of the officers, and said And[ré] and Cumble [Campbell] and Riddle [Ridsdale] with many others sent them cards and messages, and that they kept the birthdays of 6 of them by meeting together and drinking their healths in a glass of wine and that the gentlemen kept theirs in ye same manner. . . . They bragged so much of their intimacy that I was quite sick of it.

Years later, as the wife of an American officer, Peggy still spoke fondly of John André.

Yet another favorite was Becky Redman, for whom André scissored silhouettes of himself and others. His own likeness shows a comely profile, the queue done up in a jaunty ribbon. One day, at Becky's urging, he tossed off words to a German air well liked by them both. The song tells of Delia, a lost ladylove, who may have been a thinly disguised Honora — we can only guess:

Return, enraptur'd hours,
When Delia's heart was mine,
When she with wreaths of flowers
My temples wou'd entwine.

When jealousy nor care
Corroded in my breast,
But visions light as air
Presided o'er my rest.

Now nightly round my bed
No airy visions play,
No flowers crown my head
Each vernal holiday.

For far from those sad plains
My lovely Delia flies,
And, rack'd with jealous pains,
Her wretched lover dies.

Many of André's colleagues preferred less proper company than that of Becky Redman and her friends. Howe himself made no secret of his devotion to Elizabeth Loring, wife of his commissioner of prisoners. A high-ranking artillery officer paraded his doxy, decked out in the regimental colors, at a review of British troops. As the season advanced, pads sewn in the backs of dresses helped compensate for "the extraordinary natural weight which some of the ladies carry before them," according to one observer. And Becky Franks was never "half so angry" as when three officers of her acquaintance availed themselves of the charms of a Mrs. McKoy, a lady of doubtful virtue. She wrote one of the Shippen sisters about it in a great huff:

The afternoon before last I was standing at the door looking out for B. [Becky] Redman and some others I expected, when Griffen, H. Low and Mr. Cary came up to me. After talking a few minutes with me they walk'd off. There's a house next door but one that a Mrs. McKoy lives in, a lady well known to the gentlemen, and don't you think Grif and Low had the impudence to go in while I was looking right at them. Cary came back to me and said, as he was a married man, he could not take such a liberty, but they [had] gone in to look at a tube rose. . . . I never was half so angry in my life. I never think of it but I feel my face glow with rage.

It is unlikely that André indulged in anything more compromising than a playful flirtation, for he had no wish to harm his career and the consequences of a less decorous involvement could be appalling. His friend Lord Cathcart, for example, was made to marry a young lady to whom he had addressed some injudicious letters.

One day André ran into Pierre Du Simitière, the friend of his Geneva days. Du Simitière, who had come to the New World to make his way as artist and collector of random memorabilia, occupied rooms near Christ Church. He had opened a small museum on the property, with displays that included geological specimens, old coins, and Indian artifacts. His bookshelves groaned under the weight of town histories, atlases, political tracts, and the journals of bygone explorers.

Du Simitière had not been idle. He had designed the great seal for several of the states and had drawn the likenesses of more than a dozen rebel leaders, including Washington, Horatio Gates, John Jay, and Benedict Arnold. He was piecing together a history of the war from newspaper clippings. John Adams saw it.

This Mr. Du Simitière is a very curious man [he wrote his wife Abigail]. He has begun a collection of materials for an history of the Revolution. He begins with the first advices of the tea ships. He cuts out of the newspapers every scrap of intelligence, and every piece of speculation, and pastes it upon clean paper, arranging them under the head of the State to which they belong, and intends to bind them in volumes.

But Du Simitière was living from hand to mouth, with few commissions and with few visitors at his museum. To ease the situation, André commissioned a miniature of his brother, William, and arranged for a portrait of Captain Montresor, Howe's engineer. Du Simitière would not forget this.

> I received from him every mark of civility and proof of friendship that I could desire for [he says], notwithstanding the difference of ranks and the critical situation I was in at the time. I had the satisfaction of enjoying his agreeable company as often as his occupations and other engagements would admit.

Du Simitière asked if he might have one of André's own works, perhaps a miniature or a pencil sketch. He says André presented him with ˒

> a few drawings of no other value but that they were done by him and gave some idea of his superior talents, which were fully displayed in the most curious journals of his travels, which were drawn in the most lively and picturesque manner — the dresses, customs and amusements of the Canadians, Americans and Indians, the curious animals, birds in nests, all in their proper colours, with landscape prospects and plans of places.

Du Simitière was one of the very few people ever to lay eyes on his friend's private journal — missing, alas, since André's death.

It was the theater in Southwark, however, that laid claim to most of André's spare moments. Reached by a dimly lit byway, it had opened to small audiences in 1766, only to be shut down later by Congress as "a species of extravagance and dissipation." Calling themselves "Howe's Thespians," André and his associates reopened the abandoned theater, transforming what had been a murky, cavernous eyesore into an inviting playhouse. Cobwebs were swept away, seats dusted off, lamps installed to illuminate the long-neglected stage. André turned out a set of colorful backdrops with the help of Captain Oliver

De Lancey, scion of an old New York family now enrolled in a Loyalist regiment. One of their more ambitious efforts, which would edify audiences long after the war, showed a rivulet threading beneath majestic shade trees toward "a distant champagne country."

The season opened amid a dazzle of silks and satins, of scarlet coats and burnished gorgets. Tickets went for a dollar for box or pit, fifty cents for balcony. Seats were at a premium, with patrons warned not to "bribe the door-keeper." All winter the Thespians played to full houses, offering thirteen plays during a span of five months. Foote and Garrick, Shakespeare and Fielding, were produced, with the accent on comedy. André wrote prologues for several of the plays, sometimes delivering them himself. Although he is described as "a poor actor," he frequently trod the boards. Most of the Thespians were British officers, but occasionally wives of enlisted men were persuaded to take female parts, a practice that caused some unfavorable comment. "They were generally of no character," remarked a disgusted doorkeeper. "They and the officers were about the theater all day. When any piece was to be rehearsed, they would all flock around the back door or the side lot." It was so out of keeping in strait-laced Philadelphia.

Meanwhile, at Valley Forge, Washington's Continentals opened a theater of their own. Addison's *Cato*, with its preachy republicanism, was a great favorite.

While Howe's officers played onstage, American prisoners of war languished in the British Provost, a jailhouse grudgingly heated and scandalously overcrowded. Half-starved inmates devoured shoe leather, caught and ate rats, lapped soup off the floor where it had been tossed by jeering guards. Disease was rampant. Every day ten or twelve corpses were consigned to a burying ground near the prison. Nor were the men at Valley Forge less chilled or less hungry. Until makeshift huts could be erected, they were obliged to sleep in tents and brush lean-tos. Few were dressed for cold weather. Many were in rags, and some were barefoot. Deadlier than winter cold was the shortage of food supplies.

> For some days past there has been little less than a famine in the camp [Washington reported]. A part of the army has been a week without any kind of flesh, and the rest three or four days. [But the men braved it out.] Naked and starving as they are [Washington added], we cannot enough admire the incomparable patience and fidelity of the soldiery, that they have not been ere this excited by their suffering to a general mutiny and dispersion.

Military activity was limited to skirmishes between small detachments. Captain Allen McLane, with a company of Continentals and some fifty Oneida Indians, spied on enemy command posts, intercepted supply lines, and skirmished with the British Light Horse. He is said to have battled his way out of ambushes, to have penetrated to downtown Philadelphia disguised in British regimentals. So successful was his harassment of Howe's suppliers that he and his troops were dubbed "market stoppers."

John Graves Simcoe, André's friend, performed like services for the British. He had taken a nondescript Tory regiment and honed it into the Queen's Rangers, a crack unit. Attired in green and white uniforms, his troops guarded Howe's supply lines and shepherded his foraging parties. They were accused by the Continentals of raiding farmhouses and putting defenseless civilians to the bayonet. At Valley Forge, no uniform was more hated than the natty green and white.

Tory Philadelphia waited expectantly for Howe to mount a crushing attack on Valley Forge. His troops outnumbered the enemy by more than two to one. They were warmly dressed and well fed. And they were professionals, most of them, rated the best in the world. But weeks of inactivity followed, then months.

> For 7 months [fumed one observer], Gen. Washington with an army not exceeding 7 or 8,000 men has lain at Valley Forge 20 miles from here unmolested, while Sir W. Howe, with more than double his number and the best troops in the world, has been shut up in Philadelphia.

Howe maintained that to attack would court defeat, that Valley Forge was too strongly defended to justify the risk. Even Charles Grey agreed. "As affairs were then situated in America," he would testify in Howe's behalf, "I think an attack on the enemy at Valley Forge, so strongly posted as they were both by nature and art, would have been very unjustifiable." But Charles Stedman, the on-the-spot historian, blames "a long winter of riot and dissipation" for the inertia: "If disease and sickness thinned the American army encamped at Valley Forge, indolence and luxury perhaps did no less injury to the British troops in Philadelphia."

In truth, Howe had very little spirit left for his assignment. He had already tendered his resignation, accusing home authorities of failing to send him adequate reinforcements. Nor had he given up hope for a negotiated peace. At his urging, Parliament hurried off a peace commission that would offer Congress everything short of independence. With the young Earl of Carlisle as chairman, it included William Eden, a former under secretary of state, and George Johnstone, once governor of West Florida. In Philadelphia they would be joined by Howe himself and by his admiral brother, Lord Richard Howe. The commissioners were accompanied by Eden's pregnant wife and by one Anthony Storer, London's most accomplished figure skater, who had come along for the trip. Their crossing the Atlantic seems to have been festive and fraught with optimism. But they debarked to grim news. Congress had approved the French alliance and would negotiate for nothing but outright independence.

Sir William was scheduled to return home in late May. However lackluster his showing, he was idolized by his troops. "I do not believe there is upon record an instance of a commander-in-chief having so universally endeared himself to those under his command," André maintains, "or of one who received such signal and flattering proofs of their love." As the day of departure neared, André urged that a historic tribute be paid to Sir William and his admiral brother, on so lavish a scale that it would rival what General Burgoyne had staged in honor of Lord Stanley's marriage to the Duke of Hamilton's daughter. (Burgoyne had attired the wedding guests as shepherds and shepherdesses, had written a play in honor of the event, and had brought his efforts to a stirring climax with fireworks and a masque. André remembered, too, a recent regatta that had taken place on the Thames, so splendorous that it had awed those who beheld it. Both spectacles gave him ideas for what should be a dazzling salute to the Howe brothers.)

It was an incongruous sort of tribute. Sir William was to be honored with an extravaganza worthy of a conquering hero, whereas he had neither finished off the war nor brought about meaningful peace negotiations. His capture of Philadelphia had accomplished very little. His troops were separated from their base in New York, bottled up by winter weather, and confronted by an army of unyielding Continentals. He had failed to attack Valley Forge, to the disgust of local Tories. The rebels were harassing his outposts, scattering foragers, disrupting supply lines. Even with Philadelphia occupied and Congress exiled, they showed not a sign of coming to heel. Yet André would offer a mind-boggling tribute, as though the war were as good as won.

André decided to call the affair the Mischianza — or, as he put it, "a variety of entertainments." He was among the twenty-two officers who agreed to underwrite the spectacle to the amount of £3312. Four of his colleagues served as managers. Tickets, of his own design, would display a shield flanked by implements of war — cannons and cannonballs, swords, pikes, kegs of gunpowder. These would be surmounted by the Howe family crest and by the motto *Vive Vale*. The event would take place on May 18, six days before Sir William's departure.

The tribute would feature a joust staged by two teams of horsemen, the Knights of the Blended Rose and the Knights of the Burning Mountain. Each jouster would be assigned a lady, chosen for her "youth, beauty and fashion." André took charge of costumes. The Knights of the Blended Rose would be attired in French medieval dress deriving from the court of Henry IV.

> The vest was of white satin [André tells us], the upper part of the sleeves made very full, but of pink confined within a row of straps of white satin laced with silver upon a black edging. The trunk hose were exceeding wide and of the same kind with the shoulder part of the sleeves. A large pink scarf, fastened on the right shoulder with a white bow, crossed the breast and back and hung in an ample loose knot, with silver fringes, very low under the left hip; a pink and white sword belt, laced with black and silver, girded the waist, pink bows with fringes were fastened to the knees, and a wide buff leather boot hung carelessly round the ankles. The hat of white satin, with a narrow brim and high crown, was turned up in front and enlivened by red, white and black plumes, and the hair, tied with the contrasted colours of the dress, hung in flowing curls upon the back. The horses were caparisoned with the same colours, with trimmings and bows hanging very low from either ham and tied round their chest.

Squires assigned to the knights, as well as heralds and trumpeters, would be attired in matching pink and white. Heralds would flourish banners proclaiming the motto of the Blended Rose, "We droop when separated," and the group's device, two entwined roses. The Knights of the Burning Mountain, together with their squires, heralds, and trumpeters, would be arrayed in black and orange, accented with gold. Their motto, "I burn forever"; their device, a smoking volcano.

Costuming the ladies called for even greater ingenuity. André chose to attire them as Turkish maidens to give a flavor of the Crusades to the frolic.

> The dress was of the polonaise kind [he relates], and of white silk with long sleeves. The sashes, which were worn round the waist and were tied with a large bow on the left side, hung very low and were trimmed, spangled and fringed according to the colours of the knight.

Gauze turbans completed the creation, embellished with feathers, tassels, and a seductive veil.

The Mischianza would take place on the property of Joseph Wharton, an exiled patriot, whose mansion, Walnut Grove, commanded a broad view of the Delaware from its sweeping, tree-shaded elevation. André and his assistants decked the rooms with flowers, hung the hallways with ribbons, silks, and girandoles. A pavilion was constructed, its vast interior agleam with mirrors. Space was staked out for the jousters, with two small amphitheaters to accommodate their ladies. On the vast lawn that sloped majestically to the Delaware two triumphal arches were erected. But let André tell it: "The house stands at about 600 yards from the water. At the bottom of the garden a triumphal arch was erected of the Doric order, decorated with military emblems and devices." This was in honor of Sir William. "150 yards farther towards the water stood another arch of the same order but decorated with naval ornaments." This was Lord Richard's. Two grenadiers would be stationed at Sir William's arch, two pigtailed tars at Lord Richard's. Atop Sir William's arch, Fame would be portrayed; atop Lord Richard's, Neptune.

André saw to it that his friend Lord Cathcart was named Chief Knight of the Blended Rose. He himself was Third Knight, with brother William as squire. His motto would be "No Rivals," his device two fighting cocks. Selecting the maidens, a task for diplomats, was brought off to André's full satisfaction. All of his favorites were included — Becky Franks, Becky Redman, Peggy Shippen, and both her sisters. His own lady, her heart aflutter, would be Peggy Chew.

The great day dawned, bleak and threatening. "Weather overcast," Captain Montresor noted, "wind easterly." But for the Shippen girls even a downpour would not have mattered. Edward Shippen, normally an indulgent parent, had been visited that morning by a delegation of long-faced Quakers. They had reminded him that André's Turkish costumes were questionable attire for well-bred young ladies. They could not believe that a citizen of Shippen's standing in the city would countenance such scandalous trappings. Shippen may have welcomed their support. In any case, he had nodded agreement and, when they left, had announced that no daughter of his would attend the Mischianza. He was putting his foot down, more firmly than the girls had ever seen him do; and neither tears nor pleas nor tantrums could make him budge. Peggy, it is said, was "in a dancing fury." But all three daughters stayed home. The costumes were returned, untouched, to John André.

By afternoon the skies had cleared, and only the absence of the Shippen sisters would mar the festivities. "The weather was as favorable as the preparations were magnificent," André tells us. At four o'clock, the channel was cleared of pleasure craft, and three galleys set forth "in full naval pomp." First came the *Ferret*, bedecked with pennants and lined with high-ranking officers; then the *Hussar*, with the beaming Howe brothers; lastly the *Cornwallis*, with General Knyphausen and his Hessian colleagues. Accompanying the galleys were flatboats carrying military bands.

> The gaudy fleet [André writes], freighted with all that was distinguished by rank, beauty and gallantry, was conveyed down the river along the whole length of the city, whilst every ship at the wharfs or in the stream was decked in all her maritime ornaments and covered with spectators.

Abreast of the frigate *Fanny*, the fleet slowed to a stop while everyone sang "God Save the King"! "The musick," André says, "the number of spectators and the brilliancy of the gay tribe which peopled the river made the whole uncommonly solemn and striking." As the fleet bore down on Walnut Grove, the flagship *Roebuck* hailed the Howe brothers with a seventeen-gun salute.

The Wharton mansion was now in sight, its sweep of lawn accented by the two triumphal arches. The galleys docked amid the blare of military bands. André says that

> the company as they disembarked arranged themselves into a line of procession and advanced through an avenue formed by two files of grenadiers, and a line of lighthorse supporting each file. This avenue led to a square lawn of one hundred and fifty yards on each side, lined with troops and properly prepared for the exhibition of tilt and tournament, according to the customs and ordinances of ancient chivalry.

"Spectators not to be numbered darked the whole plain around," André writes. The ladies were seated first, in their special amphitheaters, while spectators massed at the jousting place. When all was ready, a herald, accompanied by three trumpeters, announced the Knights of the Blended Rose, who, when they had paid homage to the Howe brothers, hurled a challenge to the Knights of the Burning Mountain:

> The Knights of the Blended Rose, by me their herald, proclaim and assert that the ladies of the Blended Rose excel in wit, beauty and every accomplishment those of the whole world, and should any knight, or knights, be so hardy as to dispute

or deny it, they are ready to enter the lists with them and maintain their assertions by deeds of arms, according to the laws of ancient chivalry.

Thereupon the Knights of the Burning Mountain made their entrance, after their herald had flung a no less spirited challenge. The joust was on.

> The Knights then received their lances from their squires [André continues], fixed their shields on their left arm and, making a general salute to each other . . . and encountering in full gallop, shivered their spears. In the second and third encounter they discharged their pistols. In the fourth they fought with their swords.

To settle matters, the two Chief Knights challenged each other to single combat. "These, whilst fighting furiously, were parted by the interposition of the judges of the field," André says, "who doubtless deemed the ladies so fair and the knights so brave that it wou'd have been impious to decide in favour of either."

With the joust a draw, the entire company repaired to the Wharton mansion, where each knight, on bended knee, was awarded a keepsake by his lady. Dancing followed, interrupted by a display of fireworks at Sir William's arch. André says that the illuminated figure of Fame shone as if "spangled with stars." "Letters of fire" issued from her trumpet to spell out what seemed a celestial tribute: "Tes lauriers sont immortels." Sir William must have swelled.

At midnight doors were flung open on a scene of blinding splendor.

> At twelve supper was announced [André tells us], and large folding doors, hitherto artfully concealed, being suddenly thrown open, discovered a magnificent saloon of two hundred and ten feet by forty, and twenty-two feet in height, with three alcoves on each side which served as sideboards. . . . Fifty-six large pierglasses, ornamented with green

silk artificial flowers and ribbons; one hundred branches with three lights in each, trimmed in the same manner as the mirrors; eighteen lustres, each with twenty-four lights, suspended from the ceiling and ornamented as the branches; three hundred wax tapers disposed along the supper tables; four hundred and thirty covers, twelve hundred dishes; twenty-four black slaves in oriental dresses, with silver collars and bracelets, ranged in two lines and bending to the ground as the General and Admiral approached the saloon — all these, forming together the most brilliant assemblage of gay objects and appearing at once as we entered by an easy descent, exhibited a *coup d'oeil* beyond description magnificent.

André had outdone himself.

Dinner concluded with a round of toasts — to the king and queen, to "the founders of the feast," to "the ladies of each device," and, more especially, to the Howe brothers. But on the outskirts of the city Captain McLane and his troops had lined up a string of camp kettles filled with gunpowder. At the height of the festivities they ignited the kettles in swift succession, like Chinese firecrackers. Drums beat an alert, artillery was readied, and Howe's cavalry went in pursuit — but not rapidly enough to catch McLane, who vanished into the night. Within the mansion, celebrants were told that the noise was merely an impromptu fusilade honoring Sir William. "Freighted with new strength and spirits," André says, "the whole repaired to the ballroom, and daylight overtook them in all the festive mirth with which a youthful band could be animated."

André was in raptures. Even Allen McLane could not detract from the extravaganza. "Everything was as splendid and magnificent as possible," writes one observer, "and all, even those who have been in Paris and London, agree that they have never seen such a luxurious fete." But not everyone agreed. The Mischianza was a

> ridiculous farce [according to Charles Stedman]. It is really surprising that men of sense could be regaled with such non-

sense. Yet it seems to have given great satisfaction to the brothers. They were delighted at the parade. It tickled their vanity. It pleased their ambition. The exhibition of this triumphal Mischianza will be handed down to posterity, in the annals of Great Britain and America, as one of the most ridiculous, undeserved and unmerited triumphs ever yet performed.

No less vehement was Elizabeth Drinker, a citizen of Philadelphia during the British occupation.

> This day [she writes], may be remembered by many from the scenes of folly and vanity promoted by the officers of the army under the pretense of showing respect to Gen. Howe, now about leaving them. . . . How insensible do these people appear, while our land is so greatly desolated, and death and sore destruction has overtaken and impends over so many!

And a British artilleryman, when asked what distinguished the Knights of the Burning Mountain from their counterparts, merely shrugged. "The Knights of the Burning Mountain are tom fools," he said, "and the Knights of the Blended Rose are damned fools. I know of no difference between them."

André would never have understood.

In the hours of early morning, while knights and ladies still swirled across the dance floor, word came that Lafayette was encamped on nearby Barren Hill. He was posted in an exposed location, it was said, where he could easily be cut off. Howe speedily made plans to block the Frenchman's line of retreat and bag the more than two thousand men in his command. He was so confident of success that he joked about a victory dinner at which Lafayette would be the involuntary guest.

Howe struck in the dark of night. He and General Clinton stationed their troops in front of Lafayette's encampment, while General James Grant cut the line of retreat. But Howe had not reckoned on Captain McLane, who sped to headquarters and warned Lafayette in the nick of time. Keeping a cool head, the marquis withdrew his troops by way of a little-known back road. When the British closed in from opposite directions, they stared at one another across a vacant campsite.

Even Barren Hill failed to shake Howe's grip on the men's affection. He was given a lachrymose farewell:

> I am just returned from conducting our beloved general to the waterside [André writes], and have seen him receive a more flattering testimony of the love and attachment of his army than all the pomp and splendour of the Mischianza could convey to him. I have seen the most gallant of our officers, and those whom I least expected of giving such instances of their affection, shed tears while they bid him farewell. . . . On my return, I saw nothing but dejected countenances.

Before turning over the command to Sir Henry Clinton, Howe ordered the evacuation of Philadelphia. Taking the city had failed to shorten the conflict, and General Clinton must operate from bases in New York and Rhode Island. So little was expected from the peace commission that by the time Carlisle and his colleagues debarked, some of the troops had already crossed into New Jersey.

One hot morning Elizabeth Drinker and her sister woke to a city free of redcoats. "Last night it was said there was 9,000 of the British troops left in town," she says. "This morning when we arose, there was not one redcoat to be seen in town, and the encampment in Jersey had vanished." Some three thousand Loyalists jammed British transports as Continental troops poured into the city. Mrs. Drinker says that Allen McLane's men "galloped about the streets and frightened many by their appearance." On July 2, Congress returned. Two days later "a great fuss" was made — "firing of guns, sky rockets, etc.," according to Mrs. Drinker — to mark the anniversary of independence.

Howe's army had left behind it a legacy of rifled homes and desecrated public buildings.

> It would be in vain to attempt to give you an account of the devastation they committed in the environs of the city, indis-

criminately on Whig and Tory property [Du Simitière wrote a friend]. The persecution that numbers of worthy citizens underwent from the malice of the Tories, the tyranny of the police on all those they supposed to be friends to the liberties of America — all these would fill up a volume.

André had been living in Benjamin Franklin's house. Du Simitière dropped by to bid him farewell and thank him for his many kindnesses. He found André in Franklin's library removing books, musical instruments, and scientific apparatus.* A portrait of Franklin was leaning in the doorway. Du Simitière could not believe his eyes. He reminded his friend that General Knyphausen had prepared an inventory of everything not his own and had left his lodgings precisely as he had found them. But André, giving no explanation, continued to gather up books and other valuables. When he left the city, the booty went with him. Years later Franklin would speak of the portrait in a letter to a friend: "Our English enemies, when they were in possession of this city and my house, made a prisoner of my portrait and carried it off with them, leaving that of its companion, my wife, by itself — a kind of widow."

On the bicentennial of Franklin's birth, the portrait was returned to America by descendants of General Charles Grey. For more than a century it had hung in Howick House, the family's ancestral seat.** André's role in the rifling of Franklin's house now becomes clear. He was merely following orders — something he could not explain to Du Simitière.

André contributed some of his Mischianza props to Du Simitière's museum. They included the shield he had carried, a gaudily decorated lance, a tin sword.

He snipped a button from his coat and gave it to Becky Redman.

And to Peggy Chew he left this scrap of verse:

---

*André is said to have taken the multivolume *Encyclopédie* donated to the American Philosophical Society by Louis XVI.

**The portrait, painted by Benjamin Wilson in 1751, now hangs in the White House.

If at the close of war and strife
My destiny once more
Should in the varied paths of life
Conduct me to this shore;

Should British banners guard the land,
And factions be restrained,
And Clivedon's mansion peaceful stand,
No more with blood be stained,

Say! Wilt thou then receive again,
And welcome to thy sight,
The youth who bids with stifled pain
His sad farewell tonight?

Peggy would treasure it all her life.

A Different Drumbeat

NOTHING WAS RIGHT in Trenton that grim winter of 1779–80. Tallmadge was short of feed for his mounts, of clothing and proper quarters for his men.

> We have finally fixed on this place for winter quarters for the cavalry [he wrote his friend Barnabas Deane]. Am sorry to say that it is without stables or forage of any kind, and, what is still worse, the country for 10 miles round is almost stript of hay and grain. Add to this that the Navy gentlemen, about 500 in number, are billeted over the town, which makes it difficult to quarter the men.

He envied Deane his civilian status and his opportunities with the fair sex. "Don't forget me, my old friend Barna," he added, "when you ride the ladies in the sleigh this winter, and kiss them a hundred times on my account."

To ease matters, the Dragoons were transferred to Chatham, New Jersey, where Tallmadge had charge of the 5th and 6th Regiments as well as his own command. His situation was improving. He had hustled up boots and breeches for his men and had been allowed a supply of sabers taken from German prisoners of war at Saratoga. He was wholly unprepared for a stinging rebuke from the commander-in-chief, who accused the Dragoons of needlessly "galloping about the country" and permitting their mounts to be in "worse condition than those which have been kept upon constant and severe duty the whole winter." Washington implied that the Dragoons might better have stayed in Valley Forge.

Although the letter was addressed to Colonel Sheldon, Tallmadge took it personally, feeling that it reflected unfairly on his officers and men.

> I formerly had the vanity to think we were considered in a different light [he wrote in reply]. For me to apologize and answer the charges therein contained is needless since the Colonel has wrote so largely on that head. But if being commissary of forage, purchaser of boots, clothing, etc., etc., entitles the men in these several capacities to the character of being indolent and inattentive to duty, we would acquiesce in the charge.

Perhaps it was time for him to "quit a service which from principle I wish to support, and a General whose commands it has been my highest ambition to obey." If his performance did not meet with the approval of the commander-in-chief, "honour as well as inclination would urge me to impose on the public no longer." Washington, who had no wish to lose Tallmadge, hurried off a conciliatory letter. But the major had come close to tendering his resignation.

Tallmadge was transferred to Westchester County in June, to police the Neutral Ground and curb the depredations of marauding Cowboys. He also entered upon secret activities that would bring him into closer association with the commander-in-chief.

> This year [he tells us], I opened a private correspondence with some persons in New York (for General Washington), which lasted through the war. How beneficial it was to the Commander-in-chief is evidenced by his continuing the same to

the close of the war. I kept one or more boats continually employed in crossing the Sound on this business.

The "business" Tallmadge speaks of was espionage. He was in touch with a spy ring that had an operative stationed in New York — a well-regarded citizen, unsuspected by the British.

VII

"A Shy Bitch"

CLINTON WAS NOT HAPPY with his assignment. He tells us that "no officer who had the least anxious regard for his professional fame would court a charge so hopeless as this now appeared likely to be." His instructions, dictated by the recent Franco-American alliance, seemed geared to compromise and a negotiated peace. "As soon as that event was announced in form by the French court," he comments, "administration seems to have relinquished all thoughts of reducing the rebellious colonies by force of arms, and to have determined to trust the decision of the quarrel to negotiations." He must release large detachments for service in the West Indies and Florida. In the fall he must carry the war to Georgia and the Carolinas, with additional thrusts into Virginia and Maryland. If he could not prod Washington into a military showdown, he must "give up every idea of offensive operations within land" and resort to "desultory expeditions, in conjunction with the King's ships of war, for the purpose of attacking the rebel ports between New York and Nova Scotia and seizing or destroying all vessels, wharves, docks and naval and military stores along the coast." Should things go badly, he must make a last-ditch stand in Halifax.

Sir Henry was now a middle-aged widower, short and paunchy, with none of Howe's strong hold on the men's affection. But his rise through the ranks had been enviable. His family ties were of the best. He was the son of an admiral, the grandson of an earl, the cousin of a duke. He had been gazetted as a lad in the Coldstream Guards, had transferred after a few years to the Grenadier Guards, had risen to lieutenant colonel, and, during the Seven Years War, served as aide-de-camp to Prince Ferdinand of Brunswick. Wounded in action on the Continent, he had returned home with his career admirably launched. By 1775, when he joined Howe and Burgoyne aboard the frigate *Cerberus,* outward bound for Boston, he was a major general, a member of Parliament, and, on all counts, a man to watch.

No sooner had Clinton docked in Boston than he gave evidence of his tactical skills. He advised General Gage, a listless leader, to outwit the rebels by seizing Dorchester Heights. His proposal received scant attention, but a month later at Bunker Hill he disregarded the letter of his instructions and led a charge that helped win the day. On Long Island, he devised a strategy that would turn the rebels' flank and bring about their defeat. Nor was this all. In 1777, when Burgoyne faltered in his drive southward, Clinton pushed into the Hudson Highlands and seized Fort Clinton* and Fort Montgomery, a coup that failed to save Burgoyne but did credit to Sir Henry's drive and initiative. As commander-in-chief, he unquestionably had assets that Howe lacked. As the son of an admiral, he understood the importance of sea power in a war that could turn on naval support. He had been brought up in New York, where his father had been governor for ten years, and knew the temper of the colonies better than his less knowledgeable colleagues. Clinton's worst troubles derived

---

*Named for Governor George Clinton of New York.

less from the nature of his assignment than from conflicts within himself.

Sir Henry is described by one who knew him as "haughty, morose, churlish." Quick to take offense, he was edgy and standoffish with colleagues. When he crossed from England with Howe and Burgoyne he had kept mostly to himself, seldom mixing with the other two. "At first (for you know I am a shy bitch) I kept my distance," he told a friend, and "seldom spoke until my two colleagues forced me out." His relations with Howe worsened after the two set foot in Boston, nor could he get along with most of his naval colleagues. When Howe detached him in 1776 to bring the South into line, quelling opposition and establishing Loyalists in seats of power, he was paired with Commodore Sir Peter Parker in an attempt on Charleston. Through a lapse in reconnaissance, Clinton debarked his troops at a place that allowed him no access to the enemy. In the meanwhile Parker trained his guns on Fort Sullivan, a facility guarding the approaches to the city, but was driven off by the rebel garrison. The fleet was withdrawn under cover of darkness, bringing the expedition to an inglorious end.

Clinton and the commodore were promptly at each other's throats. Clinton accused Sir Peter not only of responsibility for the defeat but of submitting a lopsided and prejudicial report to the authorities at Whitehall. He acknowledged that he might have been overcautious and "fearful of a blunder." This had been, after all, his first command. But Parker — the real culprit, if we are to believe Sir Henry — had blamed him unjustly, putting him in bad odor with Lord Germain. Even the red ribbon of the Bath, awarded Clinton that April, failed to atone for the hurt. It was a behavior pattern that would be repeated. Invariably others were to blame — never Clinton — when any criticism was forthcoming.

Something deep inside Sir Henry caused him to nurse suspicions, heap blame on associates, and start a quarrel on the smallest pretext. Inevitably, he had few friends among his military equals. Even his friendship with General William Phillips of the Royal Artillery, dating back some thirty years, would cool when the two became colleagues. His relations with Sir William Howe were edgy from the start, and he would quarrel not only with Commodore Parker but with other naval men who had the bad luck to be paired with him. The few colleagues with whom he could work amicably, like Charles Grey, were with him but a short time. Only one admiral, Lord Richard Howe, would manage to collaborate harmoniously with Clinton throughout a whole campaign.

We are told that Clinton's admiral father was often away from home, that his mother was unstable, volatile, given to ruling the family with a despotic hand. The early years left him with an ambivalence toward authority, which he craved for himself but with which he could not live at peace when he had it. Always at odds with those wielding comparable powers, he was uncomfortable with his own authority and repeatedly made threats to resign. When he returned to England after the Charleston defeat he talked openly of resignation. "If I cannot serve with them I like," he is quoted as saying, "I had rather not serve at all." Although he was named Howe's second in command when he returned from England, he had very little regard for his easygoing associate. He was intensely ambitious, jealous of his powers, and chronically unsure of himself. Periodically throughout the next four years he would tender his resignation, only to rescind it before anyone at Whitehall could take action.

Clinton fared better with junior officers, who posed no threat to his uneasy psyche. He enjoyed a camaraderie with Lord Rawdon, his protégé, and with Captain Duncan Drummond, his aide-de-camp, that he could not manage with high-ranking colleagues, unless we except General Phillips. As aide to Grey, André could take Sir Henry's measure from a distance. He perceived a remote sort of chief, shy and aloof, yet accessible to an inner circle of younger men. Beneath the prickly exterior, he could sense an almost parental solicitude toward favorites. Told that Lord Rawdon discussed military matters with Clinton almost every night and that Rawdon's opinions and advice counted heavily with his chief, André wished that he, too, might be part of the inner circle. Although he had admired Howe and had extolled him to the skies in the Mischianza, André wasted no time mourning his departure. His future was with Grey — and with Sir Henry.

Clinton would travel overland with his army. His transports were filled with exiled Loyalists, and, besides, in crossing New Jersey, he might lure Washington into something more decisive than a momentary skirmish. When the troops crossed the Delaware "no shot was fired," André says, "nor did an enemy appear until the whole were on the opposite shore." But Clinton found himself in what he calls "a devoured country, inimical to man." Wells had been filled in, crops destroyed, bridges ripped apart, trees felled across roads. Warnings nailed to signposts advised him that if he continued on his course he would be "Burgoyned."*

The road forked at Allentown, one branch leading toward New Brunswick, the other striking northeast toward Sandy Hook. Clinton chose the latter, which he considered less risky. "I had also in view by this move," he says, "to draw the enemy down from the hilly country in the hope that an opportunity might offer of getting a fair stroke at him before I finally took my leave."

Clinton was vouchsafed his "fair stroke" on June 28, as hot a day as anyone could remember. He asks: "With the temperature at 96, when people fell dead in the street and even in their homes, what could be done at midday in a hot pine barren, loaded with everything that the poor soldier carries?"

*Suffer the fate of Burgoyne's army.

Some of his men shouldered packs weighing as much as a hundred pounds. All were in full uniform. But he was ready for a showdown, even though Knyphausen had gone ahead with part of the army. He caught sight of Washington's Continentals near Monmouth Court House. After some tentative skirmishing, the two sides locked in what would become a daylong test of stamina. André watched from a distance for, as at Brandywine, Grey's command was kept in reserve. In his journal he concedes that the rebels were "marching very rapidly and in good order." Although he did not know it, the change derived from Baron von Steuben's efforts to introduce European discipline and style into Washington's ranks. André describes shifting battle lines, retreats, and counterattacks by the Continentals, thrusts by the British cavalry and grenadiers — with men dropping on both sides not from wounds but from the heat. By nightfall the issue was still in doubt. The wilted armies dossed down, not far apart, but when the moon had set Clinton roused his troops and tiptoed off, giving no hint of his departure to rebel units encamped only a short way from his line of march. By daybreak he had joined Knyphausen.

Monmouth was a draw. Washington had fought the British toe to toe and had maintained his battle lines, even though his colleague, General Charles Lee, had ordered a retreat at one crucial moment. Clinton had not been turned back in his advance toward Sandy Hook. André has only praise for the way his colleagues had outwitted the rebels, who "were perplexed in their conjecture by the secrecy observed respecting our route and by false movements made to deceive them." He exults in the successful crossing of hostile terrain. "Neither could their militia or light troops, with their boasted knowledge of the country and dexterity in hovering round us, find an opportunity to give the least annoyance to a column of eight or ten miles in length."

But the last word must go to Anthony Wayne, who had a
bone to pick with "No-Flint Grey" and his redcoats.

> Tell the Phil'a ladies [he wrote a friend], that the heavenly,
> sweet, pretty redcoats — the accomplished gentlemen of the
> Guards and Grenadiers — have humbled themselves on the
> plains of Monmouth. "The Knights of the Blended Rose" and
> "Burning Mount" have resigned their laurels to *rebel* officers,
> who will lay them at the feet of those virtuous daughters of
> America who cheerfully gave up ease and affluence in a city
> for liberty and peace of mind in a cottage.

Clinton crossed to New York just in time to elude Count
d'Estaing and a French fleet. D'Estaing arrived a few days
later, standing briefly off Sandy Hook before sailing for parts
unknown. On July 27, he was reported off Rhode Island,
where a rebel army under General John Sullivan was about
to attack Newport. D'Estaing's fleet would fend off efforts to
relieve the imperiled British garrison.

Clinton went to the rescue with an army of more than four
thousand men (André puts it at 4333). His fleet was nearly as
large as d'Estaing's, but a storm off Block Island scattered all
the vessels, British and French alike. With Sullivan deprived
of naval support, Sir Henry felt confident not only of relieving
Newport but of bagging the stranded rebel army. "Most of
this, all agree, would have happened," he tells us, "but the
winds said no." He was prevented, by a shift of wind, from
scoring a major victory and "reducing General Sullivan to
something like the Saratoga business." It was a cruel run of
luck. "Our passage having been unluckily retarded by calms
and contrary winds, and time being consequently given for
alarming Sullivan by the beacons along the coast, we had the
mortification on our arrival to find that he had quitted the
island the night before."

Clinton had planned to raid the nearby coast, but head

winds caused him to leave the raiding to Grey and return with
most of the army to New York. Grey took aim at New Bedford,
a port favored by Yankee privateers. Attacking by night, he
set fire to shipyards, ropewalks, warehouses, docks, and anchored ships. Even the homes of several well-known rebels
went up in smoke. André says that "a few houses of committeemen and colonels of militia, etc., accidentally took fire
to our great mortification, as orders were only to destroy warehouses." Sailcloth and cordage, foodstuffs, ammunition, and
naval stores fed a conflagration that turned the sky a baleful
crimson, seen as far away as Newport. Subsequently Grey
would raid Falmouth and exact sheep and beef cattle from
the fishermen on Martha's Vineyard, but first he dispatched
André to report in person to the commander-in-chief. "I write
in haste and am not a little tired," he wrote Clinton. "Therefore, beg leave to refer you for the late plan of operations and
particulars to Captain André."

After his return, André was quartered in the home of Leffert
Lefferts, a third-generation Dutchman with two gossipy
daughters. Several British officers were billeted in the house,
and the two girls chattered in their native tongue about the
redcoats. André overheard some of their talk, not all of it
flattering. Taking them aside, he gave them a lecture on good
manners — spoken, to their astonishment, in the Dutch language.

André was more convinced than ever that the war was nearly
won. "The cry of the people" was for peace, he wrote home.
Their currency was so debased that four paper dollars could
be had for one of silver. Nor were they happy with the French
alliance. André claimed that "they do not in their conversations with prisoners, flags of truce and other communications
we may have with them, conceal their aversion to the French."
The Tory and Indian raids in the Mohawk Valley should
convince even the most thickheaded rebels that hostilities
could take an uglier turn, that harsh measures must follow if

surrender were long delayed. André's name was on the list of subscribers to a military manual published that same year by Captain Robert Donkin, a fellow officer.* "Dip arrows in matter of smallpox," Donkin advised, "and twang them at the American rebels in order to inoculate them. This would sooner disband these stubborn, ignorant, enthusiastic savages than any other compulsive measures. Such is their dread and fear of that disorder!"

Rumor had it that General Grey was soon to be transferred to the West Indies. In mentioning this in his letter home, André says that he was "on the figits and not without anxiety." Grey would indeed depart — not for the West Indies, but for home. But first he would join Cornwallis on a foraging expedition on the west side of the Hudson. André would be with him.

In the course of the operation Cornwallis learned that Colonel George Baylor's Continental Light Dragoons were athwart his line of march near Tappan, New York. Informants told Cornwallis that Baylor was quartered in a farmhouse and had allowed his men to bed down in some nearby barns. His sentries, few in number, were half a mile distant. It was a situation made to order for Grey, who readied his troops for a surprise attack.

Grey struck on the night of September 28. As at Paoli, he had ordered flints removed and an exclusive dependence on the bayonet. His men accomplished their task with cool dispatch, surprising many of their victims where they slept. André says that "the whole corps within six or eight men were killed or taken prisoner. . . . Amongst the prisoners were a colonel, major, a captain and three or four subalterns. The rest were killed." Actually, eleven dragoons were slain on the spot, seventeen left for dead and about forty taken prisoner. Thirty-

---

*Robert Donkin was stationed in America throughout the war. He would rise to the rank of general and, never having been absent from duty during some eighty years in the British Army, would die peaceably in his nineties.

seven made their escape. Baylor sustained a chest wound that
would contribute to his death a few years later. Although
André had had no part in the slaughter, his account of it is
matter-of-fact, nor was his high regard for Grey in the least
shaken. But others, like Judge Thomas Jones, were appalled
by what had taken place. "A merciful mind must shudder at
the bare mention of so barbarous, so inhuman and so unchris-
tian an act," Jones exclaims, "an act inconsistent with the
dignity and honour of a British general, and disgraceful to the
name of a soldier!"

Grey's services were at an end, but he made sure that his
aide suffered no setback in the transition. Upon Grey's departure, André was named aide-de-camp to Sir Henry Clinton.

Clinton's headquarters were in the Archibald Kennedy house
at Number One Broadway. The Union Jack floated majestically overhead. Rooms and hallways hummed with army business. Staff members went about their duties with crisp dispatch.
Lord Francis Rawdon, the adjutant general, was preeminent.
André remembered his lavish parties and gourmet dinners in
Philadelphia. Peter Kemble, the deputy adjutant general, and
Duncan Drummond, André's fellow aide-de-camp, were only
a notch below Rawdon. Indeed it had been Drummond who
delivered one of Clinton's letters of resignation to Lord Germain. Lord William Cathcart, a highborn Scot, shone in the
small circle of favorites, as did Banastre Tarleton, colonel of
a Tory regiment, and John Graves Simcoe, André's friend.

André's lodgings were now of the best, nor was his table
ever wanting. He dined out, sumptuously and often, at the
homes of Loyalists. He joined his chief on horseback rides to
the Beekman mansion, a country seat much favored by Sir
Henry. On one of his visits he may have heard mention of
Nathan Hale, the American spy who had been held prisoner
on the estate. Or perhaps Hale's name never came up, for he
had been hanged unceremoniously, without a fuss.

To André and his fellow officers New York must have seemed

nearly London's equal. Sir Henry relished its offerings of sport and recreation. He and André would often quit headquarters at lunchtime and gallop up Broadway to a favorite handball court, to shed the cares of office in sweaty combat. Or they would try their luck at billiards, or in a five-lane bowling alley. But fox hunting was Sir Henry's passion. "Who writes Sir H. Clinton's letters?" asks Chief Justice William Smith, a close observer. "I saw him at 3 o'clock pass my window with several horsemen, as I have often this winter, following a Hessian jaeger who dragged a bone pursued by a dog. All full speed over fences, thro' fields, etc."

Recreation in all manner of forms made life supportable for Britons far from home. Golfers were summoned to their "pleasant and healthy" pastime by the *Royal Gazette*, whose editor promised to supply golf clubs and "genuine Caledonian balls." Cricket matches were played on the parade grounds near the Jewish cemetery, and the Brooklyn Ferry House, a rendezvous for sportsmen, offered cockfights, bullbaiting, and boxing bouts. Horse races took place at the New Market race course on Hempstead Plains.

> Yesterday the grenadiers had a race at the flatlands, and in the afternoon this house swarm'd with beaux, and some very smart ones [purred Becky Franks, now an exile from Philadelphia]. How the girls wou'd have envy'd me cou'd they have peep'd and seen how I was surrounded!

Taverns were everywhere. The Bunch of Grapes, London Chop House, Shakespeare Tavern, and Faithful Irishman and Jolly Sailors were but four among so vast an array that their number had to be curtailed by edict. During the warmer months concerts were given on the mall adjoining Trinity Church.

> The walk at Trinity Church had been increased in width, so that the posts had to be sunk into the graves [writes Ewald Schaukirk, a scandalized Moravian]. The orchestra from the Playhouse, seated against the church, and another place for

the musicians erected just opposite the church, gave great offense and uneasiness to all serious and, still more, to all godly men and caused many reflections not only on the irreligious turn of the Commandant, but also on the Rector, who is said to have given his consent to it. Profaneness and wickedness prevaileth — Lord have mercy!

Nor was Chief Justice Smith any less shocked by the goings-on. "What a medley assemble here!" he writes. "A horrible contrast! Ladies in the walk, the mob in the street, and funerals crossing the company in the churchyard. The parson there officiating at the grave!"

Dinner parties commenced at four in the afternoon and continued far into the night. Balls and dancing assemblies, concerts and card parties, were held nightly throughout the city, and royal anniversaries were an excuse for all manner of celebration, including masques and fireworks. One year Baroness von Riedesel, wife of Burgoyne's German colleague, reigned over a ball in honor of the queen's birthday, giving the first toast and dancing, with her high-ranking partner, the opening minuet. Some of these arrangements got on people's nerves. General James Pattison, commandant of the city, and Cosmo Gordon, a toplofty grenadier officer and noted dandy, had charge of one such event that irked Lord Cathcart. "General Pattison takes great care of all the ladies," he sniffed, "and Cosmo Gordon torments everybody much more than usual. Bad fireworks started the evening off!"

Whenever he had time, André repaired to the Theatre Royal, a playhouse on John Street where some of his fellow officers had formed a stock company. *Macbeth*, *Richard III*, and *She Stoops to Conquer* were presented, as well as *Tom Thumb* and less discriminating fare. Some of the plays had never before been given in America. Wives of enlisted men were preferred for female parts — ladies who "followed the drum" as they were described in an appeal for their services. If they could not be had, the roles were taken by junior officers. André appeared in a number of plays, wrote and delivered prologues, and, with his friend Oliver De Lancey, painted several back-drops. But he had less time now for make-believe.

As Clinton's aide-de-camp, André could squire the most sought-after Tory belles. But he formed no lasting attach-ments and, if he listened to Becky Franks, may have consid-ered New York's offering a fickle and bold-faced lot.

> 'Tis here, I fancy, always leap year [Becky writes]. For my part, that am used to quite another mode of behavior, I cannot help shewing my surprise, perhaps they call it my ignorance, when I see a lady single out her pet to lean almost in his arms at an assembly or playhouse (which, I give my honour, I have too often seen both in married and single), and to hear a lady confess a partiality for a man who perhaps she has not seen three times. . . . They've made the men so saucy that I sin-cerely believe the lowest ensign thinks 'tis but ask and have — a red coat and smart epaulette is sufficient to secure a female heart.

André's name has been linked with a certain "Miss K" — perhaps Miss Kitty Van Horn, a much admired belle. But it was at most a passing attachment. If we are to take Becky's word for it, Kitty's teeth were already "beginning to decay, which is the case of most New York girls after eighteen."

André was the delight of Tory hostesses. At one dinner party, after expounding on "love and fashion," he entertained fellow diners with an account of a dream he claimed to have had. He had found himself in a celestial court of law, he said, where "infernal judges" had changed some of the more ob-jectionable rebels into the beasts and reptiles they most re-sembled while on earth. Chief Justice Thomas McKean of Pennsylvania, a hanging judge who had sent two Quaker Loy-alists to their deaths, was now a bloodhound. Silas Deane of Connecticut, "a trickling, hypocritical New England attor-ney" with the affectations of a French marquis, had taken on "the character of the monkey who had seen the world." General Charles Lee, a British turncoat now in the Continental ranks, had become an adder, "big with venom and ready to wound the hand that protects it or the bosom that cherishes it." John Jay, described by André as "a mixture of the lowest cunning and most unfeeling barbarity," was transformed into a serpent, while the Continental Army had assumed "the shape of the timid hare, whose disposition they already possessed." Surprisingly, General Howe was included, appearing as a gamecock "who at once began to crow and strut about as if he was meditating combat, but upon the appearance of a few cropple-crowned hens . . . dismissed his purpose." By now André was wholly in Sir Henry's corner.

André still found time for flights of playful verse. Tucked among Sir Henry's papers is a piece of ribald make-believe that surely made the rounds at headquarters. It describes the author's supposed chagrin after losing his ladylove to a triumphant rival:

The Frantick Lover

And shall then another embrace thee, my Fair?
Must envy still add to the pangs of despair?
Shall I live to behold the reciprocal bliss?
Death, death, is a refuge, elysium to this!

The star of the evening now bids thee retire;
Accurs'd be its orb and extinguish'd its fire!
For it shews me my rival, prepared to invade
Those charms which at once I admired and obey'd . . .

My insolent rival, more proud of his right,
Contemns the sweet office, that soul of delight.
Less tender, he seizes thy lips as his prey,
And all thy dear limbs the rough summons obey.

E'en now more licentious — rash mortal, forbear!
Restrain him, O Venus! Let him, too, despair!

Freeze, freeze the swift streams which now hurry to join,
And curse him with passions unsated like mine.

How weak is my rage his fierce joy to controul.
A kiss from thy body shoots life to his soul;
Thy frost, too, dissolv'd in one current is run
And all thy keen feelings are blended in one.

Thy limbs from his limbs a new warmth shall acquire,
His passions from thine shall redouble their fire,
'Till wreck'd and o'erwhelmed in the storm of delight,
Thine ears lose their hearing, thine eyes lose their sight!

Here conquest must pause, tho' it ne'er can be cloy'd,
To view the rich plunder of beauty enjoy'd;
The tresses dishevelled, the bosom display'd,
And the wishes of years in a moment repaid.

A thousand soft thoughts in thy fancy combine,
A thousand wild horrors assemble in mine.
Relieve me, kind death, shut the scene from my view,
And save me, oh save me, 'ere madness ensue!

While the rich dined and partied, less favored citizens taxed every available dwelling place in the city. The population had multiplied ten times since the Americans left, swelled by Tories fleeing their menaced homes in the surrounding countryside, by wives and children of British regulars still arriving from the mother country, and by runaway slaves taking advantage of Clinton's pledge of freedom. The fire that had smouldered when Nathan Hale was hanged had robbed the city of nearly five hundred homes, a quarter of its housing. A second fire had wiped out sixty-four additional dwelling places. Houses left empty by exiled patriots were taken over by the troops, while churches, public buildings, and warehouses were converted into hospitals and military prisons.

For the poor, there was only Canvas Town, the fire-gutted city blocks that stretched from upper Broadway to the Hudson, from a line east of lower Broadway to Whitehall. Here dwelt the city's outcasts — runaway slaves, thieves and bawds, legions of Tory refugees. Mildewed lengths of sailcloth stretched across blackened cellar holes to form crude and leaky tents. The floors were bare earth, cellar holes served as walls, and there were no windows or partitions. Meals were prepared over open fires that supplied whatever warmth there was, even in midwinter. Here mothers nursed infants, children romped, people sickened and died. Former slaves took stock of their unaccustomed freedom, bawds plied their trade, thieves reckoned up their loot. Most of what was eaten had been stolen from markets or scrounged from the army's garbage heaps. Fuel of any kind was a rare commodity. There was firewood enough for city officials and the well-to-do, but "the poor," says Baroness von Riedesel, "were obliged to burn fat."

Clinton imposed price controls on meat and flour, but many citizens could barely keep bread on the table. Even Lord Carlisle, still in America as a peace commissioner, was shocked by the prices.

> How the people exist in this town is to the greatest degree wonderful [he wrote his wife]. All the necessaries of life are dear beyond conception. Meat is from fifteen to seventeen pence a pound, and everything else in proportion. My weekly bills come to as much as the house account at Castle Howard when we have the most company.

Yet the city's upper crust — wealthier Tories, prosperous merchants, owners of privateers, highly placed officials — could still afford their pick of finery and exotic food and drink. The *Royal Gazette* carried advertisements for silk gloves and handkerchiefs, satins, laces, and "superfine broadcloths," ribbons and jewelry, "fine, fashionable hats," silk stockings and costly hair powder, smoked oxen tongues and vintage Madeira. Public officials routinely lined their pockets. Commissaries and barrack masters robbed suppliers, drovers, and woodcutters of their rightful wages, bilked farmers of what was owed them on requisitioned teams and wagons. Property owners complained that they had never been compensated for quarters taken over by the military, although the home government had been billed for the transaction. "Though the Crown was regularly charged for the hire of them in all the barrack masters' accounts, the proprietors never got a farthing," declares Judge Thomas Jones, a disenchanted Tory. While the poor burned fat, "the mistresses, the little misses and favourite dulcineas" of influential officials, if we are to take Judge Jones at his word, were "supplied with large quantities of wood, by their orders, out of the wood yards in New York, and were regaling themselves in routs, dinners, little concerts and small parties over good, warm, comfortable fires, and enjoying all the ease and luxury in life." Chief Justice Smith, equally disgusted, describes the commandant of the city, General Pattison, as "vain and weak," the lieutenant governor, Andrew Elliot, as "insidious," and Mayor David Matthews as an outright "profligate and villain."

None suffered more acutely than the American prisoners of war, who were fair game for heartless turnkeys and grafting commissaries. Packed into stone-cold churches, cavernous sugarhouses, and foul-smelling prison ships, they underwent inexpressible pain and torment. Their rations might total no more than six biscuits, half a pound of pork, and a gill of rice every three days. Although clad in rags, they were denied even a token fire on winter nights. In the French Church, designated a prison along with the Old Dutch Church, inmates ripped out pews, doors, and window frames in their frenzy for firewood. At Bridewell, a glacial keep, Hessian guards extinguished the fires every night at nine o'clock, even in the cold weather, savagely clubbing men who hung over the last embers. Prisoners succumbed in droves to cold and sickness.

Men not consigned to vacant churches and sugarhouses were taken aboard one of the five prison ships anchored in Wallabout Bay. We are told by one of their number that they resembled "walking skeletons, with scarcely any clothes to cover their nakedness and overrun with lice from head to foot." They were crammed into holds that were never aired or cleaned out. Always there was a stench, heavy and overpowering. Much of what the men ate consisted of contaminated leftovers from other British ships. Disease took a monstrous toll. It is said that more than eleven thousand prisoners died in the rat-infested holds, many within days of their arrival.

Judge Jones says that Joshua Loring, the commissioner of prisoners, appropriated "nearly two-thirds of the rations allowed to the prisoners" and "actually starved to death about 300 of the poor wretches before an exchange took place." Nor was William Cunningham, the provost marshal who had presided at Nathan Hale's execution, any less cold-blooded and avaricious. He is said to have put arsenic into the food given some of the prisoners, collecting on rations still allotted them after their demise. According to Judge Jones, these and other corrupt officials made off with "twenty millions sterling of the money raised by Great Britain for the support of the American war."

Much of the criticism found its way to headquarters. Clinton, although not accused of graft or wrongdoing, was derided as a lightweight who played favorites. General James Robertson, governor of British-occupied New York, described him as "inconstant as a weathercock." His deputy adjutant general, Stephen Kemble, deplores his "unheard-of promotion to the first departments of boys not three years in the service, his neglect of old officers and his wavering, strange, mad behavior." Chief Justice Smith rated him a "trifler" after beholding him decked out in kilts on the feast day of St. Andrew. Nor did those around Sir Henry escape censure. They were "without reputation, young and raw," Smith says. Even André was suspect, having "acted upon the stage all winter."

A Different Drumbeat

It was the letter Tallmadge was waiting for. Although it carried the signature of Samuel Culper, Senior, its author was actually Abraham Woodhull of Setauket, Long Island, where Tallmadge's father was minister of the village church. It notified Tallmadge that "a faithful friend" would spy for the Americans in British-occupied New York. Woodhull identified the "friend" as Samuel Culper, Junior, but this, too, was a fictitious name. Culper Junior was in truth Robert Townsend, a young Quaker from Oyster Bay now living in New York.

The Culpers headed a spy ring based in Setauket. It included Lieutenant Caleb Brewster, a whaleboat captain, and two or three couriers, of whom the most active and useful was a citizen named Austin Roe. False names and code numbers were used to mask identities. Tallmadge, who kept within easy reach of Long Island Sound, referred to himself as "John Bolton." But numbers were generally used. Tallmadge was assigned number 721; Culper Senior, 722; Culper Junior, 723. Austin Roe was 724; Caleb Brewster, 725. Washington was given a number — 711. Places, too, were so designated. New York was 727; Long Island, 728; Setauket, 729. Identities were so closely guarded that even Tallmadge's predecessor, General Charles Scott, was kept in the dark. In a letter to

Washington, Scott would refer to John Bolton as "the person whom Majr. Tallmadge recommended to your Excellency some time ago. . . . There will be no dainger of his being discovered. I do not know his propper name myself."

Culper Junior lived with a married couple named Underhill, not far from British headquarters. Some of Clinton's officers were billeted in the same house, but they paid scant attention to the retiring, soft-spoken Quaker. Each morning he would set forth at the same hour, ostensibly to conduct his dry goods business, but actually to eavesdrop in the vicinity of headquarters. He spent much of his time at James Rivington's coffee house, a gathering place for officers. Rivington was publisher of the *Royal Gazette,* a Tory mouthpiece, and he and Culper were close friends. Indeed, it is thought that Rivington himself may have been a spy, slipping military intelligence to the Americans. In the Culper code he was number 726.

Culper handed his information to one of the couriers, who sped it to Setauket. Here it was hidden in Culper Senior's meadow until Anna Strong, a neighbor whose house commanded an unencumbered view of the nearby shore, announced Brewster's arrival by hanging a black petticoat on her clothesline. She was the wife of Selah Strong, whose sister Zipporah was Benjamin Tallmadge's stepmother. Next to the petticoat Anna pinned from one to six handkerchiefs to indicate at which of half a dozen inlets Brewster's whaleboat was waiting. Culper Senior would then sneak the intelligence to Brewster, who would cross Long Island Sound and deliver it to Tallmadge.

Washington was much concerned for the safety of the spy ring.

> If you think you can depend on C——'s fidelity [he wrote Tallmadge], I should be glad to have an interview with him myself, in which I would endeavour to put the mode of correspondence upon such a footing that, even if his letters were to fall into the enemy's hands, he would have nothing to fear on that account.

Although the two never got together, no safeguards were overlooked. The code was employed. Messages were disguised as family letters or business communications. But nothing could quite eliminate the risk.

> I this day just saved my life [Culper Senior exclaimed after one hair-raising encounter]. Soon after I left Hempstead Plains and got into the woods I was attacked by four armed men. One of them I had frequently seen in N. York. They searched every pocket and lining of my clothes, shoes, and also my saddle, which the enclosed was in, but thank kind providence they did not find it.

Another time he was reported to Colonel Simcoe, André's chunky, powerfully built friend, who was on the lookout for rebel spies in that part of Long Island. Simcoe descended on Woodhull's residence but, finding him absent, vented his spleen on his defenseless father.

Washington urged that Culper Junior "mix as much as possible among the officers and refugees, visit the coffee houses and all public places . . . and pay particular attention to the movements by land and water in and about the city." The spy should keep check on any troop transfers and on the arrival and departure of British ships. He should learn everything he could about the fortifications rimming the city, about food supplies, forage, and firewood. Washington expressed a wish for a less hazardous route than that employed by the Culpers. Their messages often arrived too late to be of much use.

Through his friend John Jay, Washington obtained a consignment of invisible ink provided by Jay's physician brother, Sir James Jay. It involved two agents, one for writing the hidden message, the other for developing it. Washington advised Culper Junior to commit his messages to "a common pocket book," or to write them "on the leaves at each end of registers, almanacks, or any publication or book of small value." Or he might "write a letter in the Tory style with some mixture of family matters and between the lines and on the remaining part of the sheet communicate with the stain the intended intelligence."

Washington urged that Culper Junior not lay aside the dry goods business that screened his activities.

> I would imagine [he wrote Tallmadge], that with a little in-
> dustry he will be able to carry on his intelligence with greater
> security to himself and greater advantages to us under cover
> of his usual business, than if he were to dedicate himself wholly
> to the giving of information. [This should allay suspicions that]
> would become natural should he throw himself out of the line
> of his present employment.

There were tense moments. Tallmadge made a practice of crossing the Sound from time to time to confer with Culper Senior. One day he found his informant quaking in his boots. A pair of intruders had burst into his bedroom while he was testing the invisible ink. Without looking up, he had assumed that they were two of the British officers billeted in the same house. In a surge of panic he had knocked over the vial of ink — only to glance up at two convulsed female members of the household. The pair had intended merely to "surprise" him, they protested. But Culper Senior had been scared out of his wits. It was days before he regained even "tolerable health."

Like others before him, Tallmadge was Washington's dep-uty, for the commander-in-chief served as his own head of secret service. It was he who determined policy, supervised all activities, issued directives, and saw to it that spies were paid, in specie, from a fund allotted him by Congress. Al-though he knew the identity of all his informants, they were never known to one another. Nothing of consequence was delegated to colleagues. Even the wash used in developing the Culpers' messages was kept under lock and key at head-quarters. Only Alexander Hamilton, his aide-de-camp, had access to it.

In Westchester, Tallmadge had been preceded by Brigadier

General Charles Scott, a Virginian attached to West Point. Elsewhere, others had assisted Washington. Joseph Reed, for a time adjutant general of the Continental Army, had been involved in espionage, and Colonel Elias Boudinot, the commissary of prisoners, had included intelligence work among his various duties. Major John Clark and Colonel Elias Dayton both directed spy rings, Clark in the vicinity of Philadelphia, Dayton west of the Hudson. Major Alexander Clough, like Tallmadge a Continental Dragoon, had links with several New Jersey informants. Nor were the Culpers the only spies with a Long Island connection. A Lieutenant Spencer crossed regularly from Connecticut for intelligence supplied him by a counterpart of Culper Senior's, and John Fitch, a whaleboat captain, was given information by a confederate in Lloyd's Neck. Hercules Mulligan, an astute spy, resided in New York itself. Proprietor of a fashionable clothing store on Queen Street, he counted among his clients men of rank and influence who let slip much that was useful. And Lieutenant Lewis Costigan, a paroled prisoner of war, roamed the city for all of two years, posing as a Tory and eavesdropping wherever British officers were gathered.

When not dealing with the spy ring, Tallmadge combed the Neutral Ground for Cowboys and Skinners. He describes Westchester as "the most rascally part of the country I was ever in." With British cavalry and light infantry on the prowl, he was forced to shift campsites frequently, and one day near Pound Ridge his command was routed in a surprise attack. Tallmadge lost a prized mount, most of his field baggage, and what was far worse, a bundle of papers relating to espionage. This brought him a swift but fatherly rebuke from the commander-in-chief: "The loss of your papers shews how dangerous it is to keep papers of any consequence at an advanced post. I beg you will take care to guard against the like in the future."

Among the captured papers was a letter from Washington

referring to four informants, the two Culpers among them. Culper Senior was identified only by initial. Culper Junior was not named, but his services were mentioned. A third informant was referred to only as "H." "His name and business should be kept profoundly secret," Washington had written. "Otherwise we not only lose the benefits derived from it, but may subject him to some unhappy fate."

The name and whereabouts of the fourth informant had been spelled out — "a man on York Island, living on or near the North River, of the name of George Higday, who I am told hath given signal proofs of his attachment to us, and at the same time stands well with the enemy." Higday was picked up instantly by the British. He had been promised a fortune, he told them, if he would "fech information for Washington." But he had not been paid enough to buy himself "a cow or team."

> The money was so bad I could not by [buy] one [he explained]. So I returned home, for which reason I suppose he hath sent this letter that now is taken. . . . I did not think they would write to me, for Washington said my name was in the black book for being a friend of Government [the Crown] and would not trust me. . . . I beg your Excellence for the benefit of the blessed clargey.

Higday was never put to death. He was an indifferent catch, not worth hanging.

VIII

Fidus Achates

Rawdon, drummond, and kemble — each, in turn, broke with Sir Henry. But not John André. He soon made himself indispensable to his chief, handling the flood of business with praiseworthy dispatch. He scheduled appointments, screened letters, monitored requests for promotion and for leaves of absence. He was the man to reckon with at headquarters — proficient, informed, accommodating whenever possible. Amid "the jarring of parties and the conflict of interests" that swirled around Sir Henry, André "soon became the chief person," according to an observer. "His affability, his candor and his politeness gained him universal esteem." But a less admiring observer says that André so "insinuated" himself into his chief's good graces that he achieved "an absolute ascendancy."

André performed heroically in his new post, working long hours and shouldering heavy responsibilities. He was polite with everyone, the very soul of tact. For the most part he was well liked, numbering among his friends some of the brightest young officers. He reveled in his work, wore his regimentals with pride and panache. He doted on the army and was respectful at all times toward senior officers. He had idolized Sir William Howe, had made a friend and ally of General Grey. He genuinely liked Sir Henry Clinton, however standoffish he might be with high-ranking colleagues. But beneath the ready smile and unfailing courtesy lurked intense ambition. Was he driven, as a French Huguenot's son, to make his mark in a profession long identified with the British gentry? Must he prove himself, as a merchant's son, in an establishment that held trade in contempt? Must he demonstrate the rightness of his course to his skeptical mother, to his trade-minded uncles and once worshipful sisters, even to William, his halfhearted soldier brother? He seemed destined for high rank, in spite of his mercantile beginnings and lack of family connections. And he wanted it, keenly.

André showed his initiative in a report he submitted to Sir Henry on the widespread plundering by British and Hessian troops. It was an unsparing analysis that deplored the spectacle of "soldiers loaded with household utensils which they have taken for the wanton pleasure of spoil and have thrown aside soon afterwards." These stolen goods could be the belongings of "a harmless peasant," he pointed out, "a decrepit father of a family, a widow or some other person as little an object of severity." Even the homes of Loyalists had been plundered — the very persons who were "complying with what is by the General's proclamation the price of protection." Sometimes the thieving troops had been overhauled and captured by rebel patrols. During General Howe's march from Head of Elk, some two hundred British and Hessian soldiers had been taken prisoner while pillaging.

Stealing beef cattle and poultry was "pregnant with the same evils," André held.

> I have passed with the front of a brigade and seen dressing at the fires of a licentious regiment the greatest profusion of meat and poultry, whilst on their flanks other corps were living upon salt provision and inflicting a very severe punishment on such as had presumed to transgress orders.

This could lead to bitter resentments, even to mutiny. And thieving commissaries, who collected on every pound of con-

fiscated meat while paying the erstwhile owner only a fraction
of its worth, appeared, to the underpaid British regular, "in
the odious light of a vulture fattening on his blood." Even
avowed Loyalists were sometimes robbed of their livestock.
André urged that a board of safeguard, headed by a commissary of captured cattle, be established to correct the wrongs
and "spare as much as possible the property of friends." He
had spoken plainly, had trodden on toes. Clinton was impressed, filing the report with his official papers, but we are
not told what he did about it.

For Clinton it was a winter of growing despair. He called
repeatedly for reinforcements, but none arrived. He had orders to detach ten thousand men for service in the West Indies — "the very nerves of this army," he complained. He
was held to a meager military chest, barely enough to feed
the troops and pay for firewood. He felt neglected, put upon,
and he sent Duncan Drummond to England with yet another
letter of resignation. But his offer was refused.

> In short [he writes], without provisions, ships of war, or troops
> sufficient to accomplish the services which seemed to be ex-
> pected of me, or even the smallest intelligence from Europe
> for three months past, my situation was certainly not to be
> envied.

André tried to dispel his chief's glum assessment of things.
Britain had many undeclared friends in America, after all —
potential allies who would rally to her cause at the strategic
moment. André had heard that thirty escaped prisoners of
war, members of Burgoyne's army, had been conducted safely
"above 80 miles through the rebel cantonments" by friends
of Britain. Tories and Indians were on the warpath west of
Albany. They had attacked a blockhouse, killed thirty or forty
rebel soldiers, burned farms and villages. Waverers must be
having second thoughts. And the rebel army, he learned, was
in dire need of flour. André had become Sir Henry's *fidus
Achates*, offering reassurance and encouragement.

The long hours and heavy workload — what André called his "sysiphean labors" — took their toll. He seemed ever more fatigued. He had recurrent spells of fever that kept him in bed. His waning energies were not lost on Sir Henry, who advised him to repair to a country hideaway for a much-needed rest. André chose Oyster Bay on Long Island, where his friend Simcoe was stationed with the Queen's Rangers. He was given a room in the home of Samuel Townsend, a Quaker who favored the rebels but was host to Simcoe and his officers. Known as Raynham Hall, the house was a chaste saltbox that bore witness to the family's New England roots. André liked his host and, more especially, the Townsend daughters, Audrey and Sarah, both of marriageable age. Tributes to the pair still grace a window in the house, scratched with a diamond ring by Simcoe's officers. "The adorable Miss Sarah," wrote one admirer. "Miss A.T. The most accomp. young lady in Oyster Bay," wrote another. There was also a brother, Robert Townsend, who lived in New York. If André caught sight of him while at Oyster Bay he paid little attention. He had never heard of Culper Junior.

André tells us that he and Simcoe spent long hours in "sober and various occupations and conversations." Sometimes the two went on daylong expeditions, equipped with books and drawing materials. When Simcoe was on duty, André spent his time gossiping with the Townsend girls or sketching what caught his fancy. Once he persuaded Sally to pose for him in her riding habit. When he had finished, he slipped the drawing surreptitiously under her dinner plate. Another time he made off with a pan of doughnuts she had fried for an afternoon tea party. Concealing them in a cupboard, he did not reveal their hiding place until the party was almost over — apparently to everyone's amusement, even Sally's. Simcoe trod on more dangerous ground. He addressed a St. Valentine's Day poem to Sally that extolled the "powerful magic" of her eyes. Sally, who would remain unmarried all her life, cherished the tribute. She would never find Simcoe's equal.

After returning to New York, André had a recurrence of what he called his "treacherous complaint." This time Clinton sent him to a retreat closer to the city, but he would have preferred Raynham Hall.

> When we meet again [he wrote Simcoe], it must also be a holiday for you, and we must make an excursion with two or three books, ink and pencils. I should, had I been well and remained in town, have written you concerning prologues and twenty other things, but I have been so chagrined and full of ailings that I have scarce had any other than selfish cares.

In his letter, André spoke of a forthcoming "Jersey tour." He had been chosen, with Colonel West Hyde of the Foot-guards, to negotiate a prisoner exchange with representatives from Washington's army. The assignment, André recognized, was evidence of his high standing with Sir Henry and he hoped to acquit himself with distinction. Early in April he and Hyde crossed to Perth Amboy, where they sat down with their American counterparts, Colonel William Davies and Colonel Robert H. Harrison, both well-born Virginians. To their surprise, they found the Virginians easy to relate to, men of cultivation who spoke with "temper and politeness" and had nothing in common with the untutored New England louts André had encountered at St. John's. "We must acknowledge," he wrote Clinton, "that the gentlemen we have met are personally such as we could have wished to confer with." Once negotiations started, however, Davies and Harrison proved to be a quibbling, uncompromising pair. They would not consider a proposal that some of Burgoyne's troops be exchanged for an equal number of Americans, for the latter were raw recruits and should not be equated, they said, with British regulars. They had objections to everything Sir Henry proposed, arguing over minutiae and even questioning the authority of their British counterparts. They raised "obstacles to whatever we have thrown out," André reported, and showed "a minutious spirit of contention." Neither he nor Hyde could "discover any opening or even any concession" that might salvage the parley. Finally they broke off negotiations and returned to New York "with the utmost disappointment and mortification." But André had liked Davies and Harrison — especially Harrison, whom he would not forget.

With summer at hand, Clinton advanced into the Hudson Highlands, speedily taking Stony Point and Fort Lafayette. He chose André to meet with the commandant of Fort Lafayette and deliver terms. André staged the surrender on the glacis of the fort. He received the capitulation in a ceremony that would have done justice to an event of world-shaking significance, solemnly informing the commandant that there would be no honors of war. Since the surrender took place on the king's birthday, salutes were fired off, on both shores of the Hudson, followed by "vollies of musketry and every other demonstration of joy." But not everyone was edified. Fumed one critic in a public letter to Sir Henry:

> No display of ostentatious arrangements was overlooked on this occasion, and Mr. André, your aid, as if in compliance with the taste of his General, signed a capitulation, in all the pomp of a vainglorious solemnity, on the very edge of the glacis, which he had gained under cover of a flag. What, Sir Henry, could you intend by this farce? What excuse will a person of Mr. André's reputed sense find for this parade?

André could foresee a prompt wind-up of the war. He wrote a friend that Sir Henry could now "defy Mr. Washington," who must live "in dread of having his supplies intercepted in their tedious progress to him, or being himself excluded from the Jerseys." He had heard that the Continental currency was "totally depreciated," that the Continental ranks were "without prospect of being recruited." But there were distressing problems within Sir Henry's own ranks.

> It is a pity [André continued], that our generous, spirited army, or a great part of it, should think they have grounds for being somewhat dissatisfied. Every day the disgust of old and ex-

perienced officers is seen to break forth at seeing themselves,
by the new arrangements, commanded by gentlemen of very
little military experience and recently emerged from less liberal
professions.

Clinton's partiality toward younger favorites ran counter to
seniority, the mainstay of career men.

Nor was Clinton's reputation enhanced when General William Tryon, formerly a royal governor and now commander
of the 70th Foot, led a punitive raid on the Connecticut coast,
plundering New Haven, turning both Fairfield and Norwalk
to ashes. Atrocity stories abounded. It was said that an elderly
man had been burned alive, that an infant had been pitched
into the flames, that several slaves had been incinerated. Even
schools and churches went up in smoke. In Fairfield, three
churches, two schools, and more than two hundred residences
were leveled. In Norwalk, only six houses were left standing.
A proclamation that carried Tryon's signature reminded inhabitants that their property "lay within the grasp of that
power whose forbearance you have ungenerously construed
into fear, but whose lenity has persisted in its mild and noble
efforts even though branded with the most unworthy imputation." They were advised to "reflect on what gratitude requires of you — or, if that is insufficient to move you, attend
to your own interest." Chief Justice Smith believed that André
had written the proclamation. The language seemed more his
than Tryon's. Whether or not André wrote it, he might have
agreed with Judge Smith's own verdict that the burning of
Fairfield and Norwalk was "an experiment of two towns, exasperating indeed to a few but inspiring terror in many. Every
place near the sea must dread a visit and become advocates
for peace."

The raid met with no favor on the part of Clinton, who was
appalled that the "houses of individuals, much less those of
public worship," had been set afire. He asked that Tryon's

report, with "the justification in it of the burning of Fairfield and Norwalk," not be sent to Whitehall. But Judge Smith heard that the report found its way aboard the London packet anyway. He wondered if this could be André's doing.

André's optimism received an unexpected jolt when Anthony Wayne recaptured Stony Point, accomplishing it — as General Grey would have done — solely with the bayonet. Unlike Grey, however, Wayne applied his steel sparingly. "No instance of inhumanity was shown by any of the unhappy captives," General Pattison said in a letter to Lord Amherst. "No one was unnecessarily put to the sword or wantonly wounded."

A few weeks later "Light-Horse Harry" Lee led a raid on the British garrison at Paulus Hook, catching the defenders off guard and taking more than one hundred fifty prisoners. Then Rhode Island was evacuated, a move deemed essential to a more consolidated strategy. The bright outlook following the capture of Stony Point and Fort Lafayette seemed suddenly to have vanished. André was dismayed by the turn of events. To add to his distress, his friend Simcoe was taken prisoner during a raid by the Queen's Rangers and now lay under lock and key in a New Jersey jail. André appealed to American authorities for his friend's release, citing the parole given Colonel Baylor after the Tappan "massacre." He was about to approve a plan to storm the jail when Simcoe was returned in an exchange.

Although André favored a harder line than his chief, he agreed that no effort should be spared to safeguard the lives and property of the king's friends. When a group of Tories formed the Associated Loyalists, a unit organized by direction of Lord Germain to raid the New England coast, he warned them not to undercut Sir Henry "by carrying distress where he might wish to protect." Their activities must not get out of hand. They must submit full reports after each raid. They must curb hotheads and reimburse the king's friends for chance property damage. Neither he nor Clinton was happy about the association, which wished to be independent of the British military. Months passed before it received official recognition.

As André rose in Clinton's esteem, others, including Rawdon and Drummond, fell from Clinton's favor, and broke with their chief. "Neither of them go near him," Judge Smith noted in the summer of 1779. Nor was Colonel Kemble, the deputy adjutant general, on solid ground. In his journal he refers to Clinton as "despised and detested" and says that "if the Government does not remove him soon, our affairs in this country will be totally undone." Nor was Clinton on better terms with his high-ranking colleagues. Although Lord Howe had retained his respect, Clinton feuded openly with Admirals Gambier and Arbuthnot. He disliked General Robertson, the governor of New York, and he had little regard for Tryon. His relations with his old friend General Phillips would turn edgy. And he was increasingly suspicious of Lord Cornwallis, his second in command.

André was the great exception. He and Clinton, who seem never to have quarreled, had much in common. Both were driven by powerful ambition. Both found relaxation in sport — in handball and the noonday canters. Both relished the company of the fair sex, although André avoided binding commitments. And at a deeper level they saw eye to eye. Clinton was a deist. What religion he had was perfunctory. Not for him the fervor of Wesleyan preachers or even the more restrained usages of the established Church. Stirred by fine music and the spectacle of lofty peaks, he found solace in art and nature.

The same was true of André, although his love of nature was less articulated than Sir Henry's. No jotting from his pen shows more than a polite attachment to his ancestral faith. He might attend church on occasion, as when he sketched drowsing Huguenots during his early years and relished the Tory preachments of Thomas Barton while a prisoner of war in Lancaster. He might listen respectfully to the pronouncements from the pulpit, the readings from the lectern, the recitation of the Creeds, the words of ancient hymns. But he seems to have been no more given to matters of rite and doctrine than Sir Henry. Both settled for a flinty stoicism.

In other respects the two were nothing alike, but this seemed to solidify the friendship. André, unlike his chief, had no quarrel with himself or others. It was not in him to nurse grudges, harbor suspicions, blame colleagues for his own mistakes. Where he was open toward others, Sir Henry was suspicious and withdrawn. Where he was by nature affable, Sir Henry was austere and churlish. Where he attracted others to him, Sir Henry was apt to turn them off. Yet the two not only got along famously but became mutually supportive. In Clinton, André had a mentor who could assist his career, a father figure who encouraged and fostered his ambitions as his own father had failed to do. In André, Clinton had an alter ego whose sense of self-worth compensated for his own lacks. Theirs was an unlikely pairing, but it seemed to work.

Was there a homoerotic attraction that might account for their odd yoking? Of Clinton's aides, no other served him as supportively as André or complemented him more harmoniously. No one else gained so large a measure of his esteem and affection. And yet no scrap of evidence — no rumor, no bit of hearsay, no hint in diary or letter, even though New York teemed with gossip — indicates more than a fatherly attachment on Clinton's part, a filial devotion and fondness on André's. If there was a homoerotic link between the two, it would seem to have been latent and unrecognized.

Clinton was adding to André's responsibilities. Late in April 1779, he assigned him to military intelligence, although this had been the province of Colonel Stephen Kemble, the deputy adjutant general.

A Different Drumbeat

TALLMADGE ASSEMBLED HIS MEN near Stamford — a task force that included dismounted dragoons, infantry, and oarsmen to man the whaleboats. Although it was not yet October, there was a chill in the night air as he set forth for Lloyd's Neck, across from Stamford on Long Island Sound. The Tories stationed there had been raiding the Connecticut coast. Tallmadge vowed to "kill or take the whole gang of marauders and plunderers."

Tallmadge put ashore near two fortified buildings, ordering part of his command to surround the first while he and the others targeted the second. The two divisions advanced quietly, making sure that no one opened fire or spoke above a whisper. "We surrounded both houses nearly at the same time," he says, "hoping the surprise would be so great that no firing would take place." He almost succeeded, but before the buildings could be encircled a few Tories made their escape. Tallmadge burned the enemy's boats, herded his prisoners to the landing place, and got off before an alert could be sounded. He had accomplished the raid without losing a man.

Tallmadge had been informed of the Tory post by Culper Senior. "You must keep a very good lookout or your shores will be destroyed," Culper had warned. "It is a pity that company could not be destroyed at Lloyd's Neck." Tallmadge had moved swiftly. Already the spy ring had shown its worth.

IX

"Refuse None, but Mistrust All!"

Spies should be drawn "from the court to the cabin," wrote Captain Donkin in his military manual. "Statesmen, soldiers, clergy and countrymen" were good prospects all, but none should be trusted. "Sow them in the enemy's camp without their knowing each other," he advised. "Refuse none, but mistrust all! For if it be a dangerous profession, 'tis equally hazardous to him that depends on their intelligence." André's collection of spies and informants must have delighted Donkin. They came from every rank and station — old and young, rich and poor, women as well as men. Physicians, tradesmen, and farmers were among them, a judge and a divine, doughty housewives and an intrepid schoolmistress.

The intelligence service was as old as the British Army itself, but it had remained a stepchild, somehow tainted and scorned, linked to spies, informers, turncoats, and outright rogues. No training was required, for recruits came from all walks of life and included some men of note. Chaucer transmitted information to John of Gaunt, Defoe to the Earl of Oxford. Intelligence chiefs were known as "scoutmasters," or "intelligencers." These, too, might have shaky claims on their peculiar calling. At one time an Irish bishop served as scoutmaster, and in the seventeenth century George Downing, also a cleric, served as scoutmaster general for Cromwell's army.*

Notable chiefs included Sir Francis Walsingham, secretary of state to Queen Elizabeth I, Sir Samuel Luke, scoutmaster to the Earl of Essex during England's civil war, and John Thurloe, Cromwell's secretary of state. Walsingham developed a network that spread through European courts. Luke is said to have kept so close a watch on Royalists that "they eat, sleep, drink not, whisper not, but he can give us an account of their darkest proceedings." With the help of three deputies, he learned the location of enemy troops, the state of their morale, the strategy of their leaders. Thurloe served seven years in his post, fashioning a network that reached into far distant courts. He followed the plots and intrigues that flourished in such places, as well as the least doings of Britain's Royalists, even their "drinking, dancing and wenching." Cromwell allotted vast sums of money to maintain the spy ring, as much as £7000 a year. So sinister was Thurloe's influence that intelligence became, more than ever, a synonym for dark schemes.

Under James II, the duties of scoutmaster general were combined with those of quartermaster general, but the Duke of Marlborough, commander of Britain's forces, served as his own intelligence chief. His network of spies, extending into foreign courts and enemy troop encampments, provided him with both political and military intelligence. In defending the network's cost, he stressed the importance of effective espionage:

> No war can be conducted successfully without early and good intelligence. Nobody can be ignorant of this that knows anything of secret correspondence or considers the numbers of persons that must be employed in it, the great hazard they

---

*The same for whom Downing Street is named.

undergo, the variety of places in which the correspondence must be kept, and the constant necessity there is of supporting and feeding this Service — not to mention some extraordinary expenses of a higher nature, which ought only to be hinted at.

In the campaign for Quebec in 1759, General Wolfe, like Marlborough, took charge of intelligence. By reconnoitering the French position, questioning informants, and mastering all available reports, he ascertained where best to mount his attack. Much of what he learned he kept secret, known only to himself. Two decades later Washington would do the same.

Customarily the adjutant general doubled as intelligence chief, performing the duties of both offices. All reports and secret communications crossed his desk. Spies and informants were answerable to him. It was he who issued directives, saw that spies were paid, and interviewed deserters and turncoats. During the Revolutionary War, Generals Gage, Howe, and Clinton assigned the responsibility to Stephen Kemble as deputy adjutant general, although neither Howe nor Clinton placed much value on his services.

Stephen Kemble, son of a New Jersey Loyalist and brother-in-law of Gage, was a career officer who had served as Gage's aide-de-camp, been advanced through his influence to major, and, again through the good offices of his brother-in-law, been named deputy adjutant general. He seems to have been a conscientious, if undistinguished, bureaucrat, prone to self-pity and spite. By the time André became Clinton's aide, Kemble was already on the outs with Sir Henry. It is said that he maligned Clinton in secret.

As Gage's intelligence chief, Kemble had depended increasingly on spies and informants, rather than on what British officers might ascertain from deserters and prisoners of war. A certain John Howe was his most audacious operative. Disguised as a countryman, with "a small bundle tied up in a homespun checked handkerchief in one hand and a walking

stick in the other," Howe had made a survey of the roads
leading to Worcester, where local patriots had secreted military
stores. On his way back, he had persuaded trusting citizens
in Concord to show him the guns and ammunition they had
hidden away. Howe's report received instant attention at
headquarters. On April 19, 1775, less than two weeks later,
a British column set forth by way of Lexington to seize the
Concord stores.

Among Gage's informants, none quite equaled Dr. Benjamin Church. Trusted by his fellow countrymen, he had spied
for the British before hostilities began, had relayed intelligence to Gage while serving in the Provincial Congress, and
had continued on his duplicitous course after Lexington and
Concord. But not for long. By the fall of 1775 Church had
been clapped in jail, and Gage had lost an irreplaceable informant.

Benjamin Thompson, later known as Count Rumford, may
have assisted Church. He was Britain's secret friend and may
have been a paid informer. Among the Gage papers is a message from Thompson in invisible ink. It warns of a possible
attack on Castle William in Boston Harbor, reports that as
many as thirty thousand men were being recruited throughout
New England, and predicts that Congress, with an eye to
independence, would soon request foreign help. By the end
of 1775, the future scientist, diplomat, and count of the Holy
Roman Empire had joined his British allies. If he had tarried
much longer he might have followed Church to a rebel jail,
and his astonishing career might never have taken place.

Joseph Galloway of Philadelphia, a member of the First
Continental Congress and for eight years speaker of the Pennsylvania assembly, was a strategically placed spy. Early in the
war he informed the British that Benjamin Franklin favored
independence. When Howe marched on Philadelphia from
Head of Elk, Galloway supplied military intelligence of such
great value, if we are to take him at his word, that it helped

defeat Washington on the Brandywine. During the British occupation he served as superintendent of police in Philadelphia, with "upwards of eighty spies" under his direction. He kept Howe informed on what Congress was up to, even devised a plan to kidnap that historic body.

Judge John Potts, also of Philadelphia, is described by a contemporary as "one of the most confidential men Sir Wm. Howe employ'd." On one occasion he was paid nearly a thousand dollars for military intelligence. And Thomas Robinson and Peter Dubois, informants who had fled their homes to join the British, received large emoluments.

Some of Kemble's agents came to a sorry end. A Dr. John Kearsley, yet another Philadelphian, was arrested by the patriots and, like André, taken first to Lancaster, then to Carlisle. So great were his privations that he succumbed the day after his release. Two spies who may have worked for Galloway, Thomas Shanks and Thomas Church, were hanged for their exploits. On the board that condemned Shanks was Major General Benedict Arnold, the hero of Saratoga.

In 1777 a dozen spies and Tory recruiting agents were put to death by patriots. When Edmund Palmer, the previously mentioned lieutenant in Tryon's command, was hanged by General Israel Putnam's troops, Putnam informed Tryon that the hapless Tory "was taken in my camp as a spy — he was condemned as a spy — and you may rest assured, Sir, he shall be hanged as a spy." Moses Dunbar, another spy, was hanged in Hartford on land now part of the Trinity College campus. And Daniel Taylor, who carried a message from Clinton to Burgoyne inside a silver bullet, swallowed the bullet when he was stopped near Newburgh but was made to cough it up with the help of an emetic. When the bullet had been pried open, Daniel Taylor was hanged.

British intelligence, loosely organized under Gage, was stepped up under Howe and Clinton. By the time André became involved, the list of spies and informants had grown apace. None surpassed Cortlandt Skinner in diligence and ingenuity. A former New Jersey attorney general, he had tried to smuggle secret records of Congress to the British, painstakingly copied out in his own hand. When these were intercepted, he had fled to Staten Island and been made brigadier of a Loyalist regiment. His headquarters were at the Kruzer-Pelton house, where André would frequently confer with him behind locked doors.

Skinner directed a spy ring that reached across New Jersey to the Delaware. His agents had infiltrated Washington's ranks during the retreat in the fall of 1776. The next summer, when Washington's intentions were in doubt, Skinner's spies had brought word of a possible showdown at Philadelphia. More recently, they had warned of an attack on Staten Island that could have caught the British off guard. But Skinner's most enterprising spy was James Moody, who joined his regiment at the head of seventy recruits. Many of his exploits were on the western frontier, where he was liaison between British headquarters and Colonel John Butler, the Tory bushfighter who had joined with the Iroquois to spread terror and havoc. It was Moody who informed Sir Henry of the bloody Wyoming Valley massacre in midsummer 1778. Skinner says that his foremost agent "gained many articles of important intelligence concerning the movements of Colonel Butler, the real state of the rebel country, the situation and condition of the rebel armies under the command of Generals Washington, Sullivan, etc." The Reverend Charles Inglis, rector of Trinity Church, New York, describes him as "one of the most active partisans we have." He wrote a friend that Moody "perhaps has run more risque than any other man during the war. . . . The history of his adventures will entertain and astonish you."

Beverley Robinson was Skinner's counterpart. A boyhood friend of Washington's in their native Virginia, he had married into the wealthy Philipse family and acquired a country seat opposite West Point. His wife's fortune had enabled him to become one of the large landowners in the Hudson Valley and an influence in its affairs. But he was not happy with the Declaration of Independence or the break with England. John Jay advised him to make a choice — side with his own countrymen for better or for worse, or take up with the British. Robinson opted for the Crown and, repairing to New York, became colonel of a Tory regiment. He continued to keep in touch with former neighbors and tenants who thought as he did, encouraging them to spy for the British. He even tried to prevail on General Putnam to change sides — predictably, without success.

Several Hudson Valley spies were in touch with Robinson. Others operated independently. They were a venturesome lot. John Cane and John Lawson spied on West Point, Reuben Powell on the American troops near Peekskill. David Babcock and Thomas Ward reported on the location and strength of Continental regiments. Joseph McNeil set fire to some rebel barracks. A Mrs. Williams infiltrated Washington's encampment, and a Miss Barret spied on Sheldon's dragoons near Crompond. Other Hudson Valley informants included Solomon Bradbury, Manuel Elderbeck, Sylvanus Hughson, and William Jacobs. Robinson hoped to intercept communications between Washington's headquarters and Congress. "I believe I can get a man to undertake it," he wrote Clinton, "but he asks 100 guineas for the risk." Espionage was not cheap.

Elijah Hunter, also from the Hudson Valley, was a double agent, trusted by the British but apparently in league with the Americans. He made it his practice to drop in at British headquarters with bits of seemingly useful (although valueless) information, while learning what he could about the enemy's plans, strategy, troop movements, and food supplies. His role was "of too delicate a nature," as Washington puts it, to permit many missions. But he seems to have escaped detection. André trusted him implicitly. Indeed, Hunter would be one of the last spies ever brought to his attention.

Like Beverley Robinson, William Rankin of Pennsylvania broke with his patriot friends on the question of independence. A colonel in the York County militia and a former member of the provincial legislature, he is said to have rallied six thousand Loyalists to his standard. Christopher Sower, formerly editor of a German-language newspaper in Philadelphia, was his link with Clinton. Sower had accompanied the British to New York, where he founded another Tory paper for German readers, *Staats-Courier*.

Sower kept in touch with Rankin through a courier, one Andrew Fürstner, who brought word that Rankin would retain his commission in the York County militia until "ordered to appear in the King's behalf." When Sower requested a sign to safeguard their activities, he was told that a six-dollar Continental bill would be enclosed as proof of authenticity.

In midwinter 1779, Rankin joined with Colonel Butler in plans to storm the rebel magazine at Carlisle. According to his informants, the depository contained one thousand stand of arms, great quantities of gunpowder, several field pieces, and "divers other military articles" for an expedition against the Iroquois. Rankin hoped to have one of his confederates put in command of a regiment attached to the expedition. Sower pointed out that "if this can be obtained, of which they have the fairest prospects, Colonel Butler will have little to fear."

Clinton was at Southampton when Fürstner arrived with the proposal. Rather than permit any delay, Sower made an abstract of Rankin's plan and set forth on his own for the far tip of Long Island. On the way he stopped off to consult André at Oyster Bay. In perusing the abstract, André was bothered by its free use of proper names. If it were intercepted, many friends of the Crown would face imprisonment or worse. He rewrote the abstract in the form of a brief memorandum, taking care to omit names.

I have thought it proper to detail it [he explained to Clinton] and give him in its room memoranda of the heads of what he has to communicate, as it was in his own paper detailed in such a manner that should it fall into improper hands, a train of correspondence with names, etc., would have been laid open.

Although the raid never transpired, André's acumen was not lost on Sir Henry.

Samuel Wallis was a confederate of Rankin's, although he posed as a patriot and had sworn allegiance to the rebel government. His home on the West Branch of the Susquehanna was a hotbed of intrigue and secret schemes. So artfully did he conceal his activities that André, reminded of an earlier and more impulsive betrayal, gave him the code name of "Peter." Wallis, who was said to be "better acquainted with the Indian country than almost anyone else," had supplied information to General Howe and would continue his services under Clinton. He was involved in the plot to place one of Rankin's cronies in a key position in the Sullivan campaign against the Iroquois. He even handed the American commander a false map of the Iroquois country. He was involved, too, in efforts to launch an Indian offensive in western Pennsylvania under Joseph Brant, the Mohawk chieftain. John André was informed of it. He urged that local Tories furnish intelligence to Brant and support him "by a sudden meeting of loyalists at a particular place, to join and strike with him, or by intercepting convoys, burning magazines, spiking cannon, breaking down bridges, or otherwise as you shall see expedient." But the plan never came off, and André's directive went no farther than his chief's bulging file of official papers and correspondence.

Joseph Stansbury was Wallis's own link with headquarters. A Philadelphia shopkeeper who dealt in china and crockery, he had a reputable clientele and incurred little suspicion, even though he had served as a commissioner for the city watch

under Howe. When the British left Philadelphia he had taken
an oath of allegiance to the rebel cause. But he indulged a
flair for writing verse, and to give heart to those who shared
his sentiments he secretly penned lines like these:

> Think not, though wretched, poor and naked,
> Your breast alone the load sustains;
> Sympathizing hearts partake it;
> Britain's monarch shares your pains.
>
> This night of pride and folly over,
> A dawn of hope will soon appear.
> In its light you will discover
> Your triumphant day is near.

Among Stansbury's customers was Benedict Arnold, the
American commander in Philadelphia and, as of April 1779,
Peggy Shippen's husband.

Although convinced that "women in general ought not to be
trusted," Captain Donkin was not wholly averse to female
spies. They tended to attract less attention than their male
counterparts and were less apt to incur suspicion. He concedes
that "in time of war they may be very serviceable on certain
occasions and assist by their cleverness in bringing plans to
bear."

Donkin could have had no quarrel with the women spying
for the British in the spring of 1779. A Mrs. Read ascertained
the location and strength of Tallmadge's Dragoons. A Miss
Covert kept her eye on an encampment of Continentals across
the Hudson from West Point. A Mrs. Richardson brought word
that the Iroquois had destroyed a rebel magazine, that militia
in frontier communities were discouraged and prone to desert.
None, however, could match Ann Bates, a Philadelphia
schoolteacher married to an armorer in Clinton's artillery train.
Disguised as a peddler, she presented herself at Washington's
encampment ostensibly to sell combs and knives, needles,

thread, and medicinal rhubarb. She had with her five guineas
to cover expenses and a token that would identify her to a
confederate in the Continental ranks. But no sooner had she
reached the encampment than she was told that her confederate had disappeared. Unfazed, she continued on her own,
resolved to visit each of Washington's brigades.

> I then divided my little stock in different lots [she tells us],
> as near as I could form an idea of their number of brigades,
> allowing me one lot for sale in each brigade, by which means
> I had the opportunity of going through their whole army re-
> marking at the same time the strength and situation of each
> brigade and the number of cannon, with their situation and
> weight of ball.

Ann's marriage to an armorer had its practical uses.

Somewhere in the big encampment Ann happened upon a
Freemason of her acquaintance whom she could either ma-
nipulate or safely trust.

> By conversation I found he would suit my purpose [she says],
> and, being a Freemason, gave him what money I made of my
> goods that he might attend the lodge and get acquainted with
> the commissary's clerk, who was also a Freemason, and keep
> company with such as would be likely to know the state of
> affairs.

Her Freemason friend gave her information about Washington's commissary department that more than compensated for
the slight expense.

On her way back to New York, Ann was stopped by an
American patrol that searched her from head to toe. Nothing
incriminating came to light, for she had committed all she had
observed to memory, but she was robbed of her silver shoe
buckles, a silver thimble, and three dollars from her expense
account. Undeterred, she agreed to set forth on yet another
mission. This time she obtained further information about
Washington's artillery, ammunition supply, and provisions.

She even gained access to his headquarters, where she garnered some revealing facts from a loose-tongued aide-de-camp.

But time was running out, for one day Ann was recognized
by a British deserter in the Continental ranks. "Oblig'd to
make a precipitate retreat," as she puts it, she attached herself
to a brigade that was transferring to another location. She
remained with it long enough to count the artillery — "eighteen field pieces, long sixes and long tens." Near the British
lines she was stopped by a detachment of infantry under General Charles Scott, Tallmadge's predecessor as area intelligence chief. When asked to explain her business, she said
that she was an American army wife, that she had lost some
personal belongings "five or six miles below White Plains,"
and that she was now on her way to search them out. Scott
swallowed her story whole and bade her godspeed. He would
never know that he had let Clinton's most resourceful female
operative slip through his fingers.

Ann could no longer "prosecute discoveries," she tells us,
in Washington's encampment. But there were missions of a
different kind. "A friend that was in connection with General
Arnold" wished to meet with someone from British headquarters at a place some fifty miles from Philadelphia. Ann
agreed to go there, no doubt at John André's behest. Put
ashore on the New Jersey coast, she made her way inland,
traveling during the daylight hours, staying the night with
Tory confederates. When she reached the designated spot she
found, to her astonishment, that Arnold's deputy was a woman.
Ann accompanied her to New York, dropping her off at headquarters. We can only guess the purpose of the interview, for
on this subject Ann is scrupulously noncommittal.

Even Captain Donkin must have conceded that Ann far
outshone some of her male counterparts. Metcalf Bowler, chief
justice of Rhode Island, began spying for the British in 1776.
His long-winded reports, signed "Rusticus," contained little
that was new, much that was wishful thinking. He predicted

an invasion of Canada that never came off. He warned, mistakenly, of an imminent attack on Newport. While visiting Boston, he found "the people much divided, everyone wishing an end to the contest and deprecating the first authors of their misery." Their currency was "such vile trash," Bowler claimed, "that they value it not more than the dirt under their feet." Were "a B[ritish] fleet to appear and blockade the harbor," he declared, "and a land force lay siege to the town, not an hundred inhabitants would go out, for they had rather submit to B[ritish] Government than be oppressed in the manner they now are." In less euphoric moments he bemoaned the losses he had incurred at the hands of Clinton's troops.

> Not a rail left, not a single fence on the whole farm [he complained]. My only cow, the support of my children, most wantonly butchered. . . . My three horses and colt on my farm, with my cart, taken from me into the King's service.

Bowler's last communication was dated October 2, 1779. It is doubtful if Clinton even read it.

British spies were everywhere, from the Hudson to the Delaware, from Vermont to the Rhode Island coast. Samuel Shoemaker was at work in Philadelphia, Andrew Patchen in Connecticut, Robert Ferguson and Dr. John Haliburton in Rhode Island. Ferguson made a map of Providence for the British. Captain Nehemiah Marks, in charge of British espionage on Long Island Sound, linked Caleb Brewster to the Culper spy ring, but the gods smiled on Brewster and he was never caught. Joseph Chew and John Rattoon, both couriers, would risk their skins in an affair that involved John André and the fate of West Point. Of spies who were caught and hanged, one lived to tell of his ordeal. Benjamin Whitcuff, a freed slave working for the British, was hanged near Cranbury, New Jersey, and left to die. But he was saved by the timely arrival of Clinton's troops, who cut him down before he breathed his last.

Two of Clinton's agents worked secretly for the Americans. David Gray of Lenox, Massachusetts, was Beverley Robinson's courier. Before delivering Robinson's messages, Gray read through them and transmitted the information to American headquarters. Caleb Bruen, a former New Jersey minuteman, performed similar services. Although the two duped the British unconscionably, neither was found out.

Perhaps no spy was as slippery as William Heron of Redding, Connecticut, a member of the legislature, a friend of General Samuel Holden Parsons, and an enigma to fellow townsmen. He favored a reconciliation with Britain, yet he voted for the Constitution. He frequented Clinton's headquarters, using the code name "Hiram" in the course of a secret correspondence. Yet he transmitted military intelligence to Parsons, much of it picked up at British headquarters. When Tryon and his men tarried at Redding during their infamous raid, Heron served the Tory leader cakes and wine. Yet he remained the friend of Parsons.

In 1781 Heron would claim that Parsons favored the "principles of reconciliation" and could be had for a price. He told the British:

> I have on a former occasion described the man to you, his local attachments, his scruples, his prejudices and talents at intrigue; and as he had already embarked half way, your own acquaintance with the human heart will enable you to judge whether it is not probable that in time he will go through the several gradations you would wish or expect of him.

An offer was agreed upon, which Heron would urge on his friend.

> Nothing shall be wanting on my part [he promised] that may tend to beget in him a firm and perfect reliance on those offers you are pleased to authorize me to make. The ascendancy I have over him, the influence I have with him, the confidence he has already reposed in me, the alluring prospect of pecuniary as well as honorary rewards, together with the plaudits

of a grateful nation, shall all be combined together and placed in a conspicuous point of view, to engage him heartily in the cause.

No scrap of solid evidence exists to tie Parsons to so dark a plot. Although known to have been in financial straits, he served as major general until his retirement in July 1782. But what about Heron? Was he a patriot who artfully and successfully deceived the British? Or a shameless turncoat who would implicate an old friend? Or was he a double agent, committed to neither side but paid by both? The British trusted him, but so did Parsons.

Two of Clinton's officers, Captain Patrick Ferguson and Captain George Beckwith, worked closely with André. Ferguson prepared a map of the Connecticut coastline, showing channels, soundings, and strategic elevations. He urged that West Point be cut off and New Jersey invaded, pointing out that "by this measure Washington must either advance and commit himself without reserve in a general action, or lose all credit with his troops and they with themselves and the country." Ferguson's spies included both men and women. It was an anonymous woman who let him know that "an irruption of Torys and Indians" had forced Washington to detach sorely needed troops. A New Jersey spy informed him of "a magazine of forage at Westfield, another at the Scots Plains, a large one of 1500 ton at Morristown with artillery and other stores, and at Trenton a quantity of beef [and] pork brought from the South." Washington was at West Point, Ferguson learned, but would soon transfer to Morristown. He shared all of this with André.

George Beckwith, Knyphausen's aide-de-camp, was assistant adjutant general. As André's deputy, he had his own spies and informants who kept him posted on enemy troops stationed north of the city, more especially Sheldon's Horse. It was probably he who drew up guidelines for Clinton's spies. "You are to make yourself master of the state of the [American] army in general," he advised, "to know particularly the regiments, who commands them and in what manner they are brigaded, and by what generals the brigades and divisions are commanded." A spy should learn the location of magazines and obtain "an exact account of the artillery and in what manner it is placed." He should acquaint himself with "the different posts that the army occupy and where the general officers are quartered, what general officers are absent and when they are." He should ascertain "the opinion of the army relative to Congress and the prospects they have of an approaching campaign," should find out "what the French are thought to do and whether they have any movements in contemplation. Closer by, he should determine if there are any troops to be near our lines and where posted and where the militia posts are." He should "get, if possible, the standing orders of the army, an exact account of the artillery and in what manner placed, and what guns are brigaded and with what brigade." And he should learn the source of food supplies and by what route they came.

Sometimes a spy must be reassigned to other duties for his own safety. Beckwith came to the rescue of Elijah Vincent, "a young lad of uncommon bravery" who had made himself "so obnoxious to the rebels that if he falls into their hands they will certainly hang him." He asked that the youth be placed in a provincial regiment, where, as a soldier, he would not be subject to the death penalty.

Under no conditions must a spy divulge secret information to undesignated persons. William Rankin earned a rebuke for disclosing a password to one of his couriers. "We are sorry you have extended your confidence so much," André wrote him, "fearing you may be drawn into difficulties by your zeal unless tempered with much prudence." Rankin seems to have sulked, until André assured him that Clinton "shou'd be very happy to see the zeal you formerly shewed in our cause renewed and to open our communication afresh." He added that "S.H.C. [would] shew himself as sensible of the value of your service as you can desire and will treat the business with the utmost discretion and attention to your safety."

Some spies made their reports in person. David Nonsuch, an Indian from eastern Connecticut, brought word that a new fort was building at New London, that a vessel mounting thirty guns stood guard offshore. At the same time he drew attention to the plight of his people. Of the young men who joined the Continental Army not one had returned home, he said, "the whole dying of smallpox and other disorders." Only sixteen families were left in what had once been a thriving village.

Invisible ink was sometimes used for transmitting intelligence. It could be read by brushing the page with a chemical, or by holding it over a low flame. But there were risks — if a chemical were used it might be duplicated, if heat were the agent anyone could apply it. Clinton felt more comfortable with codes, or with ingeniously scissored masks. One of his codes assigns numbers to key words and proper names. It could be read by lining up the more frequently repeated numbers with commonly used words. Following are the first half dozen words with their corresponding numbers:

a	1
and	2
above	3
about	4
abscond	5
abundance	6

A more involved code begins with number 50 and continues through 200, taking us into the *D*s. Then it picks up at number 1 and goes through 30, to the end of the *E*s. Here the code returns to 201 and proceeds to its conclusion at 643. Each number represents a common word or, in some cases, a proper name. Washington is 572; Sam Adams, 592; Benedict Arnold, 597. Baltimore is 103; Boston, 119; New York, 374.

Yet another code substitutes numbers for the letters of the alphabet. Starting with number 51 for the letter *A*, it continues through 78 as *Z*, omitting J entirely, skipping numbers 56 to 59, and assigning the same number to *V* and *Y*. Or a message could be constructed from key words in a given book — perhaps the fifth edition of Blackstone's *Commentaries,* or the twenty-first and twenty-fifth editions of Bailey's *English Dictionary,* or the 1777 edition of Enteck's *New Spelling Dictionary.* The message could be found by lining up the words indicated by three numbers grouped in triplets, the first specifying the page, the second the line, the third the word's location in the line — counting from left to right. To complicate matters still more, a random figure might be added to each number in the triplet.

Sometimes only names were in code. One list, Biblically inspired, designates Washington as "James," Sullivan as "Matthew," Gates as "Andrew," Colonel John Butler as "Lazarus," and Joseph Brant as "Zebedee." Philadelphia is "Jerusalem"; the Susquehanna, the "Jordan"; the Delaware, the "Red Sea." The Indians are the "Pharisees"; Congress, the "Synagogue."

Of all secret writing the mask, or grille, was perhaps the safest. By scissoring windows in a sheet of paper, a mask was fashioned to frame each word of the message when placed over a letter or a printed page. If a letter were the medium, the hidden message was woven into it and revealed by the mask. If a printed page were used, windows were so spaced that they framed the key words. Masks with oblong windows were the easiest to make, but on one occasion, when communicating with Burgoyne, Sir Henry used a mask shaped like an hourglass, burying his message in an innocuous-sounding letter.

One spring day John André had two unexpected callers. One was Joseph Stansbury, whom he may have remembered from his winter in Philadelphia. The other was a Church of England clergyman, the Reverend Jonathan Odell. Both seemed impatient and preoccupied. They asked to meet with him behind closed doors.

Once they were alone, Stansbury opened up. General Arnold, he said, had summoned him to his home in Philadelphia. Although he had sold merchandise to Arnold, the two were not close and he was surprised at the seeming urgency of the request. When he knocked on Arnold's door he was ushered into a secluded room, where the general awaited him. Arnold seemed greatly agitated and wasted little time on preliminaries. Swearing Stansbury to the utmost secrecy, he told him that he abhorred the break with England. If allowed to continue, it would be ruinous to both countries. His voice shook as he spoke scathingly of Congress and the French alliance. He had decided, he said, to offer his services to Sir Henry Clinton. Either he would enroll at once in the British Army or, if Clinton wished, cooperate in a plan to terminate the authority usurped by Congress and restore his country to her past allegiance. He wished Stansbury to convey his offer to British headquarters.

André was told this on Monday, May 10, 1779.

A Different Drumbeat

TALLMADGE WAS PLEASED with the new code. He tried it out on Washington, notifying him that 725 (Caleb Brewster) had returned from 728 (Long Island), and the 286 (invisible ink) would be forwarded to 723 (Culper Junior).

Culper Senior used it next, in a letter to Tallmadge. His message involved Jonas Hawkins, one of the couriers:

> Dqpeu Beyocpu [Jonas Hawkins], agreeable to 28 [appointment], met 723 [Culper Junior] not far from 727 [New York] and received a 356 [letter], but on his return was under the necessity to destroy the same, or be detected, but have the satisfaction to inform you that there's nothing of 317 [importance] to 15 [advise] you of. . . . Every 356 [letter] is opened at the entrance of 727 [New York] and every 371 [man] is searched, that for the future every 356 [letter] must be 691 [written] with the 286 [invisible ink] received. They have some 345 [knowledge] of the route our 356 [letter] takes. I judge it was mentioned in the 356 [letter] taken, or they would not be so 660 [vigilant]. I do not think it will continue long so. I intend to visit 727 [New York] before long and think by the assistance of a 355 [woman] of my acquaintance, shall be able to outwit them all. The next 28 [appointment] for 725 [Caleb Brewster] is to be here the 1 of 616 [September]. . . . It may

be better times before then. I hope there will be means found out for our deliverance. Nothing could induce me to be here but the earnest desire of 723 [Culper Junior]. Friends are all well, and am your very humble servant 722 [Culper Senior].

Tallmadge had great hopes for the code. It should "render the correspondence safe," he wrote the commander-in-chief.

X

The Price of Treason

To SHIELD HIS IDENTITY, Arnold would refer to himself as "Monk," Stansbury said. André remembered that George Monk, Cromwell's general, who had conspired to thwart Parliament and restore the British monarchy, had ended up with a hefty pension and a dukedom. Arnold was indicating that he had a price.

Stansbury must return at once to Philadelphia, for he was under close surveillance and his absence would be noticed. André arranged to have him dropped off on the New Jersey coast. By taking back roads and staying the night with Crown sympathizers, he should reach home safely. Before he left, André handed him a résumé of their conversation. "On our part," he promised, "we meet Monk's overtures with full reliance on his honourable intentions and disclose to him, with the strongest assurances of sincerity, that no thought is entertained of abandoning the point we have in view." There would indeed be a financial reward commensurate with Arnold's contribution: "In case any partial but important blow shou'd by his means be struck or aimed, upon the strength of just and pointed information and cooperation, rewards equal at least to what such service can be estimated at, will be given." Should Arnold's efforts result in a military coup, "then

wou'd the generosity of the nation exceed even his most sanguine hopes." If his "every zealous attempt" should fail, he
would still have his reward, for "the cause in which he suffers
will hold itself bound to indemnify him for his losses and
receive him with the honour his conduct deserves." André
suggested the kind of services Arnold might render: supplying
military intelligence, persuading other rebel leaders to follow
his lead, or hastening the exchange of General Burgoyne's
army. "A blow of importance" on the field of battle would,
of course, be richly rewarded.

André urged the use of code or invisible ink. If code, Blackstone's *Commentaries* should be employed, or Bailey's *English
Dictionary*. If invisible ink, the letters A and F would indicate
if it should be exposed to acid or fire. When a letter was the
medium it should contain innocuous subject matter that would
arouse no suspicion, like the state of "an old woman's health."
And André had a further idea. Why not enlist Peggy Chew's
unwitting help? He would write her a letter, seemingly in all
innocence, urging her to show it to Peggy Arnold, the general's
new wife. When Peggy Chew answered his letter Peggy Arnold would add her own message, between the lines in invisible ink.

> The lady [Peggy Arnold] might write to me at the same time
> with one of her intimates [Peggy Chew, he suggested]. She
> will guess who I mean, the latter remaining ignorant of inter-
> lining [secret writing between the lines] and sending the letter.
> I will write myself to the friend and give occasion for a reply.
> This will come by a flag of truce, exchanged officer, etc., every
> messenger remaining ignorant of what they are charg'd with.
> The letters may talk of the Mischianza and other nonsense.

André's letter to Peggy Chew had every appearance of being
innocence itself:

> I hardly dare to write you after having neglected your com-
> missions and not apologized for my transgressions [he began].

I wou'd with pleasure have sent you drawings of headdresses had I been as much of a milliner as I was at Philadelphia in Mischianza times, but from occupation as well as ill health I have been obliged to abandon the pleasing study of what relates to the ladies. I should, however, be happy to resume it had I the same inducements as when I had the pleasure of frequenting yours and the Shippen family. I know besides that you have everything from Paris, the fountainhead, and therefore have less regret in neglecting your orders in this particular. I trust I am yet in the memory of the little society of Third & Fourth Street and even of the *other Peggy*, now Mrs. Arnold, who will, I am sure, accept my best respects and with the rest of the sisterhoods of both streets peruse not disdainfully this page meant as an assurance of my unabated esteem for them.

In closing, André asked after Colonel Robert H. Harrison, one of the two American negotiators with whom he and Colonel Hyde had tried to engineer a prisoner exchange.

I was never so sorry to disagree with anyone [he said]. I intended in case of agreement to have subjoined a clause that all hearts on either side shou'd be restored, or others sent in exchange. This wou'd have afforded considerable relief to many swains who still magnetically turn to the banks of the Delaware.

Either Peggy Chew never got the letter, or she failed to answer it. No reply exists, nor does André speak further of "the little society of Third & Fourth Street."

Never in their wildest dreams had Clinton or André pictured Benedict Arnold as a potential turncoat. Others maybe, but never Arnold. To be sure, he had quarreled with Congress and had his differences with colleagues; he had been harassed by certain committeemen during his command in Philadelphia. But to his countrymen he was still the shining hero of Saratoga. His patriotism seemed beyond question. As captain of the Second Company of Connecticut Footguards, he had hurried his troops to Cambridge at the first hint of armed resistance. He had stood shoulder to shoulder with Ethan Allen at the capture of Fort Ticonderoga, had attacked St. John's with a small task force, and made off with the king's sloop. He had led an army through the Maine woods to join General Montgomery in the failed attempt on Quebec. When the Americans were driven out of Canada, it was Arnold who had built a fleet and fought Carleton on Lake Champlain, gaining precious time for his countrymen. And at Saratoga he had shone, leading charge after charge until he fell, in the flush of victory, with a crippling leg wound.

Arnold had his grievances. Although advanced to major general in May 1777, he was junior to five lackluster officers promoted earlier that year. After Saratoga he had been issued a new commission that advanced the date of his promotion, giving him seniority over the less deserving five. But the hurt festered. Nor had he been reimbursed for personal debts incurred during the Canadian campaign. Assigned to the command in Philadelphia, where he might recover from his leg wound, he had clashed with Joseph Reed, head of the Supreme Executive Council, and with Reed's henchmen. They had accused him of favoritism toward Loyalists, of demeaning the sons of patriots enrolled in the militia, of using government wagons to convey privately owned merchandise, and of issuing a questionable pass to the *Charming Nancy*, a vessel in which he subsequently acquired a share. Although a committee in Congress cleared him on all counts, Reed referred four of the charges to a court-martial. Arnold must face the humiliation of being tried by a group of colleagues, none of them with a military record to compare with his.

Yet no one at Clinton's headquarters foresaw a conspiracy in the making.

It was agreed that Jonathan Odell, who lived in New York, would receive Arnold's communications and deliver them to

André. Like Stansbury, Odell was a spare-time poet, but his verses breathed a ferocity not found in those of his lay associate. Congress was one of the cleric's favorite targets, as seen in these vengeful lines:

> Joy to great Congress, joy an hundred fold;
> The grand cajolers are themselves cajol'd!
> The farce of empire will be finished soon,
> And each mock-monarch dwindle to a loon.
> Mock-money and mock-states shall melt away,
> And the mock-troops disband for want of pay . . .
> Myriads of swords are ready for the field;
> Myriads of lurking daggers are conceal'd;
> In injur'd bosoms dark revenge is nurst;
> Yet but a moment, and the storm shall burst . . .
> Now Boston trembles; Philadelphia quakes;
> And Carolina to the center shakes . . .
> Hate now of men, and soon to be the jest —
> Such is your fate, ye monsters of the West!

Stansbury notified André that Arnold would communicate in code and would be using Bailey's *English Dictionary*. His message was delivered by Odell, who had already written Arnold that André was in a hurry to start negotiations. "Lothario is impatient," he had said, using his code name for Clinton's aide-de-camp. "Convince him of your sincerity and, you may rely upon it, your most sanguine hopes will be realized." But Arnold's first letter never reached headquarters. Left at Odell's lodgings by John Rattoon, a courier given the code name of "Mercury," it had proved too much for the parson's curiosity. Odell had noticed an *F* on the communication and had held the seemingly blank page over a lighted candle — only to behold a vast splotch that obliterated all but a few disconnected words. Somehow the page had gotten wet. Moreover, it had been so "toasted" by the candle that it was now "too brittle for folding." Odell had no choice but to make a clean breast of what he had done.

I am mortified to death [he wrote André], having just received
(what I had been anxiously expecting) a letter from S——
[Stansbury] and, by a private mark agreed on between us,
perceiving it contained an invisible page for you, I assayed it
by fire, when, to my inexpressible vexation, I found that the
paper, having by some accident got damp on the way, had
spread the solution in such a manner as to make the writing
but one indistinguishable blot, out of which not the half of
any one line can be made legible.

He took occasion to point out, however, that he had spared
André "the vexation of an useless trouble."

Arnold's next letter arrived without blemish. It contained
some military intelligence — Washington was transferring his
headquarters to the Hudson Valley, the French fleet had put
to sea, the American currency was debased. What caught Sir
Henry's eye, however, was a reference to Charleston:
"C[ongress] have given up Chs. Town if attempted. They
are in want of arms, ammunition and men to defend it."
Arnold also hinted at his price — "a revenue equivalent to
the risk and services done" and indemnification for property
loss. "I cannot promise success," he said. "I will deserve it."

André, who had never laid eyes on Arnold, drafted a letter
listing ways in which the rebel hero might best serve the
British:

The most essential services for wresting this country from ruin
and oppression wou'd be in revealing the counsels of its rulers,
so as to counteract them, and in affording an opportunity to
defeat the army. Generous terms wou'd follow our success,
and ample rewards and honours wou'd be the portion of the
distinguish'd characters which wou'd contribute to so great an
end.

Then he indicated the kind of services that he and General
Clinton looked for:

Dispatches to & from foreign courts, original papers, intimation of channels thro' which intelligence passes, etc., are the

objects chiefly to be attended to, but the most brilliant and effectual blow finally to compleat the overthrow of the present abominable power wou'd be the destruction of the army. This may be effected by a grand stroke or by successive partial but severe blows.

Arnold might bring about the capture of "a considerable seaport," enabling the British to "drive away or disarm the disaffected," curb trade, and "give a spring to the just indignation of the suffering people and induce them to return to their allegiance." Could he obtain the command in the Carolinas, for example? And deliver Charleston to Sir Henry? Or might he furnish intelligence that would facilitate "intercepting a convoyed fleet to or from France or the West Indies?" On a far grander scale, Washington might be defeated in a great military showdown, with Congress seized by triumphant British troops.

> A considerable corps shall . . . march into N. England [André writes]. The consequence will be that W[ashington] will cross the North River [the Hudson] and hasten to the points attacked. He would possibly be preceded by a picked corps similar to that in Jersey under Gen. Lee ["Light-Horse Harry"], which wou'd have orders to harass, attack, awe the country, etc. Cou'd you command that corps, it might be concerted where and when it shou'd be surprised, defeated, or obliged to capitulate. . . . A chain of connivance must be very artfully laid to multiply difficulties & baffle resources. Under the circumstances, W[ashington] might be attacked, or be left to disperse from want of supplies. At such an hour, when the most boisterous spirits were with the Army and everyone intent on its fate, the seizing of Congress wou'd decide the business.

André jotted down the names of rebel leaders whom he thought might be susceptible to British overtures. First came Thomas Mifflin, the disgruntled major general said to have been involved in a plot to replace Washington with Horatio Gates. The plot had failed, and subsequently Mifflin had

resigned from the Continental Army. Could he be won over?
Was he "enterprising"? Would he help the British "seize Congress" at a propitious moment?

What about Colonel Moses Hazen? He had been Britain's
friend at the start of the Canadian campaign, had notified
Carleton when Arnold and Ethan Allen seized Fort Ticonderoga. "Hazen may be had," André wrote. "He is artful and
enterprising. He will be a good creature of [Arnold], whom
he knows and to whom he had betray'd *us* in Canada."

"Is it possible to do anything with Maxwell?" André wondered. General William Maxwell, who served honorably in
Canada, had since been accused of misconduct and drunkenness. There was talk of his being dismissed from the Continental ranks. Might he respond to an overture?

And what about General Arthur St. Clair? He had been
accused of surrendering Fort Ticonderoga in return for silver
bullets fired over the wall by Burgoyne's army. However ludicrous the story, it had been widely peddled and St. Clair
had been brought before a court-martial. He had once served
in the British Army, had been with Wolfe at Quebec. Might
he be having second thoughts?

Then there was Philip Schuyler, whom André had gotten
to know on his way southward from St. John's. In the quiet
of his family mansion, Schuyler had spoken hopefully of reconciliation. Indeed, Major John Dyke Acland, a British grenadier captured at Saratoga, quoted him as having an "aversion"
to independence and as having "assured" him that "many of
his friends and relations (naming them, and they were of the
first influence) felt as he did." Like his colleague St. Clair,
Schuyler had been blamed for the loss of Fort Ticonderoga.
Although he had been cleared by a court-martial, his good
name had suffered and his military career had been sidetracked. Clinton had discussed Schuyler's availability with
Chief Justice Smith, but Smith says he "exploded this vain
idea effectually and taught him to perceive that the converted

leaders had no safe door open to serve the Crown till the King's army drew near them." Regardless of where the king's army might be, however, Schuyler was no "converted leader." Within a year he was a delegate to Congress, firmly committed to independence.

Finally, there was the matter of Arnold's rank. Might he be given "provincial major general's rank?" André wondered. "He asks his own rank in the British Army." André's speculations were never released from Clinton's private file. But they are a clue to the hopes aroused by Arnold's overture.

Arnold was indeed a catch but, in Clinton's opinion, not a consummate one. His quarrels with Congress, his ongoing dispute with Joseph Reed and the Pennsylvania Council, had left him a reduced hero. When he asked to be admitted more fully into Clinton's long-range plans, he was advised by André to busy himself with his own contribution:

> H[is] E[xcellency] wishes to apprize you that he cannot reveal his intentions as to the present campaign, nor can he find the necessity of such a discovery, or that a want of a proper degree of confidence is to be inferred from his not making it.

Arnold should get on with what was expected of him.

> Accept a command, be surprised, be cut off [André urged]. These things may happen in the course of manoeuvre, nor could you be censured or suspected. A compleat service of this nature involving a corps of 5 or 6,000 men would be rewarded with twice as many thousand guineas.

Nor should Arnold forget the plight of Burgoyne's troops, who were anxiously awaiting their exchange:

> It cou'd be urged by none with more propriety, nor wou'd you be sorry to see this act of justice superadded to the shining revolution you may perhaps be instrumental in effecting. . . . It is service of this nature . . . which S[ir] H[enry]

looks for. It is such as these he pledges himself shall be rewarded beyond your warmest expectations.

But vague promises and talk of a "shining revolution" were not to Arnold's liking. He wanted the reward spelled out in cold cash.

On July 11 Arnold named his price. He communicated it through Stansbury, who referred to him as "Gustavus" and to André as "John Anderson" — code names that would identify them during the next year and more.

> I delivered Gustavus your letter [Stansbury said]. It is not equal to his expectations. He expects to have your promise that he shall be indemnified for any loss he may sustain in case of detection and, whether this contest is finished by sword or treaty, that ten thousand pounds shall be engaged for his services, which shall be faithfully devoted to your interest.

Arnold had slipped some military intelligence to Stansbury, none of it earthshaking. Washington had ten thousand effectives in his command, "with plenty of everything at camp, supplied from everywhere." Sullivan was said to be advancing on Detroit with fifteen hundred men. Benjamin Lincoln was in Charleston with a garrison of three thousand Continentals and five hundred militia. But this was window dressing. What Arnold wished to convey was his price — £10,000 for his services and full reimbursement for property loss.

Enclosed with Stansbury's letter were a message from Jonathan Odell and two communications from Mrs. Arnold. Odell said that Arnold "had carefully examined the letter [André's] and found by the laconic style and little attention paid to his request that the gentleman appear'd very indifferent respecting the matter." Odell tried to salvage what he deemed a "seemingly fruitless correspondence" by urging a further, more conciliatory, word from André:

> It gives me much pain to find my friend's friend [Arnold, the friend of Stansbury] had misunderstood your letter and dis-

appointed (I apprehend) your expectations. Yet, if I might take the liberty to suggest my own opinion, I could wish you to write once more at least, as it cannot do any harm and may possibly be still worthwhile.

André might assure the general that his demands would be met "in a manner that cannot fail, but through his own hesitation, to surpass his most sanguine expectations." In Odell's letter, Arnold had become "Mr. Moore," another code name.

Peggy Arnold had enclosed a shopping list and a message for Major Aquilla Giles, an American prisoner of war who had helped her with previous orders. Her list included pale pink mantua with matching ribbon, black satinet for shoes, diaper cloth for towels, and a pair of spurs. It was in Arnold's handwriting.

André reiterated that payment must hinge on services rendered. He and Clinton were accountable, after all, to the home government. He stressed this in his letter:

I am sorry any hesitation should still remain, as I think we have said all that the prudence with which our liberality must be tempered will admit. I can only add that as such sums as are held forth must be in some degree accounted for, real advantage must appear to have arisen from the expenditure, or a generous effort must have been made.

He thanked Arnold for the military intelligence but said he needed to know more about West Point.

Permit me to prescribe a little exertion. It is the procuring an accurate plan of West Point, with the new roads, New Windsor [Washington's headquarters near Newburgh], Constitution [a fort on the east side of the Hudson], etc., [as well as] an account of what vessels, gunboats or gallies are in the North River [the Hudson], or may shortly be built there, and the weight of metal they carry. [Arnold might also include] sketches or descriptions of harbours to the eastward which might be attacked, and where stores and shipping might be destroyed.

Sir Henry Clinton, an engraving by Bartolozzi, published in October 1780, from a miniature by John Smart

General Benedict Arnold, an engraving by Benoît Louis Prévost after a portrait by Pierre-Eugène Du Simitière

Major John André, an engraving by J. K. Sherwin, published in September 1784, after a self-portrait

Major Benjamin Tallmadge, from a lost drawing by John Trumbull

Above: A pencil drawing by John André of Margaret Shippen, later Mrs. Benedict Arnold

Right: Sketches of some British fellow officers by John André

Below: A pen-and-ink self-portrait of Major John André, made just before his execution

Above: A model of H.M.S. *Vulture,* starboard view, made by Bernhard Schultze from the original working drawings *Below:* An engraving from André's drawing of his longboat ride on the Hudson to meet Arnold

Above: The shore at the foot of the Long Clove on the west shore of the Hudson, where André landed en route to his rendezvous with Arnold. The remains of a wharf can be seen.
Right: The window in the Joshua Hett Smith house where André kept his vigil

Top: The Beverley Robinson house, Arnold's headquarters
Bottom: A facsimile of the pass that Arnold gave André to get
him safely through the Westchester no man's land back to
New York

Top: André's capture, from a nineteenth-century engraving
Bottom: Another portrayal of André's capture, from an undated, unsigned mezzotint. André is shown here attempting to bribe his captors by offering them his watch.

Above: The Casparus Mabie Tavern (now the '76 House) in Tappan, New York, where Major André was held until his execution

Right: A drawing of the old Dutch church at Tappan, where Major André was interrogated by a Board of General Officers

Alexander Hamilton's memo to André just before the execution, with a sketch of the innkeeper's plump wife drawn on the back by André

André proposed a parley at which he and Arnold might discuss procedures, allay any doubts or misunderstandings, and settle the payment question:

> The only method of completing conviction, on both sides, of the generous intentions of each and making arrangements for important operations is by a meeting. Would you assume a command and enable me to see you, I am convinced a conversation of a few minutes would satisfy you entirely, and I trust would give us equal cause to be pleased.

By participating in the interview, André would court risks that might better devolve on someone more expendable than he, like Beverley Robinson. But Arnold's offer, linked to a military coup, could change the whole course of events. If André took charge of the parley, attending it himself, and if it resulted in half what it promised, he must win high rank and the plaudits of the army, even of the king himself. There was that about it, too, that appealed to the actor in John André. The use of assumed names, the reliance on go-betweens, the codes and invisible ink, and now the culminating, cloak-and-dagger parley all spoke to his sense of theater. Here was high drama that could turn the war around. He must be part of it.

In acknowledging Peggy's shopping list, André spoke fondly of "the fair circle in which I had the honour of becoming acquainted with you." It was a memory "unimpaired by distance or political broils." He asked Peggy to keep him in mind for any further needs:

> You know the Mesquianza [*sic*] made me a complete milliner. Should you not have received supplies for your fullest equipment from that department, I shall be glad to enter into the whole detail of capwire, needles, gauze, etc., and, to the best of my abilities, render you in these trifles services from which I hope you would infer a real zeal to be further employed.

Was this a signal to both Arnolds of his readiness to negotiate further? And did Peggy's seemingly innocent shopping list signal that she, too, was involved? Peggy's reply was eminently discreet:

> Mrs. Arnold presents her best respects to Captain André, is obliged to him for his very polite and friendly offer to be serviceable to her. Major Giles is so obliging as to promise to procure what trifles Mrs. Arnold wanted in a millinery way, or she would with pleasure have accepted it. Mrs. Arnold begs leave to assure Captain André that her friendship and esteem for him is not impaired by time or accident.

An oddly formal communication between old friends. Was the fact that Peggy wrote it a signal that she was briefed on what was transpiring?

Arnold was still irked by André's reluctance to spell out terms. He let it be known, through Stansbury, that

> however sincerely he wished to serve his country in accelerating the settlement of this unhappy contest, he shou'd hold himself unjust to his family to hazard his all on the occasion and part with a certainty (potentially at least) for an uncertainty. [Stansbury said that Arnold hoped] to join the army in about three weeks [and] contrive an interview.

André took note of this, but he did not answer the letter or yield on his insistence that payment must depend on services rendered.

These were worrisome times for the Reverend Jonathan Odell. He received only six shillings a day as chaplain to a Tory regiment, still less as deputy chaplain to the Royal Fusiliers, and yet he had a wife and three children to support. General Howe had allowed him an extra £30 a year. What about Sir Henry Clinton? Odell took his situation to André, who arranged for a renewal of the extra payment. This was in mid-December, marking a break in the negotiations. Arnold was awaiting trial on the charges brought against him by Joseph Reed and the Pennsylvania Council. He could still call a halt to his secret overtures.

A Different Drumbeat

WHILE HE WAS AT YALE, Tallmadge had often heard the name of Benedict Arnold mentioned, though never favorably. Arnold, he was told, had prospered hugely since arriving in New Haven, without influence or wherewithal, from his native Norwich. He had started with an apothecary shop, selling pills and potions, teas, spices, and cheap watches, and had risen to become a shipowner and successful merchant. He had married the high sheriff's daughter and acquired a mansion on one of the more prestigious streets.* And yet he remained an interloper, scorned by New Haven's established families and a target for gossipy disparagement among the common folk. He had bound a seditious seaman to a post on the town green and given him forty lashes. He had nearly killed a rival in a duel. Rude and plainspoken, he was known to drive a hard bargain and to settle disputes with his fists.

As the break with Britain widened, Arnold became the leader of the more raffish patriots. His henchmen included sailors, dockhands, and assorted ne'er-do-wells, with a few hotheaded Yale students to give a touch of class to his coterie. He and

*Arnold's first wife was Margaret Mansfield, who died in 1775.

his followers harassed Loyalists, pummeled supporters of king and Parliament, and urged armed rebellion. They were rated by most citizens as lawless disturbers of the peace.

Tallmadge spent his college years reading Greek, Latin, and Hebrew, mastering rhetoric and logic. He was law-abiding, respectful of authority, although he and Nathan Hale were fined a shilling fivepence for some petty infraction. He was not among the Yale students attracted to the future traitor. In his old age he would remember Arnold as a man of no repute. "I was impressed with the belief that he was not a man of integrity," he would tell an interviewer.

XI

Laurels in the South

Although he heard nothing further from Arnold, André was learning much about West Point and its environs. A German prisoner of war sent him a list of the artillery in the fortress. Sarah Williams, wife of a British deserter, brought word of a chain stretched across the Hudson to block shipping. Elijah Hunter, the double spy, told him that General Parsons was post commander, with orders to hold out "to the last extremity." Hunter promised to do his best for the British, "as far as in my power and consistent with my honour." André was kept posted on the comings and goings of the Continental Dragoons. Moylan's troops were described as "in good order and well officered," but Sheldon's were said to be "careless and indolent, easy to be surprised." Tallmadge's personal papers, seized at Pound Ridge by a British patrol, told of a Long Island spy ring.

André again made use of Ann Bates, directing her to meet a second time with Arnold's deputy. This would be the same Philadelphia woman who had accompanied Ann to headquarters after their previous parley. André allowed Ann an expense account of $300 in paper money, not enough to meet her needs. "I found my paper dollars of small value," she says, "as I gave nine of them for a few dishes of tea without sugar for my breakfast, which I could have had for three pence hard money." She tells us nothing about the identity of Arnold's representative or the nature of their talk, but she says that she took advantage of the trip to spy on the enemy's shipping and inquire about food supplies. On her return she spent three perilous days on the New Jersey coast waiting for a British ship, "exposed to the enemy's scouting parties as well as the inclemency of the elements, nothing but a stone pillow to rest my head on." She was paid ten guineas for the mission.

Few spies were as dependable and productive as Ann Bates. Edward Fox, a civilian in British custody, told André that a Maryland patriot, whom he referred to as C, might be persuaded to change sides.* He had been in correspondence with a Loyalist of his acquaintance, Dr. Henry Stevenson, who was a friend of C's and familiar with his thinking. C was now in Philadelphia, Fox said. André suggested that he either go in person and sound out C, or remain in New York, "handsomely maintained by a private salary,'" and open a correspondence with C, as well as with "any other persons willing and capable of serving us."

Fox elected to go to Philadelphia. He was given an allowance of thirty guineas and told to get in touch with a mysterious courier, who would transmit his messages to British headquarters. André's instructions were pure melodrama, with the cloak-and-dagger dimension that he loved: "The messenger is to make a cross on the pit door of the playhouse at night, and on the next day is to find an hour and address marked over it when to call for the parcel." Fox went off as directed. But on his return he stopped in Elizabeth, where he informed the American military of British plans for a thrust into the South, "their destination said to be Virginia." What was Ed-

---

*Perhaps Samuel Chase, a signer of the Declaration of Independence accused of involvement in a shady financial deal.

ward Fox's true allegiance? Was he an American secret agent? Or a double agent, like Elijah Hunter? Or was he a keen-witted opportunist?

Alexander Brink, formerly a lieutenant in an American regiment, volunteered his services as a courier. But he turned out to be a faint-hearted operative. Given a message for the high command in Canada, he got no farther than Paulus Hook when his nerve failed him and he returned sheepishly to New York. After questioning Brink, André had him placed under arrest.

Occasionally agents brought in conflicting reports. Daniel Coxe and Joseph Chew were two of André's most trustworthy informants. Coxe was a New Jersey Loyalist. Chew, who came from New London, was now stationed in New York. Each would have a role in the Arnold negotiations. Coxe brought word that

> the rebel army by spring will not exceed three thousand men, especially should the King's troops operate to the southward and be successful. . . . The candid among them think the whole southern provinces must fall when our army arrives.

But Chew had a bleak report. He warned of a massive attack on New York, with "several hundred boats built and now building on the North River." If Chew were right, Clinton's base of operations could be in jeopardy.

Christopher Sower brought alarming news from western Pennsylvania, where Rankin's troops were on the defensive. Although the Tory colonel was "resolved to go to the extremes of fire and sword," he would need Clinton's support if driven eastward into Delaware and Maryland. André was sympathetic, but he could make no promises.

The outlook for the British was hopeful at West Point. André had up-to-date reports on the size and capabilities of the garrison. He had been told the names of the officers at the fort, the location of artillery, the whereabouts of nearby regiments. Under favorable conditions, West Point could be taken.

André had never troubled himself about money. His pay, augmented by family income, had allowed him a proper lifestyle, commensurate with his rank and status. A fair portion of his income came from the Grenada holdings acquired years ago by his father. But late in 1778 d'Estaing attacked and took Grenada. For the first time John André must get by on a captain's pay, with his mother and three sisters welcoming whatever part of it he could spare.

Then there was the problem of brother William. Bored with overseas service and inclined to easygoing associates, William had rolled up some hefty debts that must be paid promptly — by brother John. If what John sent home should turn out to be less than what was anticipated, it could be ascribed to "a little inattention in our friend William" and not to "any luxurious expenditures" of his own. He could never be accused of squandering money or of humoring "lavish" tastes. Of the £300 he had drawn from reserves, upwards of £100 had gone toward William's less-than-distinguished military career.

William was a disappointment to his brother, who had got him to join the army, arranged for his coming to America, and paved his way with senior officers. But William seemed lacking in ambition, indifferent to a military career, content to while away his days in nonproductive pastimes. He had become "rather indolent and negligent as to his person," nor was his choice of reading matter — "only plays and books of amusement" — any help to his career. "He is not otherwise extravagant than as indolence had made him so," John André wrote home, "but I hope, being sensible of the necessity of restricting himself to his pay, he will not get into difficulties." It was indeed a letdown after John André's high hopes for his younger brother.

William had had enough of war, enough of America and

the tedium of garrison duty. He keenly wanted to go back to England. To make it possible, John André proposed that they swap commissions. William would transfer to the 26th, John's regiment, which would soon leave for England. John, in turn, would enroll temporarily in William's regiment, the 44th. Since each brother was a captain, no loss of rank would be involved. But the 44th was being sent to Canada, where John would be deprived of his association with Sir Henry Clinton. So he arranged yet another transfer for himself, this time to the 54th, which would remain in New York.

In writing the family about the exchange, André pointed out that it would boost William's seniority: "I took him from the bottom of the list in the 44th and now see him on his way to England with four captains under him and in a corps of officers now become a very good one." The exchange would be much to William's advantage. But John André was penalized. In transferring to the 54th, he must lose the seniority he had acquired as a captain in the 26th. Should he fall from favor, or should Clinton be replaced, he could "stagnate," as he puts it, at "the bottom of the captains, with the retrospect of my disappointment for the amusement of my leisure hours."

Providentially, an opening occurred that could more than compensate for the loss of seniority. When he wrote his family about it, André could hardly contain his excitement:

> Whilst I lamented my disappointment the post of adjutant general became vacant by the resignation of Lord Rawdon, and the Deputy Adjt. Gen., Col. Kemble, became desirous for private reasons to withdraw himself likewise. . . . The discharge of its functions (tho' not the office itself) I conceived to be within my reach, and I saw the opportunity of getting the wished-for rank at a small expense.

The wished-for rank was that of major, with its promise of higher pay.

The elimination of Rawdon and Kemble had not come about

smoothly. Rawdon had quarreled bitterly with his chief, and Kemble's "private reasons" were no less acrimonious. Francis Rawdon-Hastings, Lord Rawdon, had served as Clinton's aide-de-camp, had participated in several campaigns, and, in 1778, had been advanced to lieutenant colonel and named adjutant general. He was impulsive and outspoken. Predictably, he had a falling-out with Sir Henry after an exchange of strong words. On September 3, 1779, he tendered his resignation, declaring that he had "no longer the honor of being upon those terms of mutual confidence in a station whose duties are most irksome to me." Clinton referred to him as "a hot-headed young one."

Stephen Kemble had been deputy adjutant general under both Gage and Howe. That he would advance to the top post seemed foreordained, but he had been known to speak slurringly of Clinton and he was no favorite of the chief's. He learned the worst when Clinton remarked that every commander "had those about him he wished to promote" and implied that Kemble was not on his list. Kemble has left us his version of their interview:

> I observed from his language I had little to expect. He repeated he had those about him he wished to serve and that I should think it hard to have a junior officer put over my head, adding that the office was of such a nature that everyone wished to fill it with a person of their own, in whom he could place implicit confidence. I then said, "I see, sir, I have nothing to expect," and thanked him for being so explicit.

Kemble would return to his old regiment, stationed in Jamaica. "What am I to do?" he groaned. "Why, wretch, grin and bear it, for you are not in a situation to kick, poor devil."

Clinton's first choice for the post had been Colonel Charles Stuart of the 26th, but Stuart, a friend of Rawdon's, declined to serve. Clinton then turned to André, naming him deputy adjutant general but assigning him all of Rawdon's duties and raising him to brevet major. André says that "to engage Col. Kemble to retire," he agreed to pay him £300 a year, with an additional £200 if he should one day "quit the office." Although he was still only a brevet major and must await approval from home authorities before becoming a major in the British line, he was delighted with the turn of events and exultantly wrote home about it: "You may well conceive how much I am flattered at being called in the space of three years from a subaltern in the Fusiliers to the employment I hold and the favour in which I live with the Commander-in-chief." Without intending to seem "arrogant" or to "betray symptoms of expectation which I have not claims to justify," he could foresee his speedy promotion to adjutant general.

> Should I continue to deserve the General's favour and he
> , continue many more months in command, should success attend the present expedition [an imminent attack on Charleston] and cheerfulness prevail, perhaps it is not unreasonable to hope to be vested with the honour of the office I shall virtually have discharged and to be appointed adjutant general. Another piece of good luck which might attend me would be the appointment of major in a regiment, which would be more satisfactory than the mere brevet I now have, as it gives addition to my pay.

André came well recommended for promotion. Not only had he Clinton's own support but General Grey spoke well of him. Indeed, Grey had written Clinton that he had never known "a more accomplished young man, with a great knowledge of his profession and the best disposition in the world." No one was prepared for the reaction of Lord Jeffrey Amherst, commander-in-chief of the king's forces and a stickler for seniority. Amherst informed Lord Germain that he was quite at a loss to know who John André was. He could find no "Captain André of the 54th Regiment" on his list — only "a Capt. John André of the 26th Regt., who has been a captain twenty

months," and "a William Lewis André, captain in the 44th
Regt., who has been a captain about a year." This was no
"old captain," Amherst huffed. "Some regard is to be had to
an officer's term of service." John André must stay a brevet
major, with no pay increase.

While awaiting the verdict, André had drawn up a mock
legal certificate, written in French and involving the Chevalier
de l'Anos, a figment of his imagination. The document declared de l'Anos a consummate rogue and was signed by André,
who listed all of his various titles. Next to his signature he
sketched a crude seal design. It showed de l'Anos dangling
from a gibbet.*

Clinton was now ready to attack Charleston. He would leave
Knyphausen in New York with ten thousand men. His thrust
southward should win Charleston, rally southern Loyalists,
and carry the war to Georgia and the Carolinas. He had enough
ships to control the sea, although he was not happy with his
admiral, Marriot Arbuthnot. Lord Cornwallis was second in
command, but he, too, left much to be desired. Nevertheless,
the timing and outlook were propitious. Already a British garrison in Savannah had dealt the rebels a crushing blow.

Clearing New York Harbor on the day after Christmas, Clinton's armada ran into mountainous seas off the New Jersey
coast. Ships were scattered like flotsam in the days that followed. One vessel foundered; another, driven far off course,
turned up on the Cornish coast. Vast quantities of food were
lost, ordnance was swept overboard, nearly all the horses perished. "One could see and hear nothing but the flags and
shots of ships in distress," a diarist relates. Forced to put in
at Savannah for repairs, Clinton did not reach Charleston until

---

*De l'Anos would resurface as "de l'Anneau," the code name given Captain George
Beckwith during the Arnold negotiations.

early February, far behind schedule. He instantly set up siege lines, to isolate the city and pound it with artillery.

André continued to direct intelligence, but he shared the work with Captain Oliver De Lancey, the same Tory officer who had helped him paint backdrops for "Howe's Thespians." The two soon had a string of spies and informants who kept them posted on the strength of the Charleston garrison, on the enemy's food and ammunition supplies, on the location of batteries and artillery. Some of their most useful spies were runaway slaves. Three slaves turned in a British deserter whom they had captured near the rebel lines. A slave named Duncan, who had fled the city in a canoe, brought word of dwindling food supplies and ebbing morale, of ships scuttled to block passage to the city while their crews manned shore-based artillery. Folklore has it that André himself entered Charleston in disguise, but there is no reason to suppose that he would have undertaken a mission that any common spy could have accomplished, with far less risk.

While André was away, Captain George Beckwith, Knyphausen's aide-de-camp, had charge of military intelligence in New York. His reports mention the shortage of food and clothing in the Continental ranks, the spiraling inflation, the shaky French alliance that had already worn thin, even with "warm partisans of rebellion." Beckwith learned that as many as twenty thousand men might be needed to take West Point. "The rocky nature of the ground" and "the great distance and difficulty in transporting cannon, mortars, stores, etc." made a frontal attack very risky. One of Beckwith's letters spoke of Benjamin Chew, Peggy's father. One wonders if this gave André pause, if he thought fondly for a moment of the long-ago splendors of the Mischianza, with Peggy, proud and adoring, at his side.

Men were beholden to André now. He was reviewing promotions and requests for sick leave. He was granting favors and issuing reprimands. And he had Clinton's ear. "I hope you will not look upon this letter as troublesome," wrote one fawning petitioner, "but will agree with me that my circumstances and disappointments in a small degree entitle me to ask for your friendship and interest." When James Rivington, publisher of the *Royal Gazette*, wished to name his infant son after Sir Henry, he turned to André in seeking Clinton's consent. Captain Donkin, our military pundit, wrote obsequiously to ask if his wife might join him in America. Would André indicate the likelihood of the request's being granted — "probable or not probable" — in a postscript to his reply? "Your p.s. will make her come out, or wait for me," Donkin said. Even Major Patrick Ferguson, a lionhearted Scot, was uncharacteristically abject: "I wish to avoid encroaching upon these moments you employ so diligently in the public service, but if anything I have said should appear worthy of his Excellency's notice, I know you will excuse me." And General Phillips, Clinton's long-time friend, declared that "the smallest intimation" on André's part could settle a dispute between himself and Knyphausen.

There were those who longed to see André stumble. His swift rise to high office and his great influence with the commander-in-chief were the envy of several older men who were still waiting for promotion after years of service. One day he obliged them, while organizing a task force at Clinton's behest. Disregarding Sir Henry's policy of restricting troops to their respective units, where they would be answerable to their own officers, André brought together a mixed force of Hessians and British regulars. When the men assembled on parade to find themselves under unfamiliar officers, they let go with a torrent of expletives. General Alexander Leslie, leader of the task force, rushed into the breach. The commander-in-chief was summoned, to reiterate his policy that duties were "in general better performed by soldiers under their own officers." André was humiliated and crestfallen. He apologized profusely for his blunder. "For my own part, I

have never suffered more anxiety," he wrote Clinton. If he
had behaved "supinely," he hoped Sir Henry would make
allowances. He had been "unacquainted with or insensible
to" the strong feelings of the men. Possibly his lapse could
be blamed on overwork, for he had been putting in long hours,
he explained, and had not slept one night in two for the past
several weeks. Clinton readily forgave the gaffe, and it is to
André's credit that so few took pleasure in his discomfiture.
He was well liked by colleagues. Lord Rawdon, in spite of
his break with Clinton, remained André's friend. Lord Cathcart wished him "glory, success and happiness" in his new
post. Even Stephen Kemble bore him no grudge.

To compensate for his lapse, André addressed himself yet
more strenuously to his tasks. He spelled out the duties of
Clinton's staff — Crosbie would have charge of the commander-in-chief's household, Wilmouski would screen Hessian promotions, Keppel would provide food and shelter for
needy Loyalists. He handled much of the official correspondence, saw to the delivery of arms and food supplies to various
units, looked after displaced Loyalists and runaway slaves.
Through Oliver De Lancey he kept abreast of military intelligence. De Lancey had learned that the Charleston garrison
consisted of sixteen hundred Continentals and some two thousand militiamen. He had gotten hold of an accurate map of
the city, showing gun positions and barricades. He had been
told the location of several nearby farms and plantations where
sheep, cattle, and farm produce could be seized. His informants were widely dispersed and capable.

Every now and then André heard from Simcoe, who was
stationed not far away with the Queen's Rangers. Simcoe's
letters were unofficial and not intended for anyone but his
friend. "I send you a very intelligent Negro boy," he says in
one. "When you dismiss him, I will be obliged to you to pass
him to the Quaker House, as I mean to keep him." Or, in a
lighthearted vein: "We hunt and barbecue in a grove of laurels

tomorrow. I wish business would permit you to partake of what I expect a novel pleasure."

André had become Sir Henry's most trusted confidant. Earlier in the year Clinton had again tendered his resignation to Lord Germain. During the long wait for Germain's reply, he had felt his authority slipping. He suspected Lord Cornwallis of plotting to replace him, and matters were not helped when junior officers played up to the earl, as though the command were already his. "So certain did his Lordship seem to be of it," Clinton says, "that he made no scruple to declare he would assume it as soon as my leave should arrive, let the siege of Charleston be ever so far advanced at the time." Clinton stopped including his second in command in staff gatherings. The two conferred only on routine matters.

Germain's letter finally came, in mid-March, saying that the king was "too well satisfied" to countenance the resignation — a royal stamp of approval that Clinton describes as "exceedingly flattering to me and perhaps not a little mortifying to the noble Earl." Cornwallis proceeded to distance himself, more than ever, from his prickly colleague.

> His Lordship's carriage toward me immediately changed [Clinton tells us], and from this period he was pleased to withdraw his counsels and to confine himself to his routine duty in the lines, without honoring headquarters with his presence oftener than that required.

Clinton wanted a record of the quarrel, to keep in his file of the campaign. He turned to André, who produced this masterpiece of diplomacy:

> From what I have understood to be Lord C[ornwallis]'s language hitherto, I think his Lordship had fallen into a belief that the command was to devolve upon him. From his apparent persuasion that this event was at hand, from the army giving symptoms that they believed it, and particularly from Lord C[ornwallis]'s having shewn that he had made up his mind on

certain parts of his conduct should your Excellency be recalled, I judge your Excellency sometimes supposed Lord C[ornwallis] had private intimations on that head.

Were there reason to expect this service [the reduction of Charleston] to be prosecuted by Lord C[ornwallis], it would behoove your Excellency to make every preparatory operation for his Lordship, lest you might be afterward criminated for his ill success. Were there *no* reason to expect you were to quit the command before this service was completed, it was essential that yourself should be sole judge of every preparatory operation, as yourself were to be responsible for the consequences.

With consummate tact, André was urging Sir Henry to assert his prerogatives as commander-in-chief and take full charge of the siege. The earl, he hinted, might be given a separate command and, at the right moment, "dispatched to a greater distance." Clinton took the advice, assigning Cornwallis to a post several miles from Charleston. But he could not trust his colleague, even at a distance, and would regret the decision. "I regret I sent him," he was heard to mutter. "He will play me false, I fear."

The siege went off like clockwork. By the end of April the garrison was nearly out of ammunition. Shells containing chunks of glass began showing up. "Every possible communication of the enemy was cut off," a diarist reports. "They could not entertain the least hope of succor. . . . Our guns and howitzers opened a murderous fire. All four embrasures were demolished to such an extent that we could not make them out any more." A cannonade brought the beleaguered garrison to its knees, and on May 12 General Benjamin Lincoln capitulated. His troops marched out of the city in seemingly endless file, "two abreast with shouldered but unloaded rifles, colors cased, to the beating of one drum per battalion." Clinton had bagged more prisoners that day than had ever before been taken on American soil.

Clinton imposed harsh terms on the conquered city. With Charleston taken, he asked André to submit a plan for expediting victory in both North and South. André's thinking on the subject would have warmed the heart of "No-Flint Grey," his erstwhile tutor. He begins by stressing the futility of peace bids. "There are three methods by which dominion over the colonies can be regained," he points out. The first, that of negotiation, had been tried to no avail. "Everything short of independence has been offered." The second, "the more mild motives of alluring offers" reinforced by the threat of armed might, had also failed. The third method, all-out conquest with no talk of negotiation, was a tactic to which Britain had "never fully appealed," André says, and one that would require large reinforcements. He urges this on Sir Henry:

> The force required to reduce America is estimated at some thousands more than we ever possessed at a time in America. Our force for the field is at the utmost 8,000 men, and yet we aspire to offensive operations. . . . I think it can be shown that were Sir William Howe's army and Burgoyne's now in America, such a portion of country might be reduced to terms as would break the knot of the rebellion.

Two divisions, on the offensive in both North and South, would "leave the rebel standing army the choice of attacking one corps and exposing their communications to the other, of starving within their stronghold, or of fighting our joint forces."

Britain should first subdue the South, André maintains. "The Carolinas, Virginia and the peninsula between Chesapeake and Delaware" embrace "a people who can and will be controlled when conquered, a people not politically, but from the ambition of a few, connected with the northern districts, and not without jealousy of the designs of France upon them." Indeed, "the fortunate capture of the whole regular force of these provinces at Charleston" leaves them ripe for conquest.

When the Delaware, the Chesapeake and the ports of Carolina shall be ours, through what channels shall trade flow? [Resistance, what there is of it, must be sternly dealt with.] Should any parishes or districts dare to remain in arms, much more should any small parties or single men infest roads and communications . . . fire and sword must cut them off, or the rigours of civil justice should bring the rebel to tbe gibbet.

Conquest of the North would follow:

The populous tracts of New England, Jersey and Pennsylvania, overspread with our most inveterate enemies and affording the enemy's army unnumbered and secure channels for supplies, are not wantonly to be invaded. . . . Perfidious thousands singly take the field against us from every tree and house and, tho' driven from our front, close in with redoubled inveteracy on our flank and rear.

Crushing these recalcitrants would complete the agenda.

Clinton studied the report, adding a few recommendations of his own. But for the moment he was less concerned with grand strategy than with plans to invade New Jersey as soon as he returned north. He assigned the southern command to Cornwallis, with orders to hold Charleston and advance into the Carolinas. He sent André on ahead, to alert Knyphausen.

André debarked to find Knyphausen already in New Jersey. Prodded by local Tories, the Hessian commander had crossed with some five thousand men, only to encounter stout resistance from both Continentals and local militia. When Clinton arrived he was aghast at what he considered an "ill-timed, malapropos move." Attempts to salvage the expedition failed. Knyphausen was turned back near Springfield, and New Jersey was cleared of British troops.

André blamed the reverse on faulty intelligence. Knyphausen had been led to believe that Washington was short of

men, that the local militia would not fight, that the Continentals would "desert and crumble" under áttack.

> The troops, after proceeding to Connecticut Farms and some
> distance beyond them, found the reports, so imprudently prop-
> agated, absolutely false [André says]. This bad move was forced
> upon poor Knyphausen by anonymous letters, by sanguine
> enthusiasts. [The British were] exposed in a march of a day
> to a loss of more men than Carolina cost us, and as we went
> to demolish an army we could not get at, so we went to receive
> the submission of a country we could not protect, and of course
> inimical.

If the incident taught nothing else, it showed the pitfalls of
hearsay and idle talk.

The time was at hand, André believed, for his attaining the
rank of major in the king's service.

> I am deputy adjutant general still [he says], and without con-
> firmation of rank. I do not, however, despair of its being granted
> me, as the Commander-in-chief has written on the subject in
> very strong terms and at a period when I think there will be
> a disposition to hear him.

Sir Henry had gained influence through his Charleston triumph.
Even the seniority question should no longer block André's
promotion.

A Different Drumbeat

FOR TALLMADGE, this had been a wretched winter. He wrote his friend Jeremiah Wadsworth that the Neutral Ground was overrun with "Tory demons" and that he would "do them as much injury as he could." "Last night a man was pursued from Middle Patent to Kingstreet," he said — one of fourteen Tories on their way to join the British Army. When finally caught, he had been "cut badly" and "half-hanged a few times" by vengeful dragoons. His confederates were still at large. "If I come across them," Tallmadge added, "I think they will get cut a little."

Tallmadge had barely been able to keep his command together. Enlistments were down, few of the dragoons had mounts, tempers had worn thin. One of his captains had been court-martialed for insulting a senior officer. He himself had spent whole weeks in Hartford trying to get a tightfisted legislature to pay his men a living wage.

To add to his troubles, Tallmadge sensed a change in Culper Junior, who had had more than his share of close calls. In the spring Culper Senior wrote that his associate wanted to cease spying. He promised to continue on his own "if any person can be pointed out by 711 [Washington] at N.Y. who can be safely relied on to supply C. Junr.'s place." But the commander-in-chief was having doubts about the spy ring. "The intelligence is so long getting to hand that it is of no use by the time it reaches me," he wrote Tallmadge. He wondered if the spy ring had served its purpose, "as C. Junior has totally declined and C. Senior seems to wish to."

When Culper Senior heard this he got off an irate letter to Tallmadge, accusing the commander-in-chief of failing to appreciate the risks taken by the spy ring and the courage of its members:

> Sorry we have been at so much cost and trouble for little or no purpose. He also mentions my backwardness to serve. He certainly hath been misinformed. You are sensible I have been indefatigable, and have done it from a principle of duty rather than from any mercenary end.

Washington quickly changed his mind. A French fleet was about to dock in Newport with reinforcements. The troops would be vulnerable to attack while disembarking, and he must learn if Clinton planned to exploit the opportunity. In an urgent letter he asked Tallmadge to reactivate the spy ring:

> As we may every moment expect the arrival of the French fleet, a revival of the correspondence with the Culpers will be of very great importance. If the younger cannot be engaged again, you will prevail upon the older to give you information on the movements and position of the enemy upon Long Island . . . in short, desire him to inform you of whatever comes under his notice.

Tallmadge managed to prevail on both Culpers. A letter from Culper Senior demonstrated their value to the American cause. He had sent Austin Roe to confer with Culper Junior, he reported. Roe had returned "in great haste" with word that a British fleet had already weighed anchor and would approach Newport "before this can possibly reach you. Also,

8,000 troops are this day embarking at Whitestone for the
before mentioned port."*

Tallmadge had won back the Culpers, but his troubles were
not over. Samuel Blagden, a Connecticut officer whom he
liked, was being replaced by Lieutenant Colonel John Jameson, a Virginian. Jameson had solid credentials — he had been
a dragoon officer since 1776 — but he was an outsider, imposed on a predominantly Yankee regiment. And then there
was West Point, always cause for concern. Tallmadge had
written Governor Trumbull,** who had charge of supplying
the garrison, that "some sudden and unexpected stroke" must
be anticipated.

> It is no secret that you have neither men nor provisions to
> garrison West Point [he said, warning that the British coveted
> the fortress]. West Point has long been an eyesore to them
> and they will risk anything in the undertaking. Depend on it,
> they will know your force and situation well, and for God's
> sake be guarded against such a movement.

---

*Actually, Clinton had assigned only 6000 men to the expedition and would call it
off before reaching Newport.
**Governor Jonathan Trumbull of Connecticut.

XII

"An Innocent Affair"

If YOUR EXCELLENCY thinks me a criminal, for heaven's sake let me be immediately tried and, if found guilty, executed. . . . Delay in the present case is worse than death!" Thus had Benedict Arnold addressed General Washington as he waited out the long months before his court-martial. But when the court finally did convene, at Christmastime, it cleared him of all charges save two: improperly issuing a pass to the *Charming Nancy* and using government wagons to convey privately owned property. His sentence was nominal — a mere reprimand from the commander-in-chief. Nevertheless, Arnold was outraged. "For what?" he fumed. "Not for doing wrong, but that I might have done wrong — or, rather, because there was a possibility that evil might have followed the good I did!" He felt shunned by the military, mistreated by Congress. He had given sacrificially of his means, had endured cold and hunger on the march through the Maine woods, had been wounded at Quebec and crippled at Saratoga. Yet promotions had been slow in coming, and he had not yet been fully reimbursed for expenses incurred in military service. He had been persecuted by "artful, unprincipled men" who had undercut him in Philadelphia and subjected him to a humiliating court-martial.

That spring Arnold reopened negotiations with the British — not with Clinton, who was still in Charleston, but with
Knyphausen and his aide-de-camp, Captain Beckwith. Arnold
made several propositions that Beckwith listed in a memorandum for André. He would "undertake the part in question," Beckwith was told,

> confiding in the former assurance made to him by his Excel-
> lency the Commander-in-chief. . . . He asks for a small sum
> of ready money to employ in a particular channel. . . . He
> particularly desires to have a conference with an officer of
> confidence. He will take a decisive part in case of an emer-
> gency, or that a capital stroke can be struck. He requests that
> a particular signature may be sent to him, that he may be
> furnished with a token to prevent any fraud, and that a regular
> mode of communication may be fallen upon. Were it not for
> his family, he declares he would join the Army without making
> any terms.

Knyphausen was loath to commit himself in Clinton's absence, but he promised to meet "any trifling expenses" Arnold
might incur and to make arrangements for a conference whenever Arnold could "point out the practicality of it." He supplied him with two duplicate rings as tokens and with two
pocket dictionaries for communicating in code. But Arnold
wanted more than this. He awaited assurances of £5000 to
cover "the loss of his private fortune" and an additional £5000
to compensate for "the debt due him by the community."
He agreed, however, to "take a decisive part in case of an
emergency," such as an "attack on Boston or Philadelphia or
any other place."

From the start, Clinton had had reservations about the hero
of Saratoga. He would allude to this in a letter written subsequently to Lord Germain:

> I was not at first sanguine in my idea of General Arnold's
> consequence, as he was said to be in a sort of disgrace, had

been tried before a general court-martial and not likely to be employed, and whatever merit this officer might have had, his situation, such as I understood it then to be, made him less an object of attention.

Arnold sensed this. To gain leverage, he must acquire a command that would make him irresistible to the British. No post, no field assignment, would quite equal West Point — the perfect bargaining chip in his negotiations with Clinton. To help him gain the command, he enlisted the support of two influential friends, Robert R. Livingston and Philip Schuyler.

Livingston wrote a letter to Washington stressing Arnold's popularity with the New York militia and his rapport with Governor George Clinton. Schuyler conferred in person with the commander-in-chief, whom he found not averse to the appointment, but reluctant to place so capable a field officer anywhere but in the lines. He notified Arnold that he might "have an alternative proposed, either to take charge of an important post, with an honourable command, or your station in the field." But field duty was the last thing Arnold wanted. He hurried to Morristown to plead in person with the commander-in-chief. Although Washington would claim that he made no commitment during their talk, Arnold promptly informed the British that West Point was as good as his.

Arnold was again slipping military intelligence to the British. He reported that a French fleet was on its way to attack Quebec, that an army under Lafayette would advance on Montreal. (Actually, nothing came of it, although there was talk of invading Canada.) Of greater interest to Clinton and his staff was what Arnold said about West Point. The garrison was under strength, he told them. Provisions were in short supply, and every ounce of flour had to be brought from Pennsylvania. He would soon be going to New Haven on private business and would visit West Point on his way back.

Four days later Arnold wrote again. He had inspected West Point and had found "only fifteen hundred soldiers" there, not enough to "half man the works." He had ascertained that "not ten days' provision" had been laid in. "If the English were to cut off the communication with Pennsylvania," the garrison "would be distressed for flour, which is not to be procured in this part of the country." He had no doubt that the great chain spanning the Hudson could be smashed by "a single ship, large and heavy loaded." He had been "greatly disappointed both in the works and the garrison," he continued.

> It is surprising a post of so much importance should be so totally neglected. The works appear to me, though well executed, most wretchedly planned to answer the purpose designed, viz., to maintain the post and stop the passage of the river. The Point is on a low piece of ground comparatively to the chain of hills which lie back of it. The highest, called Rocky Hill, which commands all the other works, is about half a mile from Fort Putnam, which is strong. On Rocky Hill there is a small redoubt to hold two hundred men and two six-pounders pointed on the other works.

The strategic fortress was a "wretchedly executed" facility. If Clinton debarked his troops three miles below West Point he would find "a good road to bring up heavy cannon."

Arnold's services had their price.

> My stock in trade (which I have before mentioned) is £10,000 sterling [he said], with near an equal sum of outstanding debts. . . . I have advanced several sums already, and risked still greater, without any profit. It is now necessary for me to know the risk I run in case of a loss.

He asked for "a clear, explicit and confidential answer in cypher," signing himself "J. Moore."

In his next letter Arnold asked for a parley

with some intelligent officer in whom a mutual confidence could be placed. [His price must be met before services could be rendered.] As life and fortune are risked by serving his Majesty, it is necessary that the latter shall be secured as well as the emoluments I give up, and a compensation for services agreed on, and a sum advanced for that purpose.

By now André was back in New York. He promptly wrote Arnold, expressing Sir Henry's keen interest in "some scheme for effecting a service of importance" in relation to West Point. But he reminded him that "the full measure of the national obligation" must depend on Arnold's "effectual cooperation." Unfazed, Arnold reiterated his terms. He must be reimbursed for his property, which he valued at £10,000. He must receive an annuity "in lieu of the pay and emoluments" he would relinquish as an American major general. And he must be paid for his forthcoming services to the British. If he turned over West Point, "twenty thousand pounds sterling" would seem "a cheap purchase for an object of such importance." In addition, he needed £1000 immediately to cover costs. A parley with an officer "in whom we can place a mutual confidence" was "absolutely necessary to plan matters." Perhaps General Phillips, Clinton's good friend, would be available. Or Captain Beckwith. Or André himself.

Arnold's letter reached headquarters on July 23. André replied at once, with Sir Henry's final offer:

Tho' West Point derives its importance from the nature of the operations of our enemy, yet shou'd we thro' your means possess ourselves of 3,000 men and its artillery and stores, with the magazine of provisions for the army which may probably be there, the sum even of £20,000 should be paid you. You must not suppose that, in case of detection or failure your efforts being known, you would be left a victim, but services done are the terms on which we promise rewards. In these you see we are profuse — we conceive them proportioned to the risk. As to an absolute promise of indemnification to the amount of £10,000 and annuity of £500, whether services are performed or not, it can never be made. Your intelligence we prize and will freely recompense it. £200 shall be lodged in your agent's hands as you desire, and £300 more are at your disposal.

The same day, through Stansbury and Odell, André notified Arnold that "Mr. Anderson is willing himself to effect the meeting, either in the way proposed or in whatever manner may at the time appear most eligible." Arnold might feign illness while at a post not far from New York, "which a flag of truce could reach and where you might be supposed to be detained." A companion letter from Jonathan Odell reminded Arnold that "essential services" would be "profusely rewarded, far beyond the stipulated indemnification," but that to request payment in advance was "highly unreasonable."

Arnold's reply never reached headquarters. He entrusted it to William Heron, the enigmatic go-between unsuspected by either side. Heron gave it to his friend General Parsons because, or so he would claim later, he felt "a jealousy or suspicion" of Arnold. Parsons glanced through the letter. In his judgment, this was a routine business communication:

> Mr. M[oor]e assures me that he is still of the opinion that his first proposal is by no means unreasonable and makes no doubt when he has a conference with you, that you will close with it. He expects when you meet that you will be fully authorized from your house, that the risks and profit of the copartnership may be fully and clearly understood.

Signing himself "Gustavus," Arnold advised against "an immediate purchase [attack]," since "there is not the quantity of goods [military stores and troops] at market [West Point] which your partner [Clinton] seems to suppose." Parsons filed the letter.

Although dealing with Arnold had first claim on his attention, André must still devote himself to routine intelligence matters. Through spies, informants, and deserters from the Con-

tinental ranks, he kept posted on the strength and whereabouts
of Washington's troops, on the shortages of equipment and
food supplies, on what the Continental strategists had in mind.
He sent a spy to Rhode Island to "learn from the inhabitants
the number and situation of the enemy's ships and troops,
what cannon they have, what works they have constructed,
and whereabouts, and what is said of their designs." Simcoe
kept him informed on the operations of the French fleet off
the Long Island coast. "The fleet I apprehend to be still
visible from Montauk," he reported on one occasion. "They
came under the lee of Block Island, not to avoid the storm as
it appeared to us, but to water."

Through information given him by Arnold, André learned
of an impending attack on New York, with American troops
advancing from the north and French troops crossing from
Long Island. Military stores for the campaign would be assembled at West Point. Clinton hoped to capture the fortress
at a strategic moment, drive the Americans back, and make
short work of the French. He was assembling boats of a draft
suitable for the Hudson when Washington called off the attack.

There were lighter moments. John McNamara Hayes, a
colleague of André's, wrote him from Charleston at the height
of a summer heat wave. "The nights are *le diable,*" he groaned.
"I have often wished for nights to give way to my desires,
but here I can entertain no such ideas. Panting for breath,
languid and half dead, I pass my hours . . . often not expecting to see another." Hayes had designs on a local heiress
but was undone by the Carolina heat.

> She has a large fortune, which I want, but the mischief is she
> must be tied in the dog days. I made some trials to see whether
> I should be equal to the enterprise. With undaunted courage,
> I made the attempt. I got so far, but all of a sudden, ashamed
> and abashed, was obliged to give the affair up and should have
> hanged myself did I not recollect the folly of so rash an action.

He had no doubt that such a calamity would never have taken place had he been "to the northward," in less debilitating climes.

André still found time for a little sketching. He drew a friend's likeness on the back of a letter, a small gunboat at the bottom of an empty page. Nor was his gift for light verse neglected. One July day Anthony Wayne led an assault on the Bull's Ferry blockhouse, a post manned by Tory refugees. He failed in the attempt and would have retreated empty-handed had he not captured a herd of cattle on Bergen Neck. The incident was made to order for André, whose mock epic, "The Cow Chace," ran as a serial in the *Royal Gazette.* He opens by reminding us of Wayne's start as a lowly tanner:

> To drive the kine one summer's morn
> The Tanner took his way;
> The calf shall rue, that is unborn,
> The jumbling of the day.

The kine would soon mock the Tanner and "call to mind, in every low, the tanning of *his* hide." But, first, Wayne harangues his "dung-born" troops:

> Oh ye, whom glory doth unite,
> Who Freedom's cause espouse,
> Whether the wing that's doomed to fight
> Or that to drive the cows,
>
> Ere yet you tempt your further way,
> Or into action come,
> Hear, soldiers, what I have to say,
> And take a pint of rum. . . .
>
> Know that some paltry refugees,
> Whom I've a mind to fight,
> Are playing hell among the trees,
> That grow on yonder height.
>
> Their fort and blockhouses we'll level,

And deal a horrid slaughter,
We'll drive the scoundrels to the devil,
And ravish wife and daughter. . . .

His daring words from all the crowd
Such great applause did gain
That every man declar'd aloud
For serious work — with Wayne.

Then from the cask of rum once more
They took a heady gill,
When, one and all, they loudly swore
They'd fight upon the hill.

But here the muse hath not a strain
Befitting such great deeds.
"Huzza!" they cried, "Huzza for Wayne!"
And, shouting, did their needs.

Wayne's retreat prompts further merriment:

Now as the fight was further fought
And balls began to thicken,
The fray assum'd, the Gen'rals thought,
The colour of a licking.

Yet, undismay'd, the chiefs command
And, to redeem the day,
Cry, "Soldiers, Charge!" — they hear, they stand,
They turn and run away.

Wayne's homespun accouterments are made fun of:

His horse that carried all his prog,
His military speeches,
His corn-stalk whisky for his grog,
Blue stockings and brown breeches.

All summer André kept adding to his epic, submitting the final canto in time for an October issue. Mockingly, he takes leave of his subject:

And now I've closed my epic strain,
I tremble as I shew it,
Lest this same warrior-drover Wayne
Should ever catch the poet!

Loyalists read the epic gleefully. There was little else to
smile at in New York that summer, for they had all but de-
spaired of Clinton and his crusty admiral, Marriot Arbuthnot.
Hopes were kindled when the two set sail with six thousand
men and an imposing fleet, intending to attack the French at
Newport. But Arbuthnot, alas, gave only grudging support.
Precious time was lost while he and Clinton bickered over
procedures. They were "blockheads alike" in the opinion of
one observer, who found it impossible to say which was "the
greatest fool." Clinton had gone only as far as Huntington
when he heard that Washington had crossed the Hudson in
an advance on New York. He hurriedly returned to the city
with all his transports, calling off the expedition. Washington
withdrew, but great was the hue and cry among New York
Loyalists. Stansbury taunted Arbuthnot in rhyme:

Of Arbuthnot, my friend, pray tell me the news;
What's done by his ships and their brave, gallant crews?
Has the old Englishman shewn old English spunk?
And the ships of the French burnt, taken or sunk?
In truth, my good sir, there has been nothing like it.
'Tis easier to threaten a blow than to strike it.

Still hoping to engage the French, Clinton scheduled a
conference with his headstrong admiral at Gardiner's Bay, at
the far tip of Long Island. He and André left New York during
an August heat wave, traveling by coach in such stifling weather
that their coachman collapsed from sunstroke. When the two
reached Gardiner's Bay a note informed them that Arbuthnot
had gone in quest of the French fleet, which was thought to
be hovering off the Long Island coast. After a few days of

irksome waiting, Clinton canceled the parley and jolted back to New York.

André was billeted at the home of Colonel Abraham Gardiner at East Hampton. Although Gardiner had a surgeon son in the Continental Army and made no secret of his staunch patriotism, he and André struck up an acquaintance that led to a friendly exchange of wine glasses. When André left, he gave his host a pair of long-stemmed glasses that would become prized heirlooms in the Gardiner family.

While at East Hampton André may have visited Gardiner's Island, where the family mansion had stood empty since a British foraging party raided the property early in the war. Quite possibly he hunted deer on the island, a favorite pastime for British officers. If wet weather discouraged hunting, he and his comrades may have pitched coins in the dining room of the mansion, using rough-edged Spanish dollars that would leave indelible scratches on the polished floor.

During his return to New York, André may have stopped off at Oyster Bay to pay his respects to Sally Townsend and have a day or two with his friend Simcoe. If he did, Sally never once, by chance remark or innuendo, betrayed her brother Robert. There is a legend that she surprised André one day as he recovered a secret message from a downstairs cupboard and that she overheard whispered talk about West Point. But these are unlikely tales. It was enough that she cast her spell over both admirers without dropping the least hint about her brother.

For three days Arnold waited anxiously for a change of orders. Washington had offered him command of the army's left wing, but Arnold insisted that his leg wound made field duty impossible. The appointment was not rescinded until after it had been officially made public. Reluctantly, and with unconcealed regret, Washington agreed to assign him the West Point command.

Arnold timed his move to perfection.

Never was an army more discontented and clamorous in the world than the Continental Army is [he was told by a Tory friend]. They are distressed for want of pay, clothing and provisions. I see no possible means of remedying their distresses. Congress has not one shilling of money nor one farthing's worth of credit, neither at home nor abroad. . . . The people at large grow every day more and more restless.

The people were indeed impatient. Some threatened to join the enemy unless a decisive blow were struck. Arnold told the British that

the mass of the people are heartily tired of the war and wish to be on their former footing. They are promised great events from this year's exertion. If disappointed, you have only to persevere and the contest will soon be at an end. The present struggles are like the pangs of a dying man, violent but of short duration.

Perhaps never, during the entire war, had morale been so low among friends of Congress. Jonathan Odell appealed to them in rhyme:

O save yourselves before it is too late!
O save your country from impending fate!
Leave those whom Justice must at length destroy —
Repent, come over, and partake our joy!

But joy was not everywhere in evidence among New York Tories, whose fate hinged on the exertions of Sir Henry Clinton. He had twice as many men as Washington, by his own reckoning. Well fed and clothed, they were rated the best troops in the world. But since taking Charleston he had succumbed to a strange inertia. "I despair of Clinton," Judge Smith said. "He will make the apprehension of a French fleet an excuse for total inactivity and recline on the pillow of the reputation acquired by the Charleston success." To all of which a Tory poet, perhaps Stansbury, has Sir Henry tossing off this blithe rejoinder:

Since Charleston is taken,
'Twill sure save my bacon —
I will live a whole year on that fame, sir!
Ride about all the day,
At night, concert or play,
So a fig for those men that dare blame, sir!

Outwardly, New York was as lighthearted as the commander-in-chief. Young and old thronged the pathways of Trinity churchyard, its gloom obliterated by the sound of music and wink of lanterns. Dinner parties abounded in Tory circles, the playhouse flourished, and cricket was played on Monday afternoons. Clinton's officers rode merrily to the hounds and shone at the weekly cotillions in the City Tavern. "Heaven preserve a nation of triflers!" fumed one observer. "Sir H. Clinton went out on horseback about noon. He returns in a phaeton this evening — probably spent the day at Beekman's villa at Turtle Bay."

André had little time now for such frivolities. Even when Peggy Chew sent her fond regards he paid scant heed and may never have acknowledged her overture. He labored long, exacting hours at Number One Broadway. "Nothing in the official way was to him a trouble," a colleague says. But the pace took its toll. "The great quantity of business which assails me sometimes affects my spirits," he wrote home. "Exercise, however, infallibly restores me." On August 27, Clinton advanced him to adjutant general, commending the promotion to Lord Germain for the king's approval:

> I have the honour to offer for his Majesty's approbation as adjutant general under my command Major John André, whose faithful discharge of the duties of that office for near a twelve-month have made me consider him as worthy of the appointment.

André wrote a euphoric letter home. "Good fortune still follows me!" he exclaimed. "The Commander-in-chief has raised me to the first office in the Army, if that of most confidence and least profit is to be styled so. I am Adjutant General." The one hitch was still the matter of rank. In the regular establishment he was rated a captain, on a captain's pay. "The rank of lieutenant colonel, which usually attends this post, is not to be given me on account of the difficulties made at giving me rank of major," he explained. The seniority problem was not yet resolved, but he had gone far in a few short years. "I am full of gratitude towards the General for so much kindness and impress'd with the greatest zeal to deserve it," he said, "but can hardly look back at the steep progress I have made without being giddy!"

André had promised to pay Colonel Kemble £200 when the latter ceased being deputy adjutant general. But André was still on captain's pay with no assurance of higher rank. He wrote Kemble that he had

> had the mortification to see my rank of major objected to, as annexed to the office of deputy adjutant general. The Commander-in-chief has now appointed me adjutant general, but what rank I am to derive, or if I am to derive any, is yet uncertain.

Kemble would have to wait.

Presently an opportunity arose that could entail such kudos that there could be no quibbling over rank. Arnold requested a parley with Clinton's deputy, to establish terms and formulate plans. He was now stationed at the Robinson house, the former residence of Colonel Beverley Robinson. The big, rambling mansion, with its spacious rooms and costly furniture, made an attractive headquarters for a command that embraced both shores of the Hudson. However, it was across the river from West Point — "surrounded on two sides by hideous mountains and dreary forests," according to one visitor — and the remote location made dependable couriers hard to come by. Arnold twice communicated with the British through his wife, Peggy, who was still in Philadelphia.

In the letter entrusted to William Heron, Arnold had referred to himself as "Mr. Moore" and had requested an interview within the next ten days. Heron, as we know, had turned the letter over to General Parsons, but Arnold was never told this. Four days later he got off a second letter that he gave to one Mary McCarthy, an army wife on her way from Canada to New York. It is now missing, but from references in other sources we know that it instructed André to communicate through Colonel Sheldon of the Continental Dragoons, who would be Arnold's unwitting liaison. Addressed to "John Anderson," it urged a prompt get-together.

In writing to Sheldon (and, through him, to Arnold), André made two stipulations. The parley must take place on neutral ground, close to the Hudson, and within reach of British vessels. André scheduled it for Dobbs Ferry on September 11. Also, he must have the protection of a flag of truce. Should he "not be allowed to go, the officer who is to command the escort, between whom and myself no distinction need be made, can speak on the affair." This put Arnold on notice that André, as a British officer, would come in uniform rather than "assume a mysterious character to carry on an innocent affair and, as friends have advised, get to your lines by stealth." By "friends" he meant Arnold, who had urged him to pose as a civilian.

Arnold was astonished when he read this. He wondered if it might be a forgery intended to trap André and himself. He dashed off a warning, addressing it to "John Anderson" and signing himself as "Gustavus":

I suspect my letter to you of the 7th has been interrupted, and the answer dictated by the enemy in hopes of drawing you into a snare, for I cannot suppose you would be so imprudent as to trust a British officer, commanding a flag, with our private concerns. . . . You must be sensible my situation will not permit my meeting or having any private intercourse with such an officer. . . . If I have been mistaken and the letter directed to Colonel Sheldon was wrote by you, I do by

all means advise you to follow the plan you propose of getting
to our lines by stealth.

But André, at Clinton's urging, would not give ground on the
uniform.

That same day Arnold started downstream in an army barge
rowed by eight unsuspecting enlisted men. He spent the night
at Haverstraw as guest of Joshua Hett Smith, brother of Chief
Justice William Smith. Next morning he continued downstream. As he approached Dobbs Ferry a British gunboat,
uninformed of the parley, streaked from shore and opened
fire. Arnold was driven back under a hail of bullets. When his
oarsmen took shelter under the guns of an American block-
house, the enemy craft put about. But it hung offshore all
afternoon, pinning him down.

At Clinton's insistence, André was accompanied by Beverley Robinson, a seasoned intelligence officer thoroughly familiar with Dobbs Ferry and its surroundings. Robinson could
explain his presence by saying that he must collect certain
personal belongings still at his former residence. Clinton would
have preferred that only Robinson meet with Arnold, but he
sent a last-minute note to André that gave grudging consent
to his attending the parley: "Col. Robinson will probably go
with the flag himself. As you are with him at the forepost
[Kingsbridge], you may as well be of the party. You will find
me on your return at General Knyphausen's." Knyphausen
was stationed at Morris House, north of the city. In awaiting
his two negotiators there, instead of downtown at headquarters, Clinton would be the first to hear how things had gone.

André and Robinson may have been taken upstream by one
of the gunboats attached to the armed sloop *Vulture*, which
lay off Kingsbridge. Or they may have journeyed north on
horseback over sparsely traveled back roads. André's heart
surely skipped a beat when he caught sight of Dobbs Ferry.
If the parley turned out favorably, if terms could be agreed

upon and a strategy devised for the surrender of West Point, his reward would be high rank and a dazzling military career. Nor was this all, for his sense of theater was involved. The risks inherent in the parley gave it an excitement he would not miss. Here was drama of a high order, with himself at center stage. He wondered what Arnold would be like — grasping and avaricious as his letters seemed to indicate, or imbued with genuine loyalty to the mother country?

André and Robinson reached Dobbs Ferry on schedule. They hid behind a row of trees and began what would turn out to be a wait of many hours. The afternoon ticked past, sultry and close, hot as midsummer. Nothing stirred on the Hudson. In their place of concealment, they could not see the British gunboat or hear its flurry of shots. They waited until nightfall, with no sign of Arnold. Then they returned, still at a loss, to their own lines.

A Different Drumbeat

ARNOLD HAD HEARD of the Culper spy ring but he did not
know the identity or whereabouts of its members. He tried
to coax the information from Lafayette, but the marquis was
noncommittal. The persons in question had confided in him,
he said, and he could not betray a trust. Arnold then approached General Robert Howe, his predecessor at West Point,
buttering him up with a gift of fine liqueurs. But Howe was
as close-mouthed as Lafayette. He explained that he had
pledged "in the most solemn manner not to inform any person
upon earth of their names." Arnold may then have turned to
Tallmadge. If he did, the answer was the same, for the dragoon major was under an equally binding pledge to the Culpers and their associates.

Tallmadge had never trusted Arnold, but he liked the
way he got things done. Many of the dragoons were still un-
mounted. Enlistments were off, and some of his best men
had transferred to other regiments. He wrote Arnold
about it. To his relief, the new commandant promised swift
results.

> If Lieutenant Colonel Jameson can find it convenient to send
> an officer to this place [Arnold wrote], I will furnish him with

orders on the Quartermaster General for as great a number of horses as he have it in his power to equip and mount properly.

In the same letter he requested an escort of two dragoons for a certain John Anderson, who would be coming through the lines on approved business.

Tallmadge thanked Arnold profusely and promised to furnish an escort for John Anderson. He also included some military intelligence. He had been told, by a strategically placed informant, that General Clinton was about to attack Rhode Island or turn southward and invade Virginia. He enclosed a list of British regiments slated for early embarkation, assuring Arnold that the information came "from the best authority and is taken on the spot." But he did not give Culper Junior's name.

XIII

The Crucial Parley

On September 15, four days later, Arnold wrote again.

> Lieut. Colonel Jameson commands in the lines in the room of Col. Sheldon [he told André]. If you think proper to pursue your former plan, you will be perfectly safe in coming to his quarters or those of Major Tallmadge of his regiment. Either of these gentlemen will immediately send an escort with you to meet me.

Should André consider this too risky, he might come by boat to Dobbs Ferry, where a deputy, whom Arnold did not identify, would await him. "It will be necessary for you to come in disguise," Arnold reiterated.

The letter also contained, in the idiom of commerce, Arnold's pledge to turn over a sizable number of American troops:

> My partner of whom I hinted in a former letter [Washington] has £10,000 cash in hand ready for speculation [ten thousand men]. I have about £1,000 [the West Point garrison] and can collect £1,500 more [fifteen hundred additional men] in two or three days. Add to this, I have some credit. From these hints you can judge purchase that can be made.

Arnold signed himself as "Gustavus." That same day he notified the British that Washington would be "at King's Ferry

Sunday evening next on his way to Hartford, where he is to meet the French Admiral and General [Rochambeau], and will lodge at Peekskill." Written in cipher, this would alert the British to Washington's schedule and let them know that if they moved swiftly they might take him prisoner in a surprise attack.

Arnold had hoped to hold the parley within his own lines, but Clinton would not hear of it. To arrange for a safer location, he sent Beverley Robinson upriver aboard the *Vulture*, an armed sloop commanded by Captain Andrew Sutherland. She dropped anchor off Teller's Point, opposite Haverstraw, where Robinson dispatched two letters, one for General Israel Putnam, the other for Arnold. The letter to Putnam, relating to the disposition of Robinson's family belongings, was a cover-up. Enclosed with it was the message for Arnold, artfully disguised:

> I have taken the liberty of enclosing my letter to General Putnam . . . and beg the favor of you to deliver it. But if he should have returned to Connecticut, I beg his letter may be returned to me. And in that case I am persuaded (from the humane and generous character you bear) that could I be so happy as to see you, you would readily grant me the same request I should make of him. But, for prudential reasons, I dare not explain the matter further until I have some assurance that it shall be secret if not granted.

In the course of the letter he threw in the name of "James Osborn," Jonathan Odell's code name. This would signal Arnold that André was involved.

That evening Arnold showed Robinson's message to the commander-in-chief. He nodded agreement when Washington warned him to have no dealings with the Tory colonel. That Washington had discouraged the interview provided Arnold with the excuse he needed to answer Robinson's message in an official communication. He got off two letters. One, which he allowed his secretary to see, loftily informed Robinson that "any application respecting your private affairs in this country ought to be made to the civil authority of this State, as they are entirely out of the line of the military." The other, enclosed in the same packet but not seen by his secretary, promised Robinson that he would "send a person to Dobbs Ferry, or on board the *Vulture*, on Wednesday night, the 20th instant, and furnish him with a boat and flag of truce." He asked that the *Vulture* "remain where she is until the time mentioned." Arnold enclosed a third document also unbeknownst to his secretary, a copy of his letter of September 15 to André. All three communications were delivered to the *Vulture* by an American artillery officer.

Everything was now in place. André had been negotiating with Arnold for sixteen months, haggling over terms through go-betweens, resorting to codes, assumed names, and invisible ink. The moment had finally come for the crucial parley, and the timing was made to order. Sir George Rodney had recently arrived with ten sail of the line, giving the British naval superiority and eliminating any serious threat to New York. He was father of the George Rodney whom André had known in Göttingen, and he would become that rare phenomenon, an admiral Sir Henry could approve of and trust. Clinton says that the cloud of sail "struck the utmost dismay into the disaffected colonists and very justly filled the minds of the King's friends with the highest joy and expectation." And in South Carolina the rebels had been handed a crushing defeat. A force of more than four thousand men had been routed at the battle of Camden in what would be described more than a century later as "the most disastrous defeat ever inflicted on an American army." Oliver De Lancey spoke of the gloom in the Continental ranks, described to him by spies and informants: "Several have resigned their commissions. Their countenances as well as their actions shew them horribly frightened, and the general cry was for peace." What better moment for Arnold's move against West Point?

To mask what was afoot, Clinton announced plans for a

thrust into Maryland and Virginia. Simcoe hoped to be given command of the light troops, but when a rival was named in his place he informed André that he wished to be spared the "disgrace" of having any part in the expedition. André wanted to relieve his friend's mind, but his reply must be circuitous and guarded. If Simcoe read between the lines he would see that something else was in the making.

> Rely on it, your alarms are in vain [André wrote him]. I should have been happy to have seen you and have hinted that apparent arrangements are not always real ones, but I beg you to seek no explanation. I should not say what I do, but cannot without concern see you in any uneasiness I can remove.

André's mission was shrouded in the utmost secrecy. Only a handful of people knew anything about it. Admiral Rodney had been told, and Knyphausen and Captain Beckwith. Jonathan Odell knew. But that seems to have been all. Troops and transports were in readiness for a dash up the Hudson, but their destination was understood to be the Chesapeake. Although Clinton gave his consent to André's going ashore for the parley, it was on condition that his adjutant general have the protection of a flag of truce.

> I could have no reason to suspect that any bad consequence could possibly result to Major André from such a mode [he tells us], as I had given it in charge to him *not to change his dress or name on any account*, or possess himself of writings by which the nature of his embassy might be traced, and I understood that after his business was finished he was to be sent back in the same way.

He also warned André never to cross enemy lines.

The day before André left, he and Clinton rode on horseback to the Beekman mansion, where Baroness von Riedesel was a house guest. She has left us her recollections of the visit.

General Clinton often came there to visit us [she says], but
dressed only in his hunting clothes and accompanied by a
single aide. . . . The last time he came he brought with him
the unfortunate Major André, [who was about to leave on a
mission] which had been assigned to another officer, too old
and too well known, whose turn it really was, and whose life,
therefore, was in greater danger and whom he wanted to save.*

André, the baroness writes, was an "excellent young man"
and "the victim of his zeal for service and his good heart."**

Next day André was sped upstream by sailboat to the *Vulture*,
which still lay at anchor off Teller's Point. He boarded the
sloop of war at about seven that night to find Beverley Robinson and Captain Sutherland awaiting him on the quarterdeck. Robinson said that Arnold's deputy was expected
momentarily. He was Joshua Hett Smith, Robinson added, a
brother of the chief justice. The name meant nothing to André,
for he had forgotten meeting Joshua Smith four years earlier
at Colonel Hay's table. Smith was a local resident, Robinson
continued, not overly bright perhaps, but a lawyer of sorts
with a fondness for rod and gun. Smith and his wife were said
to be close friends of the Arnolds. In making Smith his deputy,
Arnold had chosen a man he knew well and could trust.

The three remained on deck, pacing anxiously. Here and
there a few shore lights winked, but there was no hint of a
rowboat making its way to the dip of oars from the neighborhood of Haverstraw. The hours came and went. Then it was
midnight, with no sign of Smith. Finally André went below,
where he lay tossing until daybreak.

Early that morning André wrote two letters to Sir Henry.
One was left unsealed. It ascribed his continuing presence

*Beverley Robinson, whom Clinton would have preferred in André's place.
**Clinton gave the baroness the use of the Beekman mansion (Mount Pleasant) for
the summer of 1780, while he occupied the Cornelius Tiebout farm (Roxborough).

aboard the *Vulture* to "a very bad cold and so violent a return
of a disorder in my stomach, which had attacked me a few
days ago, that Capt. Sutherland and Col. Robinson insist on
my remaining on board until I am better." This should quiet
any suspicions among Sutherland's personnel, who might see
the letter. The other was sealed and was meant only for Sir
Henry.

> Nobody has appeared [André wrote him]. This is the second
> excursion I have made without any ostensible reason, and
> Colonel Robinson both times of the party. A third wou'd in-
> fallibly fix suspicions. I have therefore thought it best to remain
> here on pretense of sickness, as my enclosed letter will feign,
> and try further expedients.

On the previous day, one of the *Vulture*'s longboats had
been lured shoreward with a flag of truce and fired on by local
patriots. Happily, this infraction of the rules called for a protest
from Captain Sutherland that would enable André and Robinson to get a message to Arnold under the protection of a
flag. The protest, although signed by Sutherland, was in André's
hand and was cosigned by "John Anderson, Secretary," sig-
naling Arnold that André was aboard ship. Tucked into the
same packet was a message from Robinson saying that he and
André awaited Smith and would accompany him "to any con-
venient and safe place."

Smith had failed to show up because he had no way of
getting to the *Vulture*. Arnold had told him to obtain a longboat
from Major Edward Kiers, the quartermaster at Stony Point.
But Kiers had nothing he could spare, and Smith, instead of
inquiring elsewhere, had returned home to enlist one of his
tenants, a countryman named Samuel Cahoon, as oarsman for
the expedition. This turned out to be less easily arranged than
he had anticipated. "I went with him up to his room," Cahoon
tells us, "and he asked me to go with him that night a piece —
he said, down the river. I told him I had no mind to go and

did not want to go. He did not urge me hard to go." Cahoon did agree, however, to take a message to Arnold, who was still at the Robinson house. Traveling all night on horseback, he reached headquarters at sunrise and was informed that Arnold was still in bed. He left the message with an aide and started home. On the way back, Arnold passed him at a gallop. He gave no explanation for his haste and continued, without a word, toward Haverstraw.

This time Arnold himself went in search of a longboat, appealing to Kiers and to Colonel James Livingston, the commandant at Fort Lafayette. But he fared no better than his deputy. Pressed for time, he delegated the search to his barge crew and left for Smith's house, directing the men to bring the craft to Colonel Hay's landing in nearby Minesceongo Creek.

At Smith's house, Arnold closeted himself with Samuel Cahoon, only to find the tenant as balky as Smith said he would be. Cahoon said that he had been up most of the night and was too tired for the undertaking. And he made no bones of the fact that the whole idea scared him. Was he "a friend of the country"? Arnold demanded. Cahoon said he would match his love of country against that of any man but that he would not go within hailing distance of a British sloop of war. Besides, he pointed out, a longboat was too big for one man to handle. Arnold ordered him to enlist the help of his brother Joseph, also one of Smith's tenants. Samuel shuffled off, but on the way he stopped at his own house to consult his wife. She warned that under no circumstances should he get involved. Samuel went back to Smith's house and begged to be excused. Whereupon Arnold told him that if he failed in his patriotic duty he would be listed as "a disaffected man." Samuel set forth again, taking care this time to avoid his wife, and returned with brother Joseph in tow.

Joseph proved to be even balkier than Samuel. Smith met him at the front door and said they would go only "a little down the river." But Joseph did not take to the idea. "I told him I was sorry I was needed for that purpose," he tells us, "and said upon any other thing I was willing to serve him or the General." Smith stepped inside to confer with Arnold, while Joseph waited glumly in the front hall. Presently Arnold himself appeared. There was nothing to be alarmed about, he promised. The officers at guard posts along the river had been duly notified. Although "the inhabitants and common man" had not been informed, this was merely a precaution. Joseph still looked doubtful, but he seemed to nod assent.

It was past sundown when word came that a longboat had been obtained and was now tied up at Colonel Hay's landing. By now both Cahoon brothers were shaking in their boots. When Joseph muttered that he "had no mind to go" and "would rather go in the morning," Arnold threatened him with immediate arrest. There would be no further pussyfooting, he declared. Smith offered both brothers a drink, telling them that what they were about to do was for "the good of the country."

The night was "serene," Smith tells us, the tide "favorable." The previous day Arnold had issued him a pass for use at King's Ferry in case he were challenged by a sentry. He now handed him a second pass, an unsealed letter for Beverley Robinson and a very short message for "John Anderson." Before striking off through the woods for Minesceongo Creek, Smith provided each of the Cahoons with a sheepskin. To muffle the oars, he explained.

When Smith drew alongside the *Vulture* he was greeted by what he refers to as "a volley of oaths, all in the peculiarity of sea language." Crew members, who had not been forewarned of his coming, were chary of local residents after the cannonading of their longboat two days previously. Smith was hurried to the captain's quarters, where he and Sutherland exchanged small talk while Beverley Robinson went belowdecks to summon John Anderson.

André had to be roused from sleep. He hurriedly read through Arnold's letters, which Robinson had brought with him. The longer, unsealed communication, addressed to Robinson, implied that their business was in the interest of the United States.

> This will be delivered you by Mr. Smith, who will conduct you to a place of safety [Arnold had written]. Neither Mr. Smith or any other person shall be made acquainted with your proposals. If they (which I doubt not) are of such a nature that I can officially take notice of them, I shall do it with pleasure. If not, you shall be permitted to return immediately. I take it for granted Colonel Robinson will not propose anything that is not for the interest of the United States as well as himself.

The message to André contained just four words: "Gustavus to John Anderson." It signaled André that Smith's mission was authentic.

Robinson showed André the two passes — one permitting Smith, "Mr. John Anderson," and "two servants" to pass the guard at King's Ferry, the other authorizing Smith to "go to Dobbs Ferry with three men and a boy with a flag, to carry some letters of a private nature for gentlemen in New York and return immediately." André saw that Beverley Robinson's name had been omitted from both. In case they were stopped, he pointed out, this would surely create suspicion, whereas André, as "John Anderson," was covered by one of the passes and should have no difficulty getting through. He urged that Robinson remain aboard the *Vulture*, while he himself went ashore and met with Arnold. After some discussion, Robinson acquiesced.

> Upon considering all of these matters [he explains], Major André thought it best for him to go alone, as both our names was not mentioned in any of ye papers, and it appeared to him — as, indeed, it did to me — that Arnold wished to see him. I therefore submitted to be left behind.

The two proceeded to the captain's quarters, where André was introduced to Joshua Hett Smith. Having no recollection of their earlier encounter, he probably rated Smith a somewhat pompous deputy, with an obsequious way about him that could prove vexing. Robinson explained that an "indisposition" prevented his going ashore but that his colleague would represent him. "John Anderson" seemed to have "no reluctance to supply Colonel Robinson's place," according to Smith's testimony. He was wearing "a large blue greatcoat" that concealed his British regimentals. Smith took it for granted that this was a civilian on official business.

The four went on deck, to see Smith's craft hauled alongside, with the Cahoon brothers waiting anxiously at the oars. Robinson urged that one of the *Vulture*'s longboats tow the craft to midstream, but André scotched the idea. It could attract attention, he said, and raise awkward questions about their right to a flag of truce. After a quick farewell, he followed Smith down a rope ladder and took his place aft of the two oarsmen. Smith grabbed the tiller and shoved off.

André said very little as the craft drew shoreward with each dip of the muffled oars. Astern lay the *Vulture*, a spectral blur off Teller's Point. Directly ahead stretched the craggy, inhospitable-looking west bank of the Hudson. What of Arnold? What manner of man was he? What terms would he accept? What precautions had he taken for André's safety? "Very little conversation passed betwen Mr. Anderson and myself," Smith says, "excepting trivial remarks about the tide, the weather and matters of no concern." Smith was impressed by his passenger's "youthful appearance" and by "the softness of his manners." He says that Anderson seemed "fraught with the milk of human kindness."

Smith guided the craft shoreward. Overhead loomed a sheer escarpment, with thick woods dipping to the riverbank. He touched shore where an overgrown roadway led into the woods. Leaving André and the Cahoon brothers with the longboat, he scrambled up the bank and vanished. It was a moonless night, aglow with stars. André kept to himself, conscious of the lap of water, the stirrings of a light breeze, but wholly absorbed in his own thoughts. When Smith returned, he led André up a shaly hillside to the clump of evergreens where Arnold waited. Then he left immediately for the landing place.

"I went as directed," he says, "but felt greatly mortified at not being present at the interview, to which I conceived myself entitled from my rank in life and the trouble I had taken to effect the meeting."

Arnold had chosen a shadowy location, but André could see that he was a squat, thickset man, hampered by a limp. The features, dimly seen, looked coarse and jowly. The voice was rasping. Arnold seemed churlish and blunt, wasting no time on amenities. Where was Colonel Robinson? he demanded. Robinson was supposed to come too. Was André fully authorized to speak for General Clinton? There must be no quibbling over terms. Arnold must be promised his full price — £20,000 if he turned over West Point with three thousand American troops, £10,000 no matter what. He had a family to support, as André must realize. His home and personal effects would be confiscated the moment he changed sides, and he would lose his pay as major general. What he was asking was little enough for the risk he was taking. André had been instructed to offer something less, but Arnold would quote him subsequently as having agreed to his terms.

We can only guess at what was said by the two, for there was no Joshua Smith on hand to record their conversation. We know that André must be told the size of the West Point garrison, the location of nearby regiments, the whereabouts of artillery and access roads, the weak spots in the fortifications. Arnold, in turn, must be assured that a British attack would be synchronized with his own maneuvering, which must appear plausible to the garrison until the last moment. The two were still in conference when Smith clambered up the hillside to warn that it was nearly daybreak. Anderson could not be returned that night to the *Vulture*, he said. He had broached the matter to the Cahoons and found them too weary to attempt it. Arnold, who did not seem overly concerned about the change of plans, said he would take Anderson to Smith's house, while Smith and the Cahoons returned the longboat to Minesceongo Creek. He promised Anderson that they would still get him back to the *Vulture*.

Arnold led André to a clearing where three horses were tethered, watched over by a black servant from Smith's household. He assigned André one of the mounts, and the three cantered in silence along the empty road. Near Haverstraw they were stopped by a sentry who waved them on when he recognized Arnold. But André was greatly alarmed. He not only faced a whole day on shore but he had crossed enemy lines — "against my stipulation, my intention and without my knowledge beforehand," as he would testify. The three passed a few darkened farmhouses, skirted Colonel Hay's property, and ascended a steep hillside to Smith's house. The two-story residence, known as Belmont, commanded a broad view of the Hudson at Haverstraw Bay. It had a look of genteel shabbiness.

As Arnold hustled André to an upstairs bedroom, a burst of gunfire reverberated from the Hudson. Stepping to a front window, they could see smoke rising in little puffs above Teller's Point. Colonel Livingston, the commandant at Fort Lafayette, had brought up cannon, unbeknownst to Arnold, and was firing round after round at the *Vulture*, which lay immobilized by wind and tide. Beverley Robinson would describe the cannonade in his report to Clinton:

> You will remember, sir, that Arnold in his first letter to me desired the *Vulture* might continue her station at Taller's Point [*sic*] for a few days. This induced us to think we might lay there with the greatest safety and unmolested. But on Thurs-

day night they brought down on Tallers Point one six-pounder and a howitzer, entrenched themselves on ye very Point and at daylight Friday morning began a very hot fire on us . . . which continued two hours and would have been longer but, luckily, their magazine blew up. It was near high water, ye tide very slack and no wind, so that it was impossible, tho' every exertion was made, to get ye ship out of reach sooner.

The cannonade was still in progress when Smith and the Cahoon brothers arrived from Minesceongo Creek. Arnold met them in the yard, for Joseph Cahoon would remember that "he walked lame and had on a blue coat and white breeches." He sent the weary oarsmen home but ordered Smith to serve breakfast in the upstairs bedroom.

André had taken off his greatcoat. When serving breakfast, Smith beheld him, for the first time, in the uniform of a British officer. Arnold explained that Anderson had borrowed the uniform from an acquaintance in New York, that he donned it from time to time out of harmless vanity. Smith swallowed the story. He sat down with the others and joined unhesitatingly in their conversation. The talk ranged from the whereabouts of Arbuthnot's fleet and "the health and spirit of the British army" to what Smith describes as "desultory topics of no consequence." When breakfast was over he excused himself. He had a touch of ague, he said, and was bone tired after a sleepless night. Arnold hurried him out the door. No sooner were they alone than he and André were back at the front window.

The *Vulture* had begun to return the fire. She had not been severely damaged — indeed, the only wound among her crew was sustained by Captain Sutherland, who had the skin nicked from his nose by a stray splinter. "Six shots hulled us, one between wind and water," Robinson would report. "Many others struck ye sails and rigging, and boats on deck. Two shells hit us — one fell on ye quarterdeck, another near ye main shrouds." Wind and tide had shifted. As Arnold and

André watched, the sloop's longboats began inching her out of range. When her sails filled she turned downstream. To André's horror, she kept on a southerly course until she vanished from sight.

It was now ten o'clock, and Arnold must be back at headquarters. But first he must show André certain papers relating to West Point. They included a return of the garrison, an estimate of the number of troops Arnold would add to those already there, a return of ordnance, and the minutes of a recent council of war. Weak spots were itemized: Fort Putnam was in disrepair, with a gaping east wall where masons were still at work; Fort Webb was tinder dry and could be set afire; Fort Arnold was in "a ruinous condition"; outlying redoubts were short of artillery and the north redoubt could be set afire with "faggots dipt in pitch." The information should make the capture of the fortress relatively easy, especially with Arnold's secret cooperation.

André would claim that Arnold urged the papers on him.

> He made me put the papers I bore between my stockings and my feet [he would insist]. Whilst I did it, he expressed a wish, in case of any accident befalling me, that they should be destroyed, which I said of course would be the case, as when I went back to the boat I should have them tied about with a string and a stone.

In truth, however, we cannot be sure if Arnold forced the papers on André, or if André claimed this to lessen his own culpability. Both men, in parting, may have given way to impulse. That the papers were in Arnold's handwriting must expose him to instant detection if they were intercepted, and to have André try to sneak them through the lines was taking a monumental risk. In addition to the information about West Point, André would also have with him a list of local spies and informants. The name of Elijah Hunter, the double spy whom Clinton trusted, was among them.

André had twice disregarded Sir Henry's warning — he had crossed enemy lines and now he had agreed to carry treasonous papers on his person. Although he was hostage to Arnold, wholly dependent on him for his safe return, he still hoped to be taken that same day to the *Vulture*. Arnold was not so sure. On his way out, he advised Smith that his guest might have to return by land, through Westchester. The two must play it by ear, but Smith should be prepared to supply John Anderson with civilian clothes. Arnold handed him three passes — one permitting him "to pass with a boat and three hands and a flag to Dobbs Ferry on public business and to return immediately," another "to pass the guards to the White Plains and to return, being on public business by my direction." The third pass was for "John Anderson," enabling him to "pass the guards to White Plains, or below if he chooses, he being on public business by my direction." With the pass specifying "White Plains or below," André could cross into the Neutral Ground and continue southward to his own lines. Arnold also loaned Smith an army horse, with USA branded conspicuously on one shoulder. This would be John Anderson's mount.

Smith accompanied Arnold as far as Stony Point. As the two traveled the few miles on horseback, he told Arnold that if he returned Anderson by land he could come home by way of Fishkill and collect his wife and children, whom he had farmed out with relatives. Arnold raised no objections. He said he would leave the decision with the other two.

Upon his return, Smith found his guest at the bedroom window, peering downstream for some sign of the *Vulture*. To take his mind off the vanished sloop, Smith led him to the top floor of the house and showed him a panoramic view of Haverstraw Bay, shiny and pewter gray in the noontime sun. But Anderson showed no interest. "He cast an anxious look towards the *Vulture*," Smith relates, "and, with a heavy sigh, wished he was on board." Smith said he was sorry that Arnold had not ordered a flag of truce from Stony Point, so that Anderson could return directly to the *Vulture* "without the fatigue of his going to the White Plains" in the course of a "circuitous" trip by land. The remark seemed to stun Anderson. Smith says that "from this time he seemed shy, and desirous to avoid much conversation." When they returned to the bedroom for lunch Anderson no more than sampled the food before resuming his vigil at the window.

During the afternoon a drover happened by with some cattle Smith had ordered. Smith and the drover discussed the transaction directly under André's window. André could not make out what they were saying, but he was thankful when the drover finally left and Smith came back into the house. He would have breathed less easily had he known that Smith told the drover that he had a mysterious guest upstairs, a stranger from New York involved in some secret business with General Arnold.

Late that afternoon, just before sundown, Smith came to the bedroom door to remind Anderson that there was still no sign of the *Vulture*. He held a beaver hat in one hand and, over his arm, a claret-colored coat trimmed with gold lace. They must return by land, he announced. Anderson's borrowed British uniform would never get by the first sentry, and he must change into civilian clothes before leaving the house. They would travel together as far as Pine's Bridge on the Croton River, from where Anderson should have no trouble reaching New York on his own.

As surely as André had become Arnold's hostage when he crossed enemy lines and hid the papers in his boots, so he was now hostage to this chatterbox of a country lawyer. He took the hat and coat that Smith offered him, conscious of Sir Henry's warning that under no circumstances should he part with his regimentals. Very reluctantly, he removed the scarlet coat and handed it to Smith, watching as Smith tucked it, neatly folded, into a bureau drawer. Then he tried on the one

Smith had given him. It was ill-fitting, and the gold lace looked frayed and tarnished.

At sundown Smith and André, accompanied by the same servant who had been with Arnold the night before, set forth on horseback for King's Ferry, adjoining Stony Point. They had not gone far when they overtook an American officer whom Smith recognized. He introduced him as Major John Burroughs of the New Jersey line. To André's intense discomfort, Burroughs joined them, conversing airily and promising to take tea at Belmont after Mrs. Smith's return. André was acutely conscious of his borrowed clothes. He took no part in the conversation and felt a surge of relief when Burroughs turned down a side road and bade them godspeed.

Smith ran into more friends at King's Ferry, where the boat crew was sharing a comradely libation with several officers and enlisted men. They hailed Smith, who promptly joined them and entered with gusto into their banter. André could hear his voice rising above the others. "What do you think, Daddy Cooley, of being in New York in three weeks time?" he boomed. "I'm afraid not," a voice growled in reply. "Well, let it be three months then!" Smith countered. André had kept his distance. As the talk grew louder, he and the servant urged their mounts down a steep incline to the ferry. They waited at the water's edge until Smith and the boat crew finally appeared, unfazed by the delay. The horses were coaxed aboard, a crewman cast off, and the ferry nosed ponderously toward Verplanck's Point. Smith chatted with the oarsmen. At André's urging, he promised them "something to revive their spirits" if they made a fast crossing.

Smith made yet another stop, for he must pay his respects to Colonel Livingston at nearby Fort Lafayette. Although neither he nor André knew it, this was the same Colonel Livingston who had bombarded the *Vulture* off Teller's Point. André watched from a distance as Smith announced himself at Livingston's headquarters. After a short while Smith came out, all smiles. They had been invited to take supper at the fort, he said, but because of the lateness of the hour he had declined. Livingston had given him two letters to deliver, for Governor Clinton of New York and for Benedict Arnold. André breathed more easily as they turned north toward Peekskill, leaving King's Ferry behind them.

The road was thinly settled, with long stretches of uninhabited woods and only an occasional farmhouse. Smith noticed a change in his companion, who conversed readily now and seemed in better spirits. Traveling at a canter, they reached Peekskill around seven o'clock and turned east on the Crompond road. They had gone about four miles, mostly through pitch-black woods, when half a dozen militiamen blocked their path, muskets in readiness. "Friends!" Smith shouted. As the men closed in, he called for the name of their commanding officer. "Captain Ebenezer Boyd!" came the answer. Whereupon Captain Boyd strode into their midst from a nearby command post.

Boyd asked the travelers where they were from and why they were abroad at such an hour. Smith flourished the passes. He was in the service of General Arnold, he said. He and his companions needed accommodations, and he wondered if Major Joseph Strang, an acquaintance of his, might take them in. Strang was not at home, Boyd told him, nor would his wife appreciate three unannounced guests knocking at her door. What about "old Colonel Gil Drake?" Drake no longer lived here, Boyd replied. But before accommodations could be discussed, he must see the passes. He went inside to fetch a lantern. "Mr. Anderson seemed very uneasy," Smith says, "but I cheered him by saying our passes would carry us to any part of the country to which they were directed, and that no person dare presume to detain us."

When Boyd returned with the lantern he scrutinized each of the passes, noting Arnold's signature. For the first time he showed an interest in the travelers. Perhaps Andreas Miller could spare them lodging. Miller, he said, was a friend of his. He lived a short way off, on the same road. They would be wise to go no farther, for Cowboys were abroad — Tory cutthroats who had been taking prisoners and stealing cattle.

Anybody recommended by Captain Boyd was welcome to his hearth, Andreas Miller assured the travelers when they rapped on the door of his dimly lit farmhouse. He apologized, however, for what little he had to offer. He could provide sleeping accommodations, but no meals. Cowboys had raided his farm, all but emptying his cupboards, and he had barely enough to feed his wife and children. He showed André and Smith to an austere bedroom furnished with a solitary fourposter. When he left they could hear him going from room to room, bolting doors and checking windows. Neither André nor Smith undressed, and, to Smith's astonishment, André went to bed still wearing his boots. Smith slept poorly, André not at all. "I was often disturbed with the restless motions and uneasiness of mind exhibited by my bedfellow," Smith says. "He appeared in the morning as if he had not slept an hour during the night." André was up before daybreak. After helping the servant saddle the horses, he waited anxiously until Smith joined him. The three thanked Miller for their lodgings and started eastward. A thick, early morning fog shrouded the road.

Anderson seemed eager to talk and even smiled a little. He said he hoped they had passed their last sentry post and spoke appreciatively of Miller's hospitality. But at Crompond they were stopped again, this time by Captain Ebenezer Foote, a youth in his twenties who had command of a small militia unit. Foote glanced at the passes. He seemed less suspicious than Boyd and asked fewer questions. He told Smith that Sheldon's Continental Dragoons were stationed at Wright's Mills, below the Croton, and that the officer in charge, Colonel Jameson, might spare them an escort. The fog was lifting as the three travelers left Crompond and turned south toward Pine's Bridge.

A short way below Crompond the three came face to face with an American officer traveling northward on horseback. He looked familiar to André, even at a distance. As he drew closer André recognized him as Colonel Samuel Blachley Webb, a former prisoner of war whom he had known in New York. André's "hair stood erect," we are told, "and his heart was in his mouth." Webb eyed him closely as they passed but gave no sign of recognition. André would remember "ruminating on his good fortune and hair-breadth escape" after Webb had gone. He had now been stopped by local militia, had spent a night in a farmhouse along the way, and had been eyed by a Continental officer who should have remembered him on sight — and his identity was still a secret. The disguise was working.

Hilltops were emerging through wisps of ground fog. There were hints of gold and ocher in the hardwoods, and both goldenrod and purple asters bloomed by the roadside. André commented on the autumn color and on the loveliness of the wooded hillsides. "He descanted on the richness of the scenery around us," Smith says. "The pleasantry of converse and mildness of the weather insensibly beguiled the time." André spoke of the war and said that if Britain had her way, "peace was an event not far distant." But he talked mostly of the arts. Smith says that

> music, painting and poetry seemed to be his delight. He displayed a judicious taste in the choice of the authors he had read, possessed great elegance of sentiment, and a most pleasing manner of conveying his ideas by adopting the flowery colouring of poetical imagery.

Our travelers had not eaten since they left Belmont, and all three were famished. Smith spotted a farmhouse that showed signs of life. He dismounted and knocked. An old woman answered, opening the door only a crack. When Smith explained his situation, she said that Cowboys had raided the farm and driven off all but one of her milk cows. But she seemed to take pity on the travelers. Her name was Sarah Underhill, she said. She had very little food in the house but could serve them *suppon*. Smith summoned his two companions. When the *suppon* was ladled out, André took his portion to the back steps, where he sat by himself and downed what he could stomach. This was the same corn mush that had prompted his derisive reference in "The Cow Chace" to those "that eat *soupaan*."

With breakfast behind them, Smith announced that he and his servant would be turning back. Cowboys prowled the roads, he said, and he had no wish for an encounter. Besides, Pine's Bridge was only a short way from here, about two and a half miles. André raised no objections. He was probably relieved to see the last of his chatty traveling companion, and he had no fear of an encounter with Cowboys, who were friends of the Crown. But he had no money. He asked Smith for a small loan, offering a gold watch as surety. Smith would not take the timepiece, but he handed over half of what he had in his pocket. He gave André directions and a message for his brother, the chief justice. Then the two wished each other godspeed.

On his own at last, André continued southward, crossing the Croton at Pine's Bridge. He was passing through the Neutral Ground, with its forsaken homes, untended orchards, and waist-high hay fields. The few people he passed eyed him guardedly. But his spirits soared. Every hoofbeat of his borrowed mount brought him closer to his own lines, closer to the moment when he would deliver Arnold's papers to Sir Henry and tell of their parley. Tradition has it that he stopped three times on his way south — to ask directions of Jesse Thorne, a lad of twelve, to water his mount at the farm of Sylvanus Brundage, to request a drink of water at the home of Staats Hammond. He is said to have bestowed sixpence on young Sally Hammond and to have asked directions of her brother David.

At about half past nine André came to a bridge spanning a narrow, slowly meandering stream. He reined in his mount, pulled out a map he was carrying, and saw that he was on course. He was now near Tarrytown, not far from his own lines. He breathed easily. What was left of his journey should harbor few perils. He was about to cross the bridge when three men, shabbily dressed and wielding muskets, emerged from thickets bordering the road. One, wearing the green, red-trimmed coat of a German sharpshooter, pointed his gun at André and blocked the way. André took the three for Cowboys. "Gentlemen," he said, "I hope you belong to our party." "What party?" he was asked. "The lower," he replied, referring to the king's party. He held up his gold watch as proof that he was a man of substance and not to be trifled with. "I am an officer in the British service and have now been on particular business in the country," he told them. "I hope you will not detain me." The three eyed him curiously.*

---

*Accounts of the capture differ in several particulars. That of John Paulding, the only literate member of the trio, was given soon after the event and is used here.

XIV

Drumbeat for a Spy

JOHN PAULDING, Isaac Van Wart, and David Williams were three of eight local residents who had set forth that morning to waylay Cowboys and any suspicious-looking strangers. Some, but not all, may have been Skinners. Near Tarrytown the eight divided, five stationing themselves on a nearby hilltop, the other three at the bridge that John André must presently cross. The three were young men, with Williams the oldest at twenty-five. All had been enrolled in the Westchester militia, and one, John Paulding, had escaped from a British prison wearing the German sharpshooter's coat that would deceive André. A big, spare man, he was the leader of the three. He and Williams seated themselves under a tree and started a game of cards, while Van Wart kept watch from a hiding place beside the road. Several passers-by whom the three recognized were allowed to continue, but when André appeared Van Wart whispered excitedly to his companions. A stranger was approaching. His breeches and white-topped boots looked too expensive for any ordinary traveler. Paulding grabbed his musket and stepped into the road.

André had no more than declared himself an officer in the king's army than he realized that these were no friends of Britain. "My God, I must do anything to get along!" he exclaimed, trying, as Paulding puts it, "to make kind of a laugh" of the situation. He produced his pass, embellished with Benedict Arnold's signature. "My lads," he warned, "you had best let me go or you will bring yourselves in trouble, for, by stopping me, you will detain the General's business. I am going to Dobbs Ferry to meet a person there and get information for him." Paulding seemed somewhat cowed. He hoped André would not be "offended" and said that he and his companions "did not mean to take anything from him." Not so Van Wart. "Damn Arnold's pass!" he muttered. "You said you were a British officer. Where's your money?" André said he had none. "You a British officer, and no money?" exclaimed Van Wart. "Let's search him!"

The three hustled their captive into the underbrush, where he was stripped to his boots. Two watches were discovered, the gold one André had flourished to impress his captors and a silver timepiece engraved with his name. The captors kept both. The few dollars loaned him by Joshua Hett Smith were also taken. Next came André's boots. "We told him to pull off his boots," David Williams says, "which he seemed indifferent about, but we got one boot off and searched in that boot but could find nothing; and we found that there were some papers in the bottom of his stocking next to his foot, on which we made him pull his stocking off, and found there three papers wrapped up." While André watched, John Paulding unfolded the papers and pored over each in turn. He was the only member of the trio who could read. When he had finished, he looked up at his comrades. "This is a spy!" he said.

What happened next is unclear. André would give his own version the following day to Lieutenant Joshua King of the Continental Dragoons; namely, that he asked his captors their price for setting him free and offered to remain with two of them while the third took his written request to the nearest British post. King says that "the sum was agreed upon, but I cannot recollect whether it was five hundred or a thousand guineas — the latter, I think, was the sum. They held a consultation a considerable time and finally told him that if he wrote, a party would be sent out to take them, and then they would all be prisoners." Whereupon they delivered him to the Continental Dragoons.

But the captors testified that when André was asked if he would surrender his horse, bridle, watch, and 100 guineas in return for his freedom, he promised all of these, as well as any "quantity of dry goods" they might request. They maintained that they had spurned the offer. John Paulding said he told André, "No, by God! If you would give me ten thousand guineas you should not stir a step!"

Even as the versions of the capture differ, so the motive of the captors has been called in question. The three would be hailed as heroes by both Congress and the public. Each would receive a medal, and Washington would entertain them at his table. The commander-in-chief told Congress that they had refused to free André "notwithstanding the most earnest importunities and assurances of a liberal reward on his part. Their conduct merits our warmest esteem, and I beg leave to add that I think the public will do well to make them a handsome gratuity." Yet both King and his senior officer, Major Tallmadge, would maintain that the three had robbery in mind while they lurked by the bridge. Tallmadge would lump them with "that class of people who passed between both armies, as often in one camp as the other." He would have arrested them as readily as he would have taken John André into custody.

There was speculation as to why André had shown so little caution. Washington described his behavior as "an unaccountable deprivation of presence of mind in a man of the first abilities." And Thomas Paine could not understand how André "should suffer himself to be taken as a coward would have been taken — a man on horseback against three on foot had a chance of escaping, especially as the pursuit could not have been for long." But this failed to take into account that André believed he was involved with pro-British Cowboys and that by the time he realized his mistake he had three guns trained on him at close range. His chances of survival would seem much better if he let himself be taken to West Point, where Arnold would arrange his release.

Paulding and his comrades hoped to be given André's mount, saddle, watches, and pocket money in return for their catch. As they started for Wright's Mills, six miles away, one led André's horse while the other two walked beside him. Presently they were joined by their five companions, whom Paulding summoned by firing off his musket. "Big drops of sweat" fell from André's brow, Van Wart says.

> You never saw such an alteration in any man's face. Only a few moments before, he was uncommonly gay in his looks, but after we had made him prisoner, you could read in his face that he thought it was all over with him. After traveling one or two miles he said, "I would to God you had blown my brains out when you stopped me!"

Williams taunted the prisoner. Would he make a dash for freedom if given the chance? The answer was obvious — André said of course he would.

The captors seemed in no hurry, stopping to exhibit their prisoner to friends along the route. At Reed's Tavern, just east of Tarrytown, André was given some bread and milk — his first sustenance since early morning. He sat by himself in a box stairway and partook sparingly. When the group came to Wright's Mills, also known as the John Robbins house, they were told that the Dragoons had transferred their base of operations to North Castle, six miles away. It was now mid-afternoon. The group plodded northward, with André still on horseback, reaching their destination around five o'clock. To André's way of thinking, the rough-hewn barn and grist mill had a raw, countrified look, ill becoming a military post.

When André was turned over to the post commander, Lieutenant Colonel Jameson, his hopes soared. Jameson decided to send the incriminating papers to Washington, who was on his way from Hartford after a conference with Rochambeau. But André would be taken that same night to Arnold's headquarters, along with a letter acquainting Arnold with the circumstances of the capture. Once he reached the Robinson house, André's perils should be at an end. Arnold would see that he was returned promptly to New York.

André left North Castle an hour later in the custody of Lieutenant Solomon Allen and four militiamen. He was still on his borrowed mount, with his arms strapped behind him and with one of his guards holding the bridle. His spirits had risen mightily, for there was time for him to reach the Robinson house in advance of the commander-in-chief. But near Peekskill a courier overtook Allen's party with a countermand from Colonel Jameson. Allen was ordered to turn about and deliver his prisoner to Lieutenant Joshua King at South Salem.

André had a brief surge of hope when the four militiamen disputed the change of orders. They had friends they wished to see at West Point, and they urged Allen to ignore the countermand. André, who could not conceive of such behavior in the British Army, joined in the discussion and spoke eloquently in their behalf. The argument grew heated, but Allen would brook no insubordination. He ordered an about-face. Instead of proceeding directly to South Salem, however, he seems to have gone by way of North Castle, where Major Tallmadge first laid eyes on "John Anderson."

Tallmadge, who had reached headquarters soon after Allen left, had urged Jameson to issue a countermand that would prevent the prisoner from reaching the Robinson house ahead of the commander-in-chief. Jameson had complied with this, but he had insisted on dispatching the letter that would notify Arnold. Allen had the letter with him and would deliver it after he had handed over "Anderson" at South Salem.

Lieutenant King and his troops were billeted in the residence of Squire John Gilbert, whose big farmhouse was well suited to a command post. Allen's party arrived in the course of the morning, and the prisoner was confined, under heavy guard, in the bedroom of the surgeon's mate, Dr. Isaac Bronson. He warmed to Bronson and talked at length about the circumstances of his capture. He would have been set free, he claimed, if he had had "a single guinea" to pay his captors. The doctor was given to believe that

> they had ripped up the housings of his saddle and the collar of his coat and, finding no money there, were upon the point of letting him go when one of the party said, "Damn him, he may have it in his boots!" They threw him down, drew off his boots and discovered the papers, which induced the captors to think he might be a prize worth carrying in to the outposts. He offered them any sum they would name if they would let him go. . . . Their reply was, a bird in the hand is worth two in the bush.

This is what André told Dr. Bronson. All three captors would deny it.

To amuse the doctor, André drew a sketch of himself in the custody of Lieutenant Allen and his homespun militiamen, one of the rustics holding his horse's bridle. "This will give you some idea of the style in which I have had the honor to be conducted to my present abode," he quipped, handing the sketch to Bronson.

It was in Dr. Bronson's bedroom that André wrote his letter to Washington, admitting his identity and acknowledging that he had been "betrayed into the vile condition of an enemy in disguise within your posts." He wrote to clear his name, he said, and to defend his honor:

> I beg your Excellency will be persuaded that no alteration in the temper of my mind, or apprehension for my safety, induces

me to take the step of addressing you, but that it is to rescue myself from an imputation of having assumed a mean character for treacherous purposes or self-interest — a conduct incompatible with the principles that actuate me, as well as my condition in life. It is to vindicate my fame that I speak, and not to solicit security.

He asked permission to get in touch with Sir Henry Clinton and to have a change of apparel sent him from New York. And he included a threat that would not be lost on Washington. The British had in their custody several South Carolinians accused of parole violation. Their fate could be in jeopardy, for they were "persons whom the treatment I receive might affect." Retribution was not limited to either side. Before dispatching the letter, André enclosed an account of his activities up to the moment of his capture. He admitted that he had considered Tarrytown "far beyond the points described as dangerous."

With this behind him, a change came over André. He was no longer "John Anderson," to be identified with his beaver hat and ill-fitting civilian coat. He was a British officer, high in the councils of General Clinton, who had undertaken a perilous mission in the line of duty. He had come in uniform, not as a common spy paid for his demeaning work. That he had changed into civilian attire and concealed treasonous papers on his person had not been his own idea. He had acquiesced out of necessity. Those who talked with him were impressed with the confidence he had in the rectitude of his mission, however he might lament the mistakes he had made. He remained unruffled, appreciative of small favors, amiable with everyone.

While André waited out the hours in Dr. Bronson's bedroom, Benedict Arnold was busy saving his own skin. The courier who carried the treasonous papers had failed to connect with Washington and had returned with them to South Salem. He had been hurried off to the Robinson house, where Washington was due to arrive that same morning. But he was behind Lieutenant Allen, who reached headquarters first with Colonel Jameson's letter. Arnold was having breakfast with two of Washington's aides who had arrived in advance of their chief. When he read the letter he was "thrown into confusion," according to witnesses, and dashed upstairs to warn Peggy. Even as the two conferred, a knock on the door notified them that Washington was not far off. Arnold sped to the front yard, untethered his mount, and galloped down a wooded roadway to a barge kept in readiness at the riverbank. He ordered the oarsmen to hurry him to the sloop of war *Vulture*, anchored downstream. The men were perplexed, but he told them that this was official business and there must be no delay. After passing Stony Point, he tied a white handkerchief to the flag-staff as protection against American gunboats and shore batteries and as a covert signal to Captain Sutherland. He urged the oarsmen to extend themselves, promising them two gallons of rum for their exertions, but when he boarded the *Vulture* he had them placed under arrest.

Back at headquarters, Peggy Arnold was the soul of innocence. She ranted, raved, and was beguilingly tearful and distraught. "Poor, distressed, unhappy, frantic and miserable lady!" exclaimed Richard Varick, Arnold's aide-de-camp. "All the sweetness of beauty, all the loveliness of innocence, all the tenderness of a wife, and all the fondness of a mother showed themselves in her appearance and conduct," wrote Alexander Hamilton, Washington's aide and secretary. It was a performance that convinced everyone of her innocence. Joshua Hett Smith, alas, possessed no such gifts. Rousted from bed at a relative's house in Fishkill, he was marched to headquarters between fixed bayonets.

That same night André was taken to the Robinson house, guarded by one hundred Continental Dragoons. A hard rain had set in, and he was pitiful to behold as he was led into the yard and assigned a mount near the middle of the long column. As Dr. Bronson tells it,

He started up with an expression of countenance which it is impossible to describe. The rain fell in torrents, and it was the darkest and most dismal night I have ever known. On taking leave, he expressed a deep sense of the obligation he was under for the delicate and courteous deportment he had experienced from all the officers. . . . I said whatever might be in his future destiny, he would never meet them hereafter as enemies.

Like Lieutenant King, the surgeon's mate found himself sympathizing with the prisoner. Even Major Tallmadge felt a burgeoning resentment toward André's captors.

Washington had directed that strict security measures be imposed.

I would not wish André to be treated with insult [he said], but he does not seem to stand upon the footing of a common prisoner of war, and therefore he is not entitled to the usual indulgence they receive and so is to be most closely and narrowly watched.

At North Salem, Tallmadge heard that Cowboys were in the vicinity. He changed his route, passing within a short distance of where Lieutenant Allen had received Jameson's countermand.

The column reined in at headquarters just as day was breaking, with no letup in the night's downpour. Washington and Smith were already there, but André was kept apart from Smith and did not lay eyes on Washington. Throughout the week that followed, the commander-in-chief would take pains never to see the accused spy lest personal associations influence his handling of the case.

Washington notified Congress that he had arrived the day before at noontime. Finding Arnold absent, he had crossed to West Point but was told that the commandant had not been at the fort that morning. When he returned to headquarters the packet from Jameson had arrived, containing the treasonous papers and the letter from John André admitting his identity. In his report to Congress, Washington says that this was his first intimation of Arnold's treason.

> I was led to conclude immediately that he had heard of Major André's captivity, and he would, if possible, escape to the enemy, and accordingly took such measures as appeared to me most probable to apprehend him. But he had embarked in a barge and proceeded down the river, under a flag, to the *Vulture* ship of war, which lay some miles below Stony and Verplanck's Points.

Washington had sent Hamilton and Major James McHenry in pursuit, but to no avail. By then Arnold was aboard the *Vulture*, under the protection of Sutherland's artillery. Washington informed Congress that he was taking steps to forestall "the important consequences" that might ensue, implying that an attack on West Point could be forthcoming. "I do not know the party that took Major André," he added, "but it is said that it consisted of only a few militia, who acted in such a manner upon the occasion as does them the highest honor and proves them to be men of great virtue."

Hamilton and McHenry had returned with three letters sent ashore under a flag of truce. One, from Beverley Robinson, was addressed to Washington. It maintained that André had had the protection of a flag and was entitled to immediate release:

> Major André cannot be detained by you without the greatest violation of flags, and contrary to the custom and usage of all nations; and as I imagine you will see this matter in the same point of view that I do, I must desire you will order him to be set at liberty and allowed to return immediately. Every step Major André took was by the advice and direction of General Arnold, even that of taking a feigned name, and of course not liable to censure for it.

This would be Clinton's own line of reasoning.

The remaining two letters were from Arnold — one for Peggy,

which Washington transmitted to her without opening it, the other for Washington himself.

> The heart which is conscious of its own rectitude cannot attempt to palliate a step which the world may censure as wrong [Arnold wrote]. I have ever acted from a principle of love to my country since the commencement of the present unhappy contest between Great Britain and the Colonies; the same principle of love to my country actuates my present conduct, however it may appear inconsistent to the world, who very seldom judge right of any man's actions. [He requested protection for Mrs. Arnold] from every insult and injury that a mistaken vengeance of my country may expose her to. [She was] incapable of doing wrong [he said, and was] as good and innocent as an angel.

He asked that she be allowed to return to her family in Philadelphia, or to join him in New York. In a postscript he exonerated his two aides and Joshua Hett Smith, but he made no mention of John André.

Late that day the prisoners were taken separately to West Point, André to Fort Putnam, Smith to the dingy provost guardroom, where he says he was "left to choose the softest board I could find for a bed."* Major Tallmadge stayed at the Mandeville house, a private residence not far from headquarters. He wrote his friend Barnabas Deane that, although André might be the "greatest rogue that we have ever taken," he had found him "a very genteel, sensible man" nevertheless. "I wish he had been about a more honourable employment," he added.

The prisoners remained overnight at West Point, "narrowly watched," in line with Washington's directive. Smith, at the window of the provost guardroom, was taunted and reviled

---

*One tradition holds that André was kept at the Mandeville house on the east side of the Hudson, and not at West Point. Tallmadge was definitely there, and he declares that André was continually at his side.

by passers-by, whereas André was merely stared at. One observer says that André seemed to be "contemplating his fate" as he paced glumly back and forth. Next morning the two were taken in separate barges to Stony Point. André, with Tallmadge beside him, sat in the stern of the foremost barge. He talked candidly with Tallmadge and pointed out the place where the British would have launched their attack. He even pictured himself as leading a strike force, although he was not a field officer in charge of a command. "He seemed as if he were entering the fort, sword in hand," Tallmadge says. "Military glory was all he sought, and the thanks of his General, and the approbation of his King."

At Stony Point the entourage was joined by yet more dragoons, who made a formidable escort. The prisoners were assigned mounts, Smith near the front of the column, André farther back with Tallmadge by his side. At Tallmadge's order, the column set forth, clattering over country roads toward Tappan, headquarters of the Continental Army. André asked his companion what he might expect from an American military tribunal. Tallmadge brought up the name of Nathan Hale, who had been captured by the British four years previously. He asked André if he remembered "the sequel of the story." "He was hanged as a spy," André said, "but surely you don't consider his case and mine alike?" They were "precisely similar," Tallmadge replied, "and similar will be your fate."

Here and there spectators had gathered, in farmyards and on village greens. They could easily distinguish the accused spy in his beaver hat and claret-colored coat. When the party halted for a midday meal, André complained about the conspicuousness of his attire. Tallmadge offered him the loan of his dragoon cloak. André hesitated at first but, after a little persuasion, agreed to put it on. He kept it wrapped around him for the rest of the journey, hiding the shameful apparel foisted on him at Smith's house.

The column reached Tappan at sundown, drawing up in front of the old Dutch church. Onlookers jammed the town green and could be seen at every window and doorway in the tidy row of houses bordering the main street. Taunts and threats greeted the prisoners. "We were paraded before the church," Smith says. "Many of my *quondam* friends flocked around us, and from them I received the bitterest invectives." Smith was taken to a spare room in the church, cramped and meanly furnished, but André was given sleeping quarters and a separate living room in the nearby Casparus Mabie Tavern, a stoutly built stone edifice. "Every attention was paid him suitable to his rank and character," Smith allows. His own quarters were lowly indeed by comparison. But those who had come to gawp at the prisoners showed no such respect. That night, rude homemade coffins were paraded through town to remind both Smith and André of what lay in store.

During his brief service as Clinton's intelligence chief, John André had shown considerable promise. One of his assets was a fluency in French and German as well as English, along with a smattering of Dutch. These were, of course, the four principal languages of the North American continent. As a prisoner of war, he had learned much about American attitudes and modes of thinking, and, as a line officer, he had observed American troops in action. In a little more than a year (1779–80), he added both method and imagination to British espionage operations. Why, then, did he make so many egregious blunders when he himself set forth on a mission?

His primary mistake was to underestimate the complexities that faced him. The Revolutionary War was, in one sense, a civil war in which the two sides shared a common language and, except for German and French troops, came from the same genetic stock. Tories and patriots looked alike and behaved alike, differing only in their inner convictions. Thus was created a situation in which espionage was relatively easy to conduct and counterespionage was correspondingly difficult. With these favorable odds, most of the seasoned spies on both sides, such as Cortlandt Skinner, William Rankin, James Moody, and Ann Bates for the British, and David Gray, Elijah Hunter, and the "Culpers" for the Americans, escaped the hangman and survived the war.

André's most obvious mistake was his failure to obey the three directives laid down by General Clinton: always to wear his regimentals, to avoid crossing enemy lines, and to carry no papers that might incriminate him. But these were tactical mistakes that derived from a conceptual misunderstanding of secret service operations and of his role as intelligence chief.

In this late-eighteenth-century war, most of the classic instruments of intelligence were in use. There were agents-in-place, moles, double agents, codebreakers, spy networks, and codes and ciphers. Methods improved as the war lengthened. André's successor, Major Oliver De Lancey, would build on what André set in place, and the Americans would steadily update their own methods. Late in the war, for example, they would be able to decode any message they could intercept between Clinton and Cornwallis. But even as methods of gaining information became more sophisticated, the administration of the secret services remained elementary and inefficient. George Washington acted as his own intelligence chief, directing the secret service during spare moments. Benjamin Tallmadge, his deputy, had to combine intelligence work with low-level reconnaissance on the Neutral Ground. John André's time was divided between supervising intelligence and fulfilling his manifold duties as adjutant general.

In this lax atmosphere, it is not surprising that André failed to master certain basic rules. As intelligence chief, he should not have gone in person to meet with Arnold. When Arnold first intimated to the British that he might defect, André, sensing the significance of what might happen, assigned himself as case officer. In the course of a year, he developed with

Arnold the grand scheme that they hoped would culminate in the surrender of West Point. But when it came time to hold a face-to-face meeting, he did not choose the ground himself or provide alternative means for a safe return. Once on enemy terrain, he lost control to Arnold, who both saddled him with the incriminating papers and agreed that André might return by land.

In hindsight, the mistakes are glaring. André should have made sure of greater military support than the *Vulture* and her easily intimidated captain could provide. He should have insisted on a less precarious way of getting back to the British sloop. Failing this, he should have let nothing divest him of his uniform, and he should have memorized the information contained in Arnold's papers, refusing to conceal them on his person. But his most grievous blunder came at the very end, for he should never have declared himself a British officer when stopped by the three irregulars at Tarrytown. There was at least a fifty-fifty chance that the three might have been Skinners, and André should have instantly produced his pass. If the three were Cowboys, they would have taken him to the British lines and turned him in for a reward. If Skinners, or the irregulars they claimed to be, they would have hesitated to hold anyone who had been vouched for by General Arnold. André's pass lost much of its authority as soon as he declared his connection with the British Army.

That André had had little to eat since leaving the *Vulture*, had slept fitfully, and was under an inhuman strain surely impaired his judgment. But that he made so many wrong moves derived largely from his taking on a mission that should have been entrusted to a seasoned operative. He had foreseen the biggest intelligence coup of the war, involving the defection of a leading rebel and the taking of West Point. He was eager to bring it off in person, but this was not the function of a headquarters officer. His was the daring of an amateur, and it cost him the mission.

*   *   *

Washington made his headquarters at the DeWint house, a short distance from Tappan's main street. He had arrived that same day and had had his first communication from Clinton, who maintained that André had come at Arnold's bidding and had had the protection of a flag. The letter was terse, even insolent:

> I have the honor to inform you, sir, that I permitted Major André to go to Major General Arnold at the particular request of that general officer. You will perceive, sir, by the enclosed paper that a flag of truce was sent to receive Major André, and passports granted for his return. I therefore can have no doubt but your Excellency will immediately direct that this officer has permission to return to my orders at New York.

The "enclosed paper" was a letter Clinton had received from Arnold informing him of André's capture. Arnold put great stress on the flag of truce:

> I have the honor to inform you, sir, that I apprehend a few hours must return Major André to your Excellency's order, as that officer is assuredly under the protection of a flag of truce sent by me to him for the purpose of a conversation which I requested to hold with him relating to myself, and which I wished to communicate through that officer to your Excellency. Thinking it much properer he should return by land, I directed him to make use of the feigned name of John Anderson, under which he had by my directions come on shore, and gave him passports to pass my lines to the White Plains on his way to New York. This officer cannot fail of being immediately sent to New York, as he was invited to a conversation with me, for which I sent him a flag of truce, and finally gave him passports for his safe return to your Excellency.

Washington was not swayed by either letter. Flag or no flag, André had concealed treasonous papers in his boots and had disguised himself as a civilian.

Under the Articles of War, and by virtue of his commission from Congress, Washington could have dispensed summary justice, as General Howe had done in dealing with Nathan Hale. Instead, he named fourteen colleagues to a court of inquiry, known as the Board of General Officers. These would cross-examine the accused, weigh the evidence, and submit an opinion as to his innocence or guilt. Although under no legal obligation to do so, Washington chose to be guided by their findings. He appointed General Nathanael Greene president of the board. Its members included five major generals and eight brigadiers: Major Generals Lafayette, von Steuben, Robert Howe, Arthur St. Clair, and William Alexander (Lord Stirling); Brigadiers James Clinton, John Glover, Edward Hand, Jedediah Huntington, Henry Knox, Samuel Holden Parsons, John Paterson, and John Stark. John Laurance, the judge advocate, was charged with preparing the case and presenting evidence to the board. The inclusion of Knox must have awakened memories in André, reminding him of their chance introduction, four years previously, in the crowded inn near Fort Ticonderoga. He may have recollected some of their conversation about favorite authors, about their parallel careers, and how they had both forsaken trade for the military.

The board convened in the old Dutch church on Friday, the 29th, occupying seats where generations of pious folk had been preached to by their austere pastors. Only yards away Joshua Hett Smith waited fearfully for his own trial before a general court-martial. Washington's instructions to the board made it clear that he was seeking an opinion, not a verdict:

Major André, Adjutant General to the British Army, will be brought before you for your examination. . . . After a careful examination, you will be pleased, as speedily as possible, to report a precise state of the case, together with your opinion of the light in which he ought to be considered, and the punishment that ought to be inflicted.

André was brought before the board under a heavy guard. He was respectful, even courtly, and he was altogether at ease. The advocate general advised him to feel under no pressure in answering questions and requesting that they be spelled out if they seemed unclear. Had he crossed the American lines by night under an assumed name? Did he carry a pass made out to "John Anderson"? Did he have secret papers concealed on his person? Did he adopt a disguise for his journey through Westchester? Laurance produced the telltale documents — the papers, in Arnold's handwriting, that had been found in André's boots, the pass issued by Arnold to one "John Anderson," André's letter to Washington admitting his identity, the statement he had enclosed with it, and his letter to Colonel Sheldon arranging for a parley with "Gustavus" at Dobbs Ferry.

André did not deny the charges. He admitted that he had come ashore under an assumed name, that he had conferred with Arnold "somewhere under Haverstraw Mountain," that he had been unable to return to the *Vulture* that night, much to his dismay, and had been "concealed on shore in a place of safety." To the astonishment of the board, he made no claim to having had the protection of a flag. Under cross-examination he said "it was impossible for him to suppose he came on shore under a sanction, and added that if he came on shore under that sanction he certainly might have returned under it."

When questioned further, André said he had first realized that he had crossed enemy lines when he and Arnold were challenged by the sentry near Haverstraw. His letter to Colonel Sheldon indicated that he had not intended to do so, but he agreed that this had been written several days previously by order of General Clinton and might no longer be relevant. He admitted that he had changed into civilian attire, although against his wishes. Greene asked him if he had come ashore as a private citizen or as a British officer. "I wore my uniform,"

André replied, "and undoubtedly esteemed myself to be what indeed I was, a British officer."

At the end of the interrogation André thanked the board for the respect shown him. He is said to have declared, "I flatter myself that I have never been illiberal, but if there were any remains of prejudice in my mind, my present experience must obliterate them." His dignity and composure impressed all fourteen officers, but they were nonplused by his candor in admitting to the various charges. What they failed to understand was that André did not think of himself as a spy at all, but as Clinton's deputy. He was a spy by accident. Although he had crossed enemy lines, it had been against his wishes. Although he had returned by land in disguise, it had been to his "great mortification" and he had "objected much against it." The papers hidden in his boots had been pressed on him by Arnold. André saw himself as a British officer who had taken great risks in the line of duty. But the board did not concur. All fourteen members looked on him as a spy.

Not once during his testimony had André mentioned the name of Joshua Hett Smith. He had requested that he "not be interrogated concerning anything which did not immediately relate to himself and that he be excused from accusing any other." Smith would not forget this. He says of André that "with the most guarded caution and the most scrupulous nicety and circumspection, he concealed whatever might criminate others." Nor was this lost on the board. Alexander Hamilton says that "the members of it were not more impressed with the candor and firmness, mixed with a becoming sensibility, which he displayed, than he was penetrated with their liberality and politeness."

After André had left, the board was shown the letters — from Arnold, Sir Henry Clinton, and Beverley Robinson. All stressed the flag of truce. The board must decide between the word of these three and André's own admission that there had been no flag. It chose to believe André. "He put us to no proof," Baron von Steuben says, "but in open, manly manner confessed everything but a premeditated design to deceive."

No witnesses were called upon, and the investigation was concluded that same day. The fourteen officers notified Washington that in their opinion André had come ashore for his interview with Arnold "in a private and secret manner," had "changed his dress within our lines," and "under a feigned name and in a disguised habit" passed the guards at King's Ferry. In his effort to reach New York he had concealed treasonous papers on his person. Their opinion was unanimous:

> The Board, having maturely considered these facts, do also report to his Excellency General Washington that Major André, Adjutant General to the British Army, ought to be considered as a spy from the enemy; and that, agreeable to the law and usage of nations, it is their opinion he ought to suffer death.

Washington's verdict was announced a day later: on the following afternoon, Sunday, October 1, at precisely five o'clock, John André must die.

In a letter to Clinton notifying him of the verdict, Washington pointed out that, although André had been taken prisoner "under such circumstances as would have justified the most summary proceedings against him," his case had been referred to a Board of General Officers for an opinion. These had reached the unanimous decision that John André was indeed a spy and should be punished accordingly.

> From these proceedings [Washington wrote], it is evident Major André was employed in the execution of measures very foreign to the objects of flags of truce, and such as they were never meant to authorize or countenance in the most distant degree, and this gentleman confessed with the greatest candor in the course of his examination "that it was impossible for him to suppose he came on shore under the sanction of a flag."

Washington maintained that even had there been a flag, by no stretch of the law could André's actions entitle him to protection. Enclosed with the letter was a message from André himself and a communication, now missing, from Peggy Arnold to her husband. The packet was delivered to the British outpost at Paulus Hook by Captain Aaron Ogden of the light infantry.

Ogden may have carried a fourth letter, thought to have been written by Hamilton, which was slipped clandestinely to Clinton:

> It has so happened in the course of events that Major André, adjutant general to your army, has fallen into our hands. He was captured in such a way as will, according to the laws of war, justly affect his life. Though an enemy, his virtues and his accomplishments are admired. Perhaps he might be released for General Arnold, delivered up without restriction or condition, which is the prevailing wish. Major André's character and situation seem to demand this of your justice and friendship. Arnold appears to have been the guilty author of the mischief and ought more properly to be the victim, as there is great reason to believe he meditated a double treachery and had arranged the interview in such a manner that if discovered in the first instance, he might have it in his power to sacrifice Major André to his own safety. [A postscript reminded Clinton that] no time was to be lost.

Surely Clinton was tempted by the offer, but policy forbade it. No future Arnold would follow the traitor's lead if such an exchange were countenanced. Instead, Sir Henry called together some of his chief advisors. General James C. Robertson, governor of the city, was among them, and Lieutenant Governor Andrew Elliot and Chief Justice William Smith, Joshua Hett Smith's brother. All agreed that a conference, with Washington or his deputy, was imperative. Clinton chose Robertson, Elliot, and Smith to represent him. In requesting the parley, he wrote Washington that his three deputies would

present "a true state of facts." Surely the Board of General
Officers could not have been

> rightly informed of all the circumstances on which a judgment
> ought to be formed [Clinton wrote]. I think it of the highest
> moment to humanity that your Excellency should be perfectly
> apprized of the state of this matter before you proceed to put
> that judgment in execution.

His deputies would be able to confer the next day, at Sneden's
Landing opposite Dobbs Ferry, with either Washington himself or his representative. They would set forth aboard the
schooner *Greyhound* "as early as wind and tide will permit."

Although Washington put no faith in the parley, he named
General Greene as his deputy and rescheduled the execution
for Monday, October 2, at twelve noon. André's hopes may
have risen a little. He had received a message from Clinton
that offered some encouragement: "God knows how much I
feel for you in your present situation, but I dare hope you will
soon be returned from it — believe me, dear André."

According to Judge Thomas Jones, Clinton's deputies were
an ill-chosen threesome. He describes Smith as prone to "chi-
canery" and "cunning," Elliot as "a good-natured, inoffensive
person with a narrow capacity," Robertson as "a superannu-
ated, worn-out, timid, irresolute, forgetful old gentleman."
Indeed, two of them might better have stayed home. When
Greene arrived for the parley he consented to see only Robertson, a fellow soldier. Elliot and Smith could cool their heels.

What followed, if we are to take Justice Smith's word for
it, was a bootless impasse. Robertson claimed that André had
had the protection of a flag. Greene cited André's own testimony that there had been no flag. "Whether a flag was flying
or not was of no account," Robertson replied. André had
"landed and acted" under Arnold's direction. Greene disa-
greed. André, he countered, was no less involved than Arnold.
Robertson urged that Knyphausen and Rochambeau be con-

sulted. Both were "distinguished gentlemen" with "knowledge of war and nations," and, since they were neither British nor American, could be expected to take a more detached view of André's case. But Greene showed no interest. Washington would release André on one condition, he said — the surrender of Benedict Arnold. Robertson answered this "with a look," according to Justice Smith, and the parley ended.

Greene departed to consult Washington in the matter, while Clinton's deputies waited aboard the *Greyhound*. The next day Greene sent word that there had been "no alteration" in the commander-in-chief's "opinion and determination." Before returning to New York, Robertson hurried off a personal appeal to Washington, reiterating that André had had the protection of a flag and had taken "no step while on shore but by the direction of General Arnold," including "the change of clothes and name." General Clinton, he reminded the American commander, "had never put any person to death for a breach of the rules of war, tho' he had had, and has now, many in his power." If André were released, Robertson promised to "have any person you would please to name set at liberty."

Robertson enclosed a further communication from Arnold, who was now safely in New York. The traitor warned his erstwhile commander-in-chief that if André's sentence were carried out, he would feel "bound by every tie of duty and honor to retaliate on such unhappy persons in your army as may fall within my power, that the respect due to flags and the law of nations may be better understood and observed." He made specific reference to the forty South Carolinians in custody for parole violation, warning that "a scene of blood at which humanity will revolt" must surely follow unless André were released. Washington, he said, would be "justly answerable" for this "torrent of blood."

While negotiations faltered, Simcoe hatched a plan to rescue André. He believed that Congress must review the evidence and that, if André were needed to give testimony, the Queen's Rangers might waylay his guard between Tappan and Philadelphia. He wrote a mutual friend, Colonel William Crosbie, about it: "I have forty cavalry, as gallant men as ever were in the field, and horses capable of marching seventy miles without halting." Never had "attachment to my General, private friendship and public duty" been more interlocked. He was prepared to take whatever risk was required to deliver André to his own lines. What Simcoe did not know was that Washington, in the case of a spy, was under no obligation to consult Congress.

If all else failed, Simcoe still had hopes for an exchange with Arnold. He sounded out an American acquaintance, Major "Light-Horse Harry" Lee, who was in touch with the situation. Lee's reply gave grounds for hope — until Simcoe reached the postscript Lee had subsequently added. There was indeed "a possibility of Major André's being restored to his country and the customs of war being fully satisfied," Lee had written. But before dispatching the letter he heard differently. "I find that Sir Henry Clinton's offers have not come up to what was expected," he said in his postscript.*

André might have blamed others for his situation, especially Arnold. The traitor had allowed him to cross enemy lines, had caused him to spend a perilous day at Smith's house, had urged that he carry incriminating papers through the lines. Nor was Smith without blame. By choosing to cross through Westchester, he had compelled André to change into civilian clothes. But André made no mention of either. It was he, after all, who had yielded to their urging, who had been too accommodating, much too trusting. That the mission had been

---

*In 1791 John Graves Simcoe would become the first lieutenant governor of Upper Canada. A town, a county, and a lake, all in Ontario, have been named for him.

badly planned and recklessly carried out had been his own doing as well as theirs. His silence in the matter, bespeaking an innate gallantry, made its impact on American officers who got to know him at the Mabie Tavern, especially Tallmadge and Hamilton. Both attest to his politeness, his affability, his charm of manner, which had captivated Tory hostesses and which he now maintained in his relations with guards and others. "Had he been tried by a court of ladies," Tallmadge said, "he is so genteel, handsome and polite a young gentleman that I am confident they would have acquitted him." In a letter to his fiancée, Hamilton expressed admiration for André, and envy for his unfailing charm: "I wished myself possessed of André's accomplishments for your sake, for I would wish to charm you in every sense."*

It was through Hamilton's good offices that André gained permission to write General Clinton.

> There is only one thing that disturbs my tranquillity [he told Hamilton]. Sir Henry Clinton has been too good to me — he has been lavish of his kindness. I am bound to him by too many obligations and love him too well to bear the thought that he should reproach himself, or that others should reproach him, on the supposition of my having conceived myself obliged by his instructions to run the risk I did. I would not for the world leave a sting in his mind that should embitter his future days.

At this, André broke down and wept. Hamilton transmitted the request to Washington, who readily allowed it.

André's letter urged Sir Henry to feel no blame for the mission's failure. His wish was

> to remove from your breast any suspicion that I could imagine that I was bound by your Excellency's orders to expose myself

---

*Hamilton was engaged to Elizabeth Schuyler, daughter of Philip Schuyler.

to what has happened. The events of coming within an enemy post and of changing my dress, which led me to my present situation, were contrary to my own intentions, as they were to your orders; and the circuitous route which I took to return was imposed (perhaps unavoidably) without alternative upon me.

He went on to express his devotion and gratitude to the chief who had so advanced his military career:

I am perfectly tranquil in mind and prepared for any fate to which an honest zeal for my King's service may have devoted me. In addressing myself to your Excellency on this occasion, the force of my obligations to you and of the attachment and gratitude I bear you, recurs to me. With all the warmth of my heart I give you thanks for your Excellency's profuse kindness to me, and I send you the most earnest wishes for your welfare which a faithful, affectionate and respectful attendant can frame.

He was concerned for his mother and sisters, hard hit by their Grenada losses, and asked that they receive the money due on his commission. "I am persuaded of your Excellency's goodness," he said in closing. "I receive the greatest attention from his Excellency General Washington and from every person under whose charge I happen to be placed."

André was resigned to suffering a spy's fate, but he hoped to die in a manner that would do honor to British arms. He told Hamilton that "since it was his lot to die, there was still a choice in the mode that would make a material difference to his feelings." With Hamilton's approval, perhaps at his urging, he wrote Washington requesting that he be shot as a soldier, not hanged as a spy. His letter was both short and eloquent:

Buoy'd above the terror of death by the consciousness of a life devoted to honourable pursuits and stained with no action that can give remorse, I trust that the request I make of your

Excellency at this serious period, and which is to soften my last moments, will not be rejected. Sympathy towards a soldier will surely induce your Excellency, and a military tribunal, to adapt the mode of my death to the feelings of a man of honour. Let me hope, Sir, that if aught in my character impresses you with esteem towards me, if aught in my misfortune marks me as the victim of policy and not of resentment, I shall experience the operation of these feelings in your breast by being informed that I am not to die on a gibbet.

Out of respect for André's feelings, Washington did not answer the letter. But, as Hamilton sensed, this was in itself a form of answer. Policy ordained the gibbet for convicted spies. The commander-in-chief would leave no doubt in anyone's mind of John André's status.* But Hamilton could not agree. In a letter to his fiancée, he deplored what he considered a heartless rigidity:

I urged a compliance with André's request to be shot, and I do not think it would have had an ill effect. But some people are only sensitive to motives of policy, and sometimes from a narrow disposition mistake it. When André's tale comes to be told, and present resentment is over, the refusing him the privilege of choosing [the] manner of death will be branded with too much obduracy.

André himself did not interpret Washington's silence as an outright refusal. He continued to hope for a soldier's death, commensurate with the sensibilities and good name of a British officer.

There was still talk of an exchange for Arnold. Hamilton was asked to enlist André's help in urging it on General Clinton. But Hamilton would have no part of this.

---

*In notifying Congress of his decision, Washington said that, although André had asked to be shot, "the practice and usage of war, circumstanced as he was, were against the indulgence."

As a man of honor, he could not but reject it [he says of André],
and I would not for the world have proposed to him a thing
which must have placed him in the unamiable light of sup-
posing him capable of such meanness, or of not feeling myself
the impropriety of the measure.

A personal matter weighed on André, involving an association of long standing. He had willed the more valuable of
his two watches to Walter Ewer, an old friend. Both watches
had been taken from him. Could the one bequeathed to Ewer,
the silver timepiece engraved with André's name, possibly
be recovered? A search was initiated by Colonel Robert H.
Harrison, Washington's secretary. This was the same Colonel
Harrison who had met with André and Colonel West Hyde
to negotiate a prisoner exchange and whom both British officers had found so compatible. André felt sure that Harrison
would make every effort to recover the missing watch.

Harrison found the inferior gold watch in the possession of
the three captors, who asked thirty guineas for its return. The
money was advanced on condition that André arrange to have
it refunded by British authorities. "One instance of littleness
must not be forgot," fumed Andrew Elliot, New York's lieutenant governor. "Major André wished to leave the watch to
a friend. It was refused him till an officer of the name of
Harrison paid thirty guineas for it." Harrison failed to recover
the engraved silver timepiece intended for Walter Ewer.*

Surely André wrote his family during his last hours, but no
farewell letter survives. However, a note to Lieutenant Colonel William Crosbie, like Simcoe a cherished friend, still exists.

The manner in which I am to die at first gave me some uneasiness [André wrote him], but I instantly recollected that it is
the crime alone that makes any mode of punishment igno-

---

*It turned up in New York in 1923.

minious — and I could not think an attempt to put an end to a civil war, and to stop the effusion of human blood, a crime.

To pass the hours, André turned out three pen-and-ink drawings relating to his capture. One shows a plump, matronly woman, perhaps the innkeeper's wife, seated primly in a straight-back chair. André sketched it on the back of a message from Hamilton. Another depicts Smith's longboat pressing shoreward from the *Vulture*, André and Smith hunched in the stern, the Cahoon brothers pulling valiantly at the oars — all of them dwarfed by the towering sweep of the escarpment. A third is a self-portrait done on a scrap of paper. It shows the artist in his place of confinement, seated at a table, neatly attired, his expression contemplative and drained of hope.*

André's servant, Peter Laune, had now arrived from New York with clean linen and a set of regimentals. A surgeon was on hand — by coincidence Dr. Nathaniel Gardiner, son of the Abraham Gardiner with whom André had exchanged wine glasses at East Hampton. But no chaplain was present. Unlike Nathan Hale, who had called for a Bible and the ministrations of a chaplain, André requested neither. He had long kept dogma and ritual at arm's length. His death would mark no exception. He would meet it stoically — "like a Roman," as Thomas Paine would describe it.

André slept little, if at all, on his last night. At one point his servant brought him tea. "Can I do anything else?" Peter Laune inquired. André seemed on the verge of tears. "No, Peter," he replied, waving him away. "You have done well. You have done well." By morning he had regained his composure. He was shaved, given fresh linen, and, as a mark of

---

*The sketch of the innkeeper's wife is the property of J. Robert Maguire, an engraving of the longboat is in the New York Public Library, the self-portrait is in the Yale University Art Gallery. There may have been a fourth sketch, now missing, showing a view of West Point from the Hudson.

respect, served breakfast from Washington's table. He is said to have donned his regimentals "with as much composure as though he were going to a ball," the scarlet coat, with popinjay green facings, proclaiming him an officer of the 54th Regiment. During the morning Colonel Alexander Scammell, Washington's adjutant, came to notify him that the execution would take place at twelve noon. Laune broke into sobs. "Leave me until you can show yourself more manly!" André ordered. There must be no show of weakness during these last hours. Just before twelve o'clock he thanked his guards for their services — especially the two who had been continually at his side, Captain John Hughes and Ensign Samuel Bowman — and calmly announced, "I am ready at any moment, gentlemen, to wait upon you."

Tappan swarmed with troops. Some five hundred were stationed outside the Mabie Tavern. Onlookers from far and wide flooded the village — "many hundreds, if not thousands," according to one who was there. At the stroke of twelve André was brought out. The weather was summery, with a slight yellowing in the hardwoods. He smiled faintly as he faced the captain's escort drawn up before the tavern, with a fife and drum corps at one side, and he is said to have "run down the steps as quickly and lively as though no execution were taking place." He linked arms with Hughes and Bowman. Close by was Captain John Van Dyk of Lamb's Artillery. A command was shouted, drums and fifes broke into the "Dead March," and the column swung past the old Dutch church, where Joshua Hett Smith's court-martial had convened that very morning. Turning left, it toiled up a long hill toward the place of execution. André managed a "most agreeable smile," a witness says, and acknowledged whomever he recognized with a courtly bow. "I am much surprised to find your troops under so good a discipline, and the music is excellent," he remarked to those nearest him. But he was pale as death. Washington was nowhere in sight. He had remained at the De Windt house in deference to André, but he may have heard the throb of drums, the wail of fifes.

Near the top of the hill the column turned into an open field. André beheld, for the first time, the stark framework of the gibbet. He recoiled visibly, Captain Van Dyk would remember. "Gentlemen, I am disappointed!" he exclaimed. "I expected my request would have been granted." But he recovered himself in an instant. "I am reconciled to my death but not to the mode," he said as he continued walking.

A great hush descended as André was led to the cleared space surrounding the gibbet. On one side stood a two-horse baggage cart holding a black coffin. Near it was an open grave. The hilltop was packed with onlookers, including rank on rank of Continental troops. "The guard formed three circles around the gallows, with their backs towards it and bayonets fixed," says Private Daniel Roberts, an infantryman. As André passed the Board of General Officers, stationed in a group on horseback, he bowed respectfully to each. "Such fortitude I never was witness of," says Dr. John Hart, a medical inspector familiar with such proceedings. "To see a man go out of time without fear, but all the time smiling, is a matter that I could not conceive of." General John Glover, the officer of the day, waited on horseback near the scaffold, with Colonel Scammell beside him. The three captors stood close by, like honored guests. And Peter Laune was in evidence, weeping shamelessly.*

At André's request, Major Tallmadge stepped forward, and the two shook hands like old friends. "I became so deeply attached to Major André," Tallmadge would declare in his memoirs, "that I can remember no instance where my affections were so fully absorbed in any man." After he had with-

---

*It had been agreed that after André's death Laune would remove the uniform and take it back to New York.

drawn, Colonel Scammell read the death sentence. André listened impassively, although Dr. James Thacher, an army surgeon, noticed that he was "placing his foot on a stone and rolling it over, and choking in his throat as if attempting to swallow." Captain Van Dyk observed "a small flush moving over his left cheek," and André was seen by others to glance upward at the gibbet. Major Tallmadge let his eyes wander over the crowd. "All the spectators seemed to be overwhelmed by the affecting spectacle," he says, "and many were suffused in tears."

When Scammell finished, André was ordered to take his place in the wagon. Hoisting himself onto the tailboard, he stepped to the coffin, stood on top of it and, with his hands on his hips, paced back and forth. He removed his hat and laid it on the coffin, revealing, as one witness recalls, a "long and beautiful head of hair, which, agreeable to the fashion, was wound with a black ribbon and hung down his back." Then he removed his neckcloth and tucked it inside a pocket. With a forefinger, he turned back his shirt collar. "It will be but a momentary pang," he told himself, audibly enough to be overheard by Dr. Thacher.

To hide his identity, the hangman had smeared his face and hands with soot.* He was about to adjust the halter when André snatched it from him, lowered it over his own head, and knotted it under the right ear. Removing a handkerchief from his pocket, he tied it across his eyes. "Major André," he was told, "if you have anything you would wish to say more, you now have the opportunity." André raised the blindfold and looked at Glover and Scammell. "I have nothing more than this," he said, "that I would have you gentlemen bear me witness that I die like a brave man."

---

*He was a Tory named Strickland, who had been promised his freedom in return for hanging André.

Glover ordered André's arms pinioned. Amid what many would remember as a deathly stillness, André brought out a second handkerchief, which the hangman knotted above the elbows. Glover caught the hangman's eye and signaled. André stood waiting, motionless as stone. Then the whip cracked, like a pistol shot, and the wagon lurched from beneath John André's feet.

Afterword

JOHN ANDRÉ would lie in his hilltop grave for more than forty years. In 1821, at the behest of the Duke of York, his bones would be dug up and returned to England, to be buried in Westminster Abbey among kings and poets. A pension would be awarded his mother not long after his death, and brother William would be made a baronet.

General Clinton is said to have been crushed by André's death. It "struck poor Sir Henry to the heart," General Phillips says. Clinton's fortunes would not improve, and he would be made the scapegoat for Yorktown. He would never relinquish his belief that had André made it to the British lines, England need not have lost America.

General Washington agonized over André, whom he considered "more unfortunate than criminal." It is said that when he signed the death sentence his hand shook uncontrollably. Major Tallmadge maintains that Washington could not have let André be shot without casting doubt on the validity of the sentence, "the universal usage of nations having affixed to the crime of a spy, death by the gibbet."

Benedict Arnold would be paid handsomely for his treason and be commissioned a brigadier in the British Army. But he would disappoint his military superiors, drift into exile, and would die heavily in debt. Peggy would settle most of the debts before following him to the grave two years later.

Joshua Hett Smith would conduct his own defense and win acquittal. He would flee to England but would return, in the end, to his native New York.

Benjamin Tallmadge would serve with distinction throughout the war and would become a congressman from his district. He would not forget André. When John Paulding asked for a larger pension in 1817, Tallmadge would oppose the application. But of course he was prejudiced. His high regard for André had not diminished in nearly forty years.

In her *Monody on Major André*, Anna Seward would bemoan her subject's "ill-starred passion" for Honora and his "pangs of inauspicious love." Honora would never lay eyes on the poem. She died in 1780, a few months before John André. But by then the two had lost track of each other and were linked only in Anna's busy imagination.

Acknowledgments
Notes
Bibliography
Index

Acknowledgments

IN TELLING John André's story, I have been hugely indebted to the late Brigadier James R. G. André and to James W. André of Millicent, South Australia, for allowing me access to André's letters to his family. James W. André has also provided me with photographs of family portraits taken by his son, Roger André. I am indebted to him not only for these but for his friendship, encouragement, and steadfast support.

I owe much, very much, to J. Robert Maguire, who has in his possession several drawings by John André, as well as letters relating to him. He has permitted me to use two of the drawings in this book, together with certain letters. In addition, he has given painstaking scrutiny to the book while it was still in manuscript and has made many crucial suggestions. I am indebted also to Emanuel Teitelman, an authority on André, for his knowledgeable and penetrating answers to my questions. Both have been mainstays.

I shall be ever grateful to my editor, Robie Macauley, for his guidance, incisive criticisms, and many apt suggestions in the making of this book.

I wish to thank the manuscript editor, Lois M. Randall, for invaluable assistance, and my meticulous secretary, Phyllis Hinchman. Of the many who have helped me with source material, I owe special thanks to the following: Benjamin Andrews, John D. Babington, Joan H. Baldwin, Mrs. Robert Jenkins Clark, Eliza Cope, John C. Dann, Peter Decker, Josephine Feagley, James T. Flexner, John C. Foley, Sebastian Gaeta, David Hamilton-Russell, John T. Hayes, Richard J. Koke, David Light, John W. W. Loose, Richard Maass, Thomas Mahoney, C. F. William Maurer, Broadus Mitchell, Mrs. Earl A. Mosley, Ruth Neuendorffer, Howard H. Peckham, John H. G. Pell, Mrs. Donald G. Raymer, Edward F. Sayle, Arlene Shy, Paul G. Sifton, Adelaide R. Smith, Martin P. Snyder, the late William B. Willcox, and Galen R. Wilson.

I am indebted to the staffs of the following: American Antiquarian Society, American Jewish Historical Society, Boston Athenaeum, British Museum, William L. Clements Library, Colonial Williamsburg, Connecticut Historical Society, Dietrich Brothers Americana Corporation, East Hampton Historical Society, Frick Art Reference Library, Friends of Raynham Hall, Historical Society of Pennsylvania, Historical Society of the Tarrytowns, Houghton Library, Huntington Library, Lancaster County Historical Society, Library of Congress, Litchfield Historical Society, Long Island Historical Society, New-York Historical Society, New York Public Library, Public Archives of Canada, Public Records Office, Rosenbach Museum and Library, Joseph Rubinfine Company, Somerset House, Tappan Historical Society, Universitätsbibliothek Göttingen, University of Nottingham, and Yale University Art Gallery.

I must single out for special thanks the staff of the William L. Clements Library, particularly John C. Dann and Arlene Shy, whose many kindnesses made Sir Henry Clinton's vast correspondence a pleasure to wade through, even in the heat of summer.

R.M.H.

Notes

Item Title

AP — André Papers

Repository Titles

CHS — Connecticut Historical Society
CL — Clements Library
HL — Houghton Library
LC — Library of Congress
LHS — Litchfield Historical Society
PRO — Public Records Office

COUNTERMAND

page

2   *"Dirty traffic"*   Tallmadge to George Clinton,
                         September 23, 1780, HL.

3   *Anderson letter*   Jared Sparks, ed., *Writings of
                         Washington*, VII, pp. 522–23.

page

33 *Percy comment* — "Letters of Earl Percy," *Bulletin of Boston Public Library,* January 1892, p. 318.

33–34 *New York situation* — Thomas Jones, *History of New York,* p. 37.

35–36 *André at Quebec* — John André to Louisa André, December 1, 1774; John André to Mary André, March 5, 1775, AP.

CHAPTER III

37–38 *Reactions to capture of Fort Ticonderoga* — *Journal of the Continental Congress,* May 18, 1775; Peter Force, *American Archives,* 4, II, pp. 773, 776–77.

39–40 *Reactions to Quebec Bill* — Charles H. Metzger, *The Quebec Act,* pp. 100–110; Harold C. Syrett and Jacob E. Cook, eds., *Papers of Alexander Hamilton,* 1, pp. 68, 175; E. C. Burnett, ed., *Letters of Members of the Continental Congress,* August 29, 1775–July 4, 1776, p. 113.

40 *Address to French Canadians* — *Journal of the Continental Congress,* October 26, 1774, and May 29, 1775.

41 *Schuyler appeal* — Public Archives of Canada, Q, XI, p. 258.

42 *André letter* — *Parke-Bernet Catalogue,* December 6, 1938, p. 3.

43 *Fassett statement* — H. P. Ward, *Follett-Dewey-Fassett-Safford Ancestry,* p. 216.

43 *André's statement* — André's journal of the siege of St. John's, September 17, 1775. This and subsequent quotations from the journal are from *Report of Public Archives for 1914–15,* Ottawa, 1916, App. B, pp. 18–25.

page

43	*André on climate*	André journal, September 17, 1775.
44	. . . *on siege*	Ibid., September 19–21, 1775.
45	. . . *on folly of war*	Ibid., September 18, 1775.
45–46	. . . *on bombardment*	Ibid., September 22–29, October 6, 12, 14–16, 1775.
46–47	. . . *on Lt. Hunter*	Ibid., September 30, 1775; *Report of Public Archives for 1914–15,* Hunter to Preston, October 17, 1775, p. 12.
47	. . . *on cattle and pigs*	André journal, October 8, 23, 30, 1775.
47	. . . *on lack of ammunition*	Ibid., October 23, November 1, 1775.
48	*Montgomery warning*	*Report of Public Archives for 1915–16,* Montgomery to Preston, November 1, 1775, pp. 12–13.
48	*André on accepting terms*	André journal, November 2, 1775.
49	*Carleton statement*	Public Archives of Canada, Q, XI, p. 274.
50	*American chaplain's statement*	Benjamin Trumbull, "A Concise Journal or Minutes of the Principal Movements Towards St. John's," *Connecticut Historical Society Collections,* VIII, p. 162.
50	*Plundering by Americans*	Anna Seward, *Monody on Major André.*
50	*André on heroism of garrison*	André journal, November 3, 1775; John André to Marie Louise André, December 17, 1776, AP.

A DIFFERENT DRUMBEAT

52	*Tallmadge to Hale*	Charles S. Hall, *Benjamin Tallmadge,* Talmadge to Hale, May 9, 1775, p. 12; Morton Pennypacker, *General Washing-*

page
52   *ton's Spies on Long Island and in New York,* Tallmadge to Hale, July 4, 1775, p. 19.

CHAPTER IV

55   *Schuyler on reconciliation* — Peter Force, ed., *American Archives,* 4, III, pp. 1603–4.

55–56   *Charges against Cuyler* — Ibid., VI, pp. 1772–73.

57   *André parole* — *Pennsylvania Magazine of History and Biography,* I, no. 1, p. 54.

57   *Enlisted men* — Force, IV, pp. 371, 561, 619, 801–2; Ibid., 5, I, pp. 103–4.

58   *Eberhart Michael statement* — *Lancaster County Historical Society Papers,* XVIII, pp. 134–35.

58   *Landlord's demands* — Force, IV, pp. 848–50.

59   *Reasons for transfer* — Ibid., pp. 1213–14.

59   *Officers' transfer* — *Pennsylvania Archives,* Series 2, XIII, pp. 513–14.

60   *André on Carlisle* — John André to Marie Louise André, December 17, 1776, AP.

61   *Riflemen* — Justin H. Smith, *Our Struggle for the Fourteenth Colony,* I, p. 511.

61   *Smith's kindness* — John André to Marie Louise André, December 17, 1776, AP.

61   *André to Eberhart Michael* — *Lancaster County Hist. Soc. Rpts.,* XVIII, p. 133.

62   *André to Caleb Cope* — *Notes and Queries,* X, Series 1, pp. 77–78.

65–66   *Thomas Cope's statement* — Eliza Cope Harrison, *Diary of Thomas P. Cope,* pp. 68, 141–44, 184.

66   *André at Pottstown Inn* — *A Centennial Memorial of Christian and Ann Wolff,* pp. 42–45.

66   *Infiltration suspected* — John C. Fitzpatrick, ed., *Writings of Washington,* VI, pp. 326–27.

67   *André to mother* — John André to Marie Louise André, December 17, 1776, AP.

A DIFFERENT DRUMBEAT

page
68–69   *Death of Hale*   Henry P. Johnston, *Nathan Hale.*

CHAPTER V

70–71   *André to mother*   John André to Marie Louise
                                   André, December 17, 1776,
                                   AP.
71–72   *"Boxed about"*   Troyer Anderson, *Command of the Howe Brothers*, p. 236.
72   *Rebel tactics*   André journal, pp. 30, 33.
72   *"A little mischief"*   John André to Charles Pres-
                                   ton, July 16, 1777, collection
                                   of David S. Light.
73   *André on Charles Grey*   John André to Marie Louise
                                   André, August 28, 1777, AP.
73   *Howe to attack Phila-*   Anderson, p. 218.
        delphia
73–74   *André's will*   *Collection of New-York Historical Society*, 1900, pp. 138–39.
74   *André on brother Wil-*   John André to Marie Louise
        liam   André, December 17, 1776, AP.
74–75   *Chesapeake and Elk*   Friedrich von Muenchhausen,
        River   *At General Howe's Side*, pp. 24,
                                   26; Anderson, p. 279; André
                                   journal, pp. 38–43.
75–76   *Howe's battle plan*   Ibid., pp. 45–46; John André,
                                   manuscript journal of cam-
                                   paign; John André to Marie
                                   Louise André, September 28,
                                   1777, AP.
76   *Washington report*   John D. Fitzpatrick, ed., *Writings of Washington*, IX, p. 220.
77   *Massacre of Wayne's*   André journal, pp. 49–51;
        troops   manuscript journal of cam-
                                   paign; John André to Marie
                                   Louise André, September 28,
                                   1777, AP.

page

78–79	*André to mother*	Ibid.
79–80	*Battle of Germantown*	André journal, pp. 54–57; manuscript journal of campaign; John André to Marie Louise André, September 28, 1777, AP.
80–81	*Mud Island*	John André to Louisa André, November 30, 1777, AP.
81	*Whitemarsh*	André journal, p. 70; Fitzpatrick, X, p. 149.
82	*André for harsh measures*	André, manuscript journal of campaign.
82	*André to Louisa*	John André to Louisa André, November 30, 1777, AP.

A DIFFERENT DRUMBEAT

84	*Washington on Dragoons*	John D. Fitzpatrick, ed., *Writings of Washington*, VI, pp. 386–88.
84	*Tallmadge on Howe's withdrawal*	Tallmadge to Washington, March 16, 1777, LHS.
84	*Duties of Dragoons*	Tallmadge to Jeremiah Wadsworth, December 9, 1777, CHS.
85	*Rescue of female spy*	Benjamin Tallmadge, *Memoir*, pp. 26–27.
86	*Tallmadge on Congress*	Tallmadge to Wadsworth, December 30, 1777, CHS.

CHAPTER VI

87–88	*Becky Franks*	*Pennsylvania Magazine of History and Biography*, XVI (1892), pp. 216–18.
88	*Gambling*	Charles Stedman, *History of the American War*, 1, p. 309.
89	*André on William's prospects*	John André to Louisa André, November 30, 1777, AP.

page

89 *André's appearance*   Extract from a letter by James Green, 62nd Foot, December 23, 1780, National Army Museum, London.

90–91 *Poems for Peggy Chew*   *Century Magazine*, XLVII (March 1894), p. 686.

91 *Grace Galloway*   *Penn. Mag. Hist. & Bio.*, LV (1931), p. 78.

91–92 *Song for Delia*   *American Bibliopolist*, I (1869), p. 339.

92 *Pregnancies*   Elizabeth Evans, *Weathering the Storm*, p. 189.

92–93 *Becky Franks disgusted*   June Avery Snyder and Martin P. Snyder, *The Story of the Naomi Wood Collection and Woodford Mansion*, p. 71.

93 *John Adams on du Simitière*   L. H. Butterfield, *The Book of Abigail and John*, pp. 154–55.

94 *André's lost journal*   Du Simitière Letterbook, du Simitière to George Clinton, November 1780, LC, Peter Force Collection.

94 *Congress closes theater*   A. R. Quinn, *History of American Drama*, p. 32.

95 *Bribing of doorkeepers*   *Pennsylvania Ledger*, May 2, 1778.

95 *Criticism of female parts*   Thomas C. Pollock, *The Philadelphia Theater in the Eighteenth Century*, pp. 34–35.

96 *Washington on fidelity of troops*   John C. Fitzpatrick, ed., *Writings of Washington*, XI, p. 469.

97 *Tory fumes*   *Ohio State University Bulletin*, XXIV (April 1920), no. 23, p. 48.

97 *Grey's testimony*   William Howe, *Narrative*, p. 106.

97 *Winter of dissipation*   Stedman, p. 308.

98 *André lauds Howe*   "Particulars of the Mischianza," *The Gentleman's Magazine*, XLVIII (1778), pp. 353–57.

page

98–101	*Plans for Mischianza*	"Major André's Story of the Mischianza," *Century Magazine*, XLVII (March 1894), pp. 684–91.
101	*Weather overcast*	"Journals of Captain John Montresor," New-York Historical Society Collection, 1881, p. 492.
101–104	*Mischianza*	*Century Magazine* and *The Gentleman's Magazine*.
104	*Observer's reaction*	Friedrich von Muenchhausen, *At General Howe's Side*, p. 52.
104–105	*Criticisms of Mischianza*	Stedman, pp. 385–86; "Journal of Mrs. Henry Drinker;" *Penn. Mag. Hist. & Bio.*, XIII (1889), p. 306; Winthrop Sargent, *Life of Major André*, p. 181.
106	*André on Howe's send-off*	*The Gentleman's Magazine.*
106	*Mrs. Drinker on evacuation*	"Journal of Mrs. Henry Drinker," pp. 307–8.
107	*Du Simitière on pillaging of Franklin's home*	Du Simitière to John Lamb, November 24, 1778, New-York Historical Society, Albert Myers Cook Collection; "The Wilson Portrait of Franklin," *Penn. Mag. Hist. & Bio.*, XXX, no. 4, p. 409; VIII, no. 4, p. 430; XXX, no. 2, p. 242.
108	*Poem for Peggy Chew*	*Century Magazine*, p. 687.

A DIFFERENT DRUMBEAT

109	*Tallmadge's frustration*	*Coll. of Conn. Hist. Soc.*, XXIII (1930), p. 125, Tallmadge to Barnabas Deane, January 12, 1778.
109–110	*Washington's rebuke*	John C. Fitzpatrick, *Writings of Washington*, XI, pp. 244–45.

page
110   *Tallmadge's reply*   Tallmadge to Washington,
                                      May 3, 1778, LHS.
110–111 *Tallmadge sets up spy*   Benjamin Tallmadge, *Memoir*,
         ring   p. 29.

CHAPTER VII

112   *Clinton on war*   Sir Henry Clinton, *The Ameri-
                                     can Rebellion*, pp. 85–87.
114   *Clinton "haughty"*   Thomas Jones, *History of New
                                     York*, p. 319.
114–16 *Clinton's personality*   William B. Willcox, *Portrait of
                                     a General*, pp. 492–524.
117   *Battle of Monmouth*   Clinton, pp. 94–97; André
                                     journal, pp. 78–81.
118   *Wayne remark*   *Anthony Wayne Papers*, V, p.
                                     58, Wayne to Richard Peters,
                                     Jr., July 12, 1778, Penn. Hist.
                                     Soc.
118   *Clinton delayed*   Clinton to Benjamin Carpen-
                                     ter, September 21, 1778, CL,
                                     Clinton Papers; Clinton, p.
                                     103.
119   *André on New Bedford*   John André to his uncle, Sep-
      raid   tember 12, 1778, AP.
119   *Grey's message to Clin-*   Grey to Clinton, September 8,
      ton   1778, CL, Clinton Papers.
119   *André on plight of reb-*   John André to his uncle, Sep-
      els   tember 12, 1778, AP.
120   *Donkin recommendation*   Robert Donkin, *Military Collec-
                                     tions and Remarks*, p. 190.
120   *André on Baylor mas-*   André journal, p. 98.
      sacre
121   *Criticism of Grey*   Jones, p. 286.
122   *Clinton seen riding*   William Smith, *Memoirs*, p. 78.
122   *Golfers*   *Royal Gazette*, April 21, 1779.
122   *Becky Franks and*   June A. and Martin P. Snyder,
      beaux   *The Story of the Naomi Wood
                                     Collection and Woodford Man-
                                     sion*, p. 78.

page

122–23 Schaukirk comment   Penn. Mag. Hist. &. Bio., X, pp. 429–30.

123 Funerals   Smith, p. 152.

123 Cathcart grumbles   Cathcart to Mrs. William Eden, October 10, 1779, J. Robert Maguire collection.

124 Becky Franks on New York belles   June A. and Martin P. Snyder, pp. 77–78.

124–25 "A political dream"   Royal Gazette, January 23, 1779; I. N. Phelps Stokes, Iconography of Manhattan Island, V, p. 1081.

125–26 "The Frantick Lover"   Reprinted in pamphlet form with an introduction by Howard H. Peckham, CL, Clinton Papers.

127 Baroness von Riedesel on the poor   Baroness von Riedesel, Letters and Journals, p. 173.

127 Earl of Carlisle's complaints   Stokes, p. 1075.

127 Advertisements   Royal Gazette, December 9, 1778, May 17, 1780.

127–128 Criticism of public servants   Smith, pp. 173, 251, 166.

128–129 Prisoners   Corey Ford, A Peculiar Service, pp. 157–59, 253–55.

129 Graft   Jones, pp. 337, 341, 351–52.

129 Criticism of Clinton and aides   Smith, pp. 9, 97, 181, 187, 189; New-York Hist. Soc. Coll., 1883, p. 188.

A DIFFERENT DRUMBEAT

130–131 Culpers   Morton Pennypacker, General Washington's Spies, pp. 32–33.

131 Washington's anxiety   John C. Fitzpatrick, Writings of Washington, XIII, p. 355.

132 Narrow escape   Pennypacker, p. 62.

132–33 Washington's instructions   Ibid., p. 49; Fitzpatrick, XVI, pp. 330–31, and XVII, p. 493.

page
143 *Pattison to Amherst* — William B. Willcox, *Portrait of a General*, p. 278.

143–44 *Associated Loyalists* — Henry Barry to André, November 13, 1779, CL, Clinton Papers; André on regulations for Associated Refugees, enclosed with letter from William Franklin to André, November 10, 1779.

144 *Colleagues break with Clinton* — Smith, pp. 154, 163; "Kemble Journals," *New-York Hist. Soc. Coll.*, 1883, p. 188.

A DIFFERENT DRUMBEAT

146 *Information from Culper Senior* — Morton Pennypacker, *General Washington's Spies*, pp. 45–46.

CHAPTER IX

147 *Donkin on spies* — Robert Donkin, *Military Collections and Remarks*, pp. 119, 232–34.

147–49 *History of British intelligence* — Jock Haswell, *British Military Intelligence*, pp. 11–19; B. A. H. Parritt, *The Intelligencers*, pp. 1–32.

152 *Skinner and Inglis on Moody* — Charles I. Bushnell, *Narrative of Lieut. James Moody*, pp. 62–63, 69.

152–54 *Beverley Robinson and others* — Robinson intelligence, March 9, 1779; ibid. from John Lawson, April 3, 1779; ibid. from Reuben Powell, July 20, 1779; Thomas Barclay to Robinson, July 22 and 24, 1779; ibid. from David Babcock and Thomas Ward, November 9, 1779; Robinson intelligence,

page

162   *Rankin rebuked*   André to Rankin, July 31, 1779, CL, Clinton Papers.

163   *Nonsuch report*   Intelligence from David Nonsuch and David Carrol, April 11, 1779, CL, Clinton Papers.

163–64   *Codes and secret writing*   Code for use in the British Army, CL, Clinton Papers; cipher in which numbers stand for words, 1778; code names given American posts and generals; Howard H. Peckham, *British Secret Writing in the Revolution.*

164–65   *Stansbury interview with Arnold*   J. G. Taylor, *Some New Light on the Later Life and Last Resting Place of Benedict Arnold and His Wife Margaret Shippen,* p. 55.

A DIFFERENT DRUMBEAT

166–67   *Code letters*   Tallmadge to Washington, July 25 and 28, 1779, LHS; Morton Pennypacker, *General Washington's Spies,* p. 252.

CHAPTER X

168–70   *André letters to Clinton, Stansbury, and Peggy Chew*   Carl Van Doren, *Secret History of the American Revolution,* André to Stansbury, May 10, 1779; to Clinton, May 10, 1779; to Margaret Chew, May 1779, pp. 439–41.

172   *Odell poem*   Winthrop Sargent, *Loyal Verses,* p. 48.

172   *Stansbury and Odell*   Van Doren, Stansbury to Odell, June 9, 1779; Odell to Stansbury, June 9, 1779, pp. 444–45.

page
173 *Odell on damaged letter*   Ibid., Odell to André, May
                                31, 1779, pp. 442–43.
173 *Arnold intelligence*   Ibid., Arnold to André, May
                                23, 1779, pp. 441–42.
173–76 *André speculates*   Ibid., André to Arnold, June
                                (?), 1779, pp. 446–47. Never
                                sent.
175–76 *Smith on Schuyler*   William Smith, *Memoirs*, pp.
                                109, 228.
176–77 *André advises Arnold*   Van Doren, André to Arnold,
                                June 1779, p. 448.
177 *Stansbury on Arnold's*   Ibid., Stansbury to André,
     expectations   July 11, 1779, pp. 449–50.
177–78 *Odell note*   Ibid., Odell to André, July 18,
                                1779, pp. 450–51.
178 *Peggy's shopping list*   Ibid., shopping list, July 18,
                                1779, pp. 451–52.
178–79 *André on Arnold's ser-* Ibid., André to Arnold, July
     vices   1779, p. 453.
179 *André replies to Peggy*   Ibid., André to Margaret Ar-
                                nold, August 16, 1779, p. 454.
180 *Peggy's answer*   Ibid., Margaret Arnold to
                                André, October 13, 1779, p.
                                455.
180 *Arnold not assuaged*   Ibid., Stansbury to André,
                                July 1779, pp. 453–54.
180 *Odell's financial straits* Ibid., Odell to André, Decem-
                                ber 18, 1779, pp. 456–57.

A DIFFERENT DRUMBEAT

182 *Tallmadge comment on*   *Magazine of American History*,
     Arnold   III, no. 12, p. 754.

CHAPTER XI

183 *Hunter letter*   Elijah Hunter to Clinton, June
                                6, 1779, CL, Clinton Papers.
183 *Report on Dragoons*   Intelligence, late 1778, CL,
                                Clinton Papers.

page

183–84   *Ann Bates*   Petition of Ann Bates, PRO,
                                    Treasury Papers, 1785.

184–85   *Edward Fox*   Carl Van Doren, *Secret History
                                    of the American Revolution*, pp.
                                    224–28; André to Henry Ste-
                                    venson, September 15, 1779,
                                    CL, Clinton Papers.

185   *Chew and Coxe*   Joseph Chew to André, Octo-
                                    ber 30, 1779; intelligence from
                                    Daniel Coxe, December 10,
                                    1779, CL, Clinton Papers.

186–87   *André letter*   André to family member,
                                    probably his uncle John Lewis
                                    André, November or Decem-
                                    ber 1779, AP.

187   *Rawdon resignation*   Mark M. Boatner, *Encyclopedia
                                    of the American Revolution*, p. 919.

188   *Kemble by-passed*   *New-York Hist. Soc. Coll.*, I,
                                    1883, "Journals of Lieutenant
                                    Colonel Stephen Kemble,"
                                    pp. 150 ff.

189   *Grey commendation*   Grey to Clinton, December
                                    29, 1779, CL, Clinton Papers.

189–90   *Amherst opposition*   Amherst to Germain, Decem-
                                    ber 4, 1779, CL, Clinton Pa-
                                    pers.

190   *Mock certificate*   Mock legal certificate with pro-
                                    phetic seal, November 10,
                                    1779, CL, Clinton Papers.

190   *Storm at sea*   Bernhard A. Uhlendorf, *Siege
                                    of Charleston*, Diary of Captain
                                    Hinrichs, p. 119.

191–92   *Appeals to André*   Alexander Sutherland to
                                    André, April 20, 1780; James
                                    Rivington to André, Decem-
                                    ber 24, 1779; Robert Donkin
                                    to André, March 14, 1780;
                                    Patrick Ferguson to André,
                                    December 10, 1779; William
                                    Phillips to André, February
                                    23, 1780, CL, Clinton Papers.

page

202   *Arnold rails*   Willard M. Wallace, *Traitorous
                                Hero*, p. 191.

203   *Knyphausen memo*   Carl Van Doren, *Secret History
                                of the American Revolution*,
                                Knyphausen's notes, pp. 458–
                                59.

203–204 *Clinton on Arnold*   Clinton to Germain, October
                                11, 1780, CL, Clinton Papers.

204   *Arnold and Schuyler*   Van Doren, pp. 258–59, 265–
                                66.

204–205 *Arnold on West Point* Ibid., Arnold to Beckwith,
                                June 7, 1780; to Beckwith or
                                André, June 12, 15, 16, 1780,
                                pp. 459–61.

205–207 *Arnold and André on* Ibid., Arnold to André, July
        terms   12, 1780; Arnold to André,
                                July 15, 1780; André to Ar-
                                nold, July 12, 1780; André to
                                Arnold, July 24, 1780, pp.
                                462–66.

207   *Letter entrusted to Wil-* A. B. Hart, *Varick Court of In-
        liam Heron   quiry*, pp. 100–101.

208   *French fleet*   André to Tobias Wrightman,
                                July 28, 1780; Simcoe to
                                André, August 1, 1780, CL,
                                Clinton Papers.

208–209 *Hayes*   John McNamara Hayes to
                                André, July 18, 1780, CL,
                                Clinton Papers.

209   *Gunboat doodle*   Sketch of fortification on
                                blank page; William St. Leger
                                to André, July 24, 1780, CL,
                                Clinton Papers.

209–211 *"Cow Chace"*   *Royal Gazette*, August 16 and
                                30, September 23, 1780.

211   *"Blockheads"*   William Smith, *Memoirs*, p. 285.

211   *Stansbury poem*   Winthrop Sargent, *Loyal
                                Verses*, p. 66.

213   *Intelligence from Tory* Intelligence from Philadel-
        friend; Arnold on plight phia, September 24, 1780, CL,
        of rebels; Odell poem Clinton Papers; Van Doren,

page

222–23	*Robinson letters*	Van Doren, Robinson to Arnold, September 17, 1780; Arnold to Robinson, September 18, 1780; Arnold to André, September 18, 1780, pp. 482–84.
223	*Fleet arrives*	Sir Henry Clinton, *The American Rebellion*, p. 213.
223	*De Lancey letter*	Oliver De Lancey report and letter, September 19, 1780, CL, Clinton Papers.
224	*Simcoe*	Simcoe to André, September 11, 1780, CL, Clinton Papers; André to Simcoe, September 12, 1780, Joseph Rubinfine catalogue, list 64, item 1.
224	*Clinton's warning*	Clinton, p. 216.
224–25	*Baroness von Riedesel*	Baroness von Riedesel, *Letters and Journals*, pp. 179–80.
226	*Feigned illness*	Van Doren, André to Clinton, September 21, 1780, pp. 484–85.
226	*Robinson message*	Ibid., Robinson to Arnold, September 24, 1780, p. 474.
226–27	*Cahoon statement*	*Historical Magazine*, X, Supplement, pp. 2–3.
228	*Cahoons engaged*	Ibid., pp. 4–5.
228	*Weather and tide*	Joshua Hett Smith, *Authentic Narrative*, pp. 25–26.
229	*Arnold to Robinson and André; Robinson to Clinton*	William Abbatt, *Crisis of the Revolution*, p. 5; Van Doren, Robinson to Clinton, September 24, 1780, p. 474.
230–31	*Smith comments*	Smith, pp. 27–33.
232	*André crosses lines*	Henry B. Dawson, *Papers of Major André*, p. 21.
232–34	Vulture	Van Doren, Robinson to Clinton, September 24, 1780, pp. 474–75.
233	*Smith and André*	Smith, pp. 34–48.
234	*Secret papers*	New York State Library, "André Papers."

page

251–52 *Washington to Congress*   Fitzpatrick, pp. 91–93.
252   *Robinson blames Arnold*   Sparks, pp. 533–34.

253   *Arnold to Washington*   Ibid., p. 533.
253–54 *Smith in guardroom*   Joshua Hett Smith, *Authentic Narrative*, p. 66.
253   *Tallmadge to Deane*   Tallmadge to Deane, September 27, 1780, J. Robert Maguire collection.
253–54 *André at Fort Putnam*   Richard J. Koke, *Accomplice in Treason*, p. 128.
254   *Hale and André*   *Magazine of American History*, III, no. 12, pp. 755–56.
255   *Arrival in Tappan*   Smith, p. 82.
258   *Clinton and Arnold letters* Carl Van Doren, *Secret History of the American Revolution*, Clinton to Washington, September 26, 1780; Arnold to Clinton, September 26, 1780, pp. 486–87.
259   *Instructions to board*   Fitzpatrick, p. 101.
260   *André testimony*   Theodore Woodbridge diary, LC; Edward Boynton, *History of West Point*, pp. 149–51; Smith, pp. 89–90.
260–61 *André examined*   Sargent, pp. 390–400.
261   *Hamilton on André's conduct* Syrett and Cook, p. 466.
262   *Von Steuben*   Abbatt, p. 61.
262   *Board's opinion*   Boynton, p. 139.
262   *Washington's verdict*   Fitzpatrick, pp. 109–10.
262–63 *Washington notifies Clinton* Boynton, Washington to Clinton, September 30, 1780, p. 141.
263   *Secret letter*   Syrett and Cook, pp. 445–46.
263   *Clinton requests parley*   Van Doren, Clinton to Washington, September 30, 1780, p. 448.
264   *Clinton to André*   Clinton to André, October 1, 1780, J. Robert Maguire collection.

page

264   *Jones criticizes negotiators*   Thomas Jones, *History of New York*, p. 376.

264–65   *Parley*   William Smith, *Memoirs*, pp. 337–38; Van Doren, Robertson to Clinton, October 1, 1780, pp. 488–89.

265   *Greene's message*   Abbatt, p. 68.

265   *Robertson's reply*   Van Doren, Robertson to Washington, October 2, 1780, p. 490.

265   *Arnold's warning*   Ibid., Arnold to Washington, October 1, 1780, pp. 490–91.

265–66   *Simcoe's efforts*   Simcoe to William Crosbie, 1780, CL, Clinton Papers; John Graves Simcoe, *Military Journal*, Appendix, pp. 292–93.

267   *Tallmadge on André's charm*   James W. Webb, *Reminiscences of General Samuel B. Webb*, Tallmadge to Samuel B. Webb, September 30, 1780, p. 297.

267   *Hamilton to Elizabeth Schuyler*   Syrett and Cook, Hamilton to Elizabeth Schuyler, October 2, 1780, pp. 448–49.

267–68   *André and Hamilton*   Ibid., p. 466.

267–68   *André's farewell to Clinton*   Van Doren, André to Clinton, September 29, 1780, pp. 475–76.

268–69   *André's plea*   Boynton, André to Washington, October 1, 1780, p. 147.

269   *Washington on reason for his decision*   Fitzpatrick, p. 131.

269   *Hamilton protests*   Syrett and Cook, p. 468.

270   *Hamilton refuses to embarrass André*   Ibid., pp. 448, 468.

270   *The two watches*   Charles H. Roe, *Major André's Watches*, Harrison to André, September 30, October 1, 1780, J. Robert Maguire col-

page
270

270–71 *André to Crosbie*
271 *Thomas Paine remark*

271–72 *André's composure*

274 *Scammell reads death
sentence*

274–75 *Contemporary accounts
of André's execution*

lection; Andrew Elliot comment, October 5, 1780, British Museum.
Abbatt, p. 68.
Paine to Nathanael Greene, October 17, 1780, Sotheby Parke Bernet catalogue.
Fanny Smith Cowles, *Diary*, quotation from Captain Ebenezer Smith.
Death warrant signed by Scammell, Richard Maass collection.
John W. Barber and Henry Howe, *Hist. Coll. of State of New Jersey*, anonymous account of execution, pp. 77–78; testimony of Nathan Beers to Theodore Woolsey, February 12, 1834, HL; Abbatt, testimony of Samuel Bowman, pp. 73–74; Samuel Dewees, *Life and Services*, pp. 219–20; *Knickerbocker Magazine*, XVI, no. 4, testimony of Dr. Hall, pp. 366–67; *New England Hist. and Genea. Register*, LXIX, July 1915, testimony of John Hart, pp. 224–26; *Penn. Mag. of Hist. and Bio.*, XX, 1896–97, letter-books of Enos Reeves, p. 314; pension application of Daniel Roberts, August 30, 1832; Benjamin Tallmadge, *Memoir*, pp. 38–39; James Thacher, *Military Journal*, pp. 269–75; *Historical Magazine*, Fifth Series, VII, Letter of Col. John Van Dyk, pp. 250–52; Theodore Woodbridge diary, LC.

AFTERWORD

page
276   *Phillips on Clinton's grief*   Phillips to Duke of Newcastle, October 14, 1780, Univ. of Nottingham collection.

276   *Washington on André*   John C. Fitzpatrick, *Writings of Washington*, XX, Washington to Rochambeau, October 10, 1780, p. 151.

276   *Tallmadge on execution*   Benjamin Tallmadge, *Memoir*, p. 38.

Bibliography

NOTE ON SOURCES

The André papers, so designated by James T. Flexner in *The Traitor and the Spy*, consist of letters written by John André to members of his family during his years of military service in America. They were sold by the family a few years ago and are now scattered among various libraries and private collections. Through the kindness of the late Brigadier James R. G. André, they were made available to me in copy and have been indispensable in the preparation of this book.

The journal that John André kept at the behest of Major Charles Preston, "Narrative of the Siege of St. John's," is in the Public Archives of Canada and has been printed in the *Report* for 1914–15.

Sir Henry Clinton's papers are at the William L. Clements Library at the University of Michigan. Sir Henry had a squirrel's instincts, saving every scrap that crossed his desk, and his papers are a priceless resource. Arnold's treasonous correspondence with the British, part of the collection, has been printed in full in Carl Van Doren's *Secret History of the American Revolution*. Sir Henry's own book about the war, *The American Rebellion*, edited by William B. Willcox and published in 1954, throws light on the hapless commander at whose side John André served.

Further correspondence relating to the conspiracy may be found in the Library of Congress, which has a large collection of Arnold source material. Jared Sparks's correspondence with Benjamin Tallmadge and Dr. Isaac Bronson is in the Houghton Library at Harvard University. Several Tallmadge letters are at the Litchfield Historical Society in Litchfield, Connecticut, where Tallmadge resided throughout most of his working life. Others are at the Connecticut Historical Society in Hartford.

An Authentic Narrative of the Causes Which Led to the Death of Major André is Joshua Hett Smith's account of his connection with André and their fateful journey through Westchester.

Abbatt, William. *The Crisis of the Revolution: Being the Story of Arnold and André.* New York, 1899.

Abbott, Wilbur C. *New York in the American Revolution.* New York, 1929.

Alexander, R. O. "Fort of St. John's on the River Richelieu," *Journal of the Society for Army Historical Research*, II, no. 10, October 1923, pp. 186–88.

Allen, Asa W. *Genealogy of the Allen and Witter Families.* Salem, Ohio, 1872.

American Bibliophist, I and II.

Anbury, Thomas. *Travels Through the Interior Parts of America.* New York, 1969.

Anderson, Enoch. *Personal Recollections.* Wilmington, Del., 1896.

Anderson, Troyer S. *The Command of the Howe Brothers during the American Revolution.* New York, 1936.

André, John. *Journal from June, 1777, to November, 1778.* Tarrytown, N.Y., 1930.

———. "The Mischianza, Humbly Inscribed to Miss Peggy Chew," *Century Magazine*, XLVII, 1893, pp. 687–91.

———. "Narrative of the Siege of St. John's," *Report of Public Archives of Canada, 1914–15*, pp. 18–25.

———. Papers. Unpublished and now in various libraries and private collections.

———. "Particulars of the Mischianza . . . A Letter from an Officer in Philadelphia," *Gentleman's Magazine*, XLVIII, 1778, pp. 353–57. Attributed to André.

Armes, Ethel, ed. *Nancy Shippen, Her Journal Book*. Philadelphia, 1935.

Arner, Robert D. "The Death of Major André, Some Eighteenth Century Views," *Early American Literature*, XI, no. 1, Spring 1976.

Arnold, Isaac. *The Life of Benedict Arnold*. Chicago, 1880.

Ashmun, Margaret. *The Singing Swan, an Account of Anna Seward and Her Acquaintance with Dr. Johnson, Boswell, and Others of Their Time*. New Haven, 1931.

Atkinson, C. T. "British Forces in North America, 1774–1781," *Journal of the Society for Army Historical Research*, XVI, no. 61, Spring 1937, pp. 3–22.

———. "Two Hundred and Fifty Years Ago: James II and His Army," *Journal of the Society for Army Historical Research*, XIV, no. 53, Spring 1935, pp. 1–12.

"Authentic Account of that Greatly Lamented Officer, Major John André . . . Solely composed from material supplied by the late Major's most intimate friends both in this Country and America," *Political Magazine*, II, London, 1781, pp. 171–73.

Ayling, Stanley. *George the Third*. London, 1972.

Bakeless, John. *Turncoats, Traitors and Heroes*. New York, 1959.

Barck, Oscar T. *New York City During the War for Independence*. New York, 1931.

Barnett, Correlli. *Britain and Her Army, 1509–1970*. London, 1970.

Bates, Ann. Petition. Public Records Office, Treasury Papers, 1785.

Bayne-Powell, Rosamond. *Eighteenth-Century London Life*. New York, 1938.

Benson, Egbert. *Vindication of the Captors of Major André*. New York, 1865.

Besant, Walter. *London in the Eighteenth Century*. London, 1901.

Biddle, Charles J. "The Case of Major André," *Memoirs of the Historical Society of Pennsylvania*, VI, pp. 319–416.

Biddulph, H. "The Era of Army Purchase," *Journal of the Society for Army Historical Research*, XII, no. 48, Winter 1933–34, pp. 221–23.

Bolton, Robert. *A History of the County of Westchester from Its First Settlement to the Present Time*. New York, 1848.

314   BIBLIOGRAPHY

Boynton, Edward C. *History of West Point*. New York, 1871.

Brooks, Noah. *Henry Knox, A Soldier of the Revolution*, New York, 1974.

Burnett, Edmund, ed. *Letters of Members of the Continental Congress*. Washington, D.C., 1921–36.

Campbell, Charles A. "Bibliography of Major André," *Magazine of American History*, VIII, pp. 61–72.

Carleton, Sir Guy. Papers, including files of the British Headquarters in America. Colonial Williamsburg.

Case of Major André. New York, 1780.

Chester, Joseph Lemuel. "Some Particulars Respecting the Family of Major John André," *Proceedings of the Massachusetts Historical Society*, 1875–76.

Clark, Jane. "Metcalf Bowler as a British Spy," *Rhode Island Historical Society*, XXIII, no. 4, October 1930.

Clinton, George. *Public Papers*. Albany, 1899 ff.

Clinton, Sir Henry. *The American Rebellion*, William B. Willcox, ed. New Haven, 1954.

————. Papers, including files of the British headquarters in America. William L. Clements Library, University of Michigan.

Connecticut Historical Society Collections.

Cope Gilbert. *A Record of the Cope Family*. Philadelphia, 1861.

Cowles, Fanny Smith. *Diary*, containing an account of André's execution as told by her father, Captain Ebenezer Smith.

Crary, Catherine Snell. "The Tory and the Spy: The Double Life of James Rivington," *William and Mary Quarterly*, XVI, no. 1, January 1959.

Crawford, Mary C. *The Romance of the American Theater*. Boston, 1913.

Curtis, Edward E. *The Organization of the British Army in the American Revolution*. New Haven, 1926.

Dawson, Henry B., ed. *Papers Concerning the Capture and Detention of Major John André*. Yonkers, N.Y., 1866.

————. *Record of the Trial of Joshua Hett Smith*. Morrisania, N.Y., 1866.

Day, Sherman, ed. *Historical Collections of the State of Pennsylvania*. Philadelphia, 1843.

Decker, Malcolm. *Ten Days of Infamy*. New York, 1969.

Donkin, Robert. *Military Collections and Remarks*. New York, 1777.

Dunlap, William. *A History of the American Theater.* New York, 1832.

Du Simitière, Pierre-Eugène. Du Simitière Letterbook. Library of Congress, Peter Force Collection.

Eberlein, Harold D. *Manor Houses and Historic Homes of Long Island and Staten Island.* Philadelphia, 1928.

Edgeworth, Richard Lovell. *Memoirs.* London, 1844.

Egle, William H. *History of the Commonwealth of Pennsylvania.* Philadelphia, 1883.

Ellis, Franklin, and Samuel Evans. *History of Lancaster County, Penna.* Philadelphia, 1883.

Emmett, Thomas A. "Sir Henry Clinton's Original Secret Record of Private Daily Intelligence," *Magazine of American History,* X.

Faris, John T. *The Romance of Old Philadelphia.* Philadelphia, 1918.

Farmer, John, and Jacob B. Moore. *Collections Historical and Miscellaneous and Monthly Literary Journal.* Concord, N.H., 1824.

Fisher, Sydney G. *The Struggle for American Independence.* Philadelphia, 1908.

Fitzpatrick, John C., ed. *The Writings of George Washington from the Original Manuscript Sources, 1745–1799.* Washington, D.C., 1931–44.

Flexner, James T. *The Traitor and the Spy, Benedict Arnold and John André.* New York, 1953.

Flick, Alexander C. *Loyalism in New York During the American Revolution.* New York, 1901.

Flower, Milton E., and Lenore E. Molton. *This Is Carlisle.* Carlisle, Pa., 1944.

Force, Peter, ed. *American Archives.* Washington, D.C., 1837–53.

Ford, Corey. *A Peculiar Service.* Boston, 1965.

Ford, Worthington C., ed. *Correspondence and Journals of Samuel Blachley Webb.* New York, 1893.

———. *Journals of the Continental Congress, 1774–1780.* Washington, D.C., 1904–37.

Fortescue, Sir John W. *A History of the British Army.* London, 1899–1930.

Foucher, Antoine(?). *Journal tenu pendant le Siège du Fort St. Jean en 1775.* Public Archives of Canada.

Friedman, Lee M. *Jewish Pioneers and Patriots.* New York, 1943.

Fuller, J. F. C. *British Light Infantry in the Eighteenth Century.* London, 1925.

Futhey, J. Smith, and Gilbert Cope. *History of Chester County, Pa.* Philadelphia, 1881.

Gentleman's Magazine.

Goodrich, Samuel G. *Recollections of a Lifetime, or Men and Things I Have Seen.* New York, 1856.

Greene, Francis Vinton. *General Greene.* New York, 1893.

Hall, Charles Swain. *Benjamin Tallmadge, Revolutionary Soldier and American Businessman.* New York, 1943.

Hall, Charles S. *Life and Letters of Samuel Holden Parsons.* Binghamton, N.Y., 1905.

Hand, Julianna F. *Westchester Treasure Hunt Tour — West Point.* Croton, N.Y., 1980.

Harris, Alex. *A Biographical History of Lancaster County.* Lancaster, Pa., 1872.

Harrison, Eliza Cope, ed. *Philadelphia Merchant: The Diary of Thomas P. Cope.* South Bend, 1981.

Hart, Albert Bushnell. *The Varick Court of Inquiry to Investigate the Implication of Colonel Richard Varick in the Arnold Treason.* Boston, 1907.

Haswell, Jock. *British Military Intelligence.* London, 1973.

Hayes, John T. *Connecticut's Revolutionary Cavalry: Sheldon's Horse.* Chester, Conn., 1975.

Hensel, W. U. *Major John André as a Prisoner of War at Lancaster, Pa., 1775–76.* Lancaster, Pa., 1904.

Historical Magazine and Notes and Queries.

Hopkins, Mary Alden. *Dr. Johnson's Lichfield.* New York, 1952.

Howe, John. *Journal.* Concord, N.H., 1827

Howe, Sir William. *The Narrative of Lieut. Gen. Sir William Howe in the Committee of the House of Commons, April 29, 1779.* London, 1781.

Hufeland, Otto. *Westchester County During the American Revolution.* White Plains, N.Y., 1926.

Huguenot Society of London. *Proceedings,* X; Publications, XXXVII.

Johnston, Henry P. *Nathan Hale.* New York, 1901.

———. "The Secret Service of the Revolution," *Magazine of American History,* VIII, pp. 95–105.

Johnston, S. H. F. *The History of the Cameronians (26th and 90th Regiments)*. Aldershot, England, 1957.

Jones, Thomas. *History of New York During the Revolutionary War*. New York, 1879.

Journal of Lancaster County Historical Society.

Journal of the Society for Army Historical Research.

Kemble, Peter. "Journals." *New-York Historical Society Collections*, 1883–84.

Knollenberg, Bernhard. *Growth of the American Revolution*. New York, 1975.

Koke, Richard J. *Accomplice in Treason, Joshua Hett Smith and the Arnold Conspiracy*. New York, 1973.

Krause, Ernst. *Erasmus Darwin*. London, 1879.

Lamb, Roger. *An Original and Authentic Journal of Occurrences During the Late American War from Its Commencement to the Year 1783*. Dublin, 1809.

Lancaster County Historical Society Papers.

Landis, Charles I. *Major John André's German Letter*. Lancaster, Pa., 1914.

Leake, Isaac Q. *Memoir of the Life and Times of General John Lamb*. New York, 1857.

List of the General and Field-Officers, 1771, 1772, 1778, 1779, 1780.

Literary World, XII, 1881.

Lossing, Benson J. *The Pictorial Field-Book of the Revolution*. New York, 1859–60.

——. *The Two Spies, Nathan Hale and John André*. New York, 1886.

Lucas, E. V. *A Swan and Her Friends*. London, 1907.

Mackenzie, Frederick. *Diary*. Cambridge, Mass., 1930.

Magazine of American History.

Marshall, Dorothy. *Eighteenth Century England*. London, 1962.

Martin, Joseph P. *Private Yankee Doodle*. George E. Scheer, ed. Boston, 1962.

Massachusetts Historical Society Proceedings.

Metzger, Charles H. *The Quebec Act, A Primary Cause of the American Revolution*. New York, 1936.

Millis, Wade. *A Spy Under the Common Law of War*. Detroit, 1925.

Minutes of a Court of Inquiry upon the Case of Major John André with Accompanying Documents. Albany, 1865.

Mombert, J. I. *An Authentic History of Lancaster County.* Lancaster, Pa., 1869.

Monk, Samuel H. "Anna Seward and the Romantic Poets: A Study in Taste," in *Wordsworth and Coleridge*, Earl L. Griggs, ed. Princeton, New Jersey, 1939.

Montresor, John. "Journals," G. D. Skull, ed. *New-York Historical Society Collections*, 1881.

Montross, Lynn. *The Reluctant Rebels: The Story of the Continental Congress, 1774–1789.* New York, 1950.

Moody, James. *Narrative of the Exertions and Sufferings of Lieut. James Moody.* London, 1783.

Moore, Frank. *Diary of the American Revolution from Newspapers and Original Documents.* New York, 1858.

Mowat, Robert B. *England in the Eighteenth Century.* London, 1932.

Namier, Lewis B. *England in the Age of the American Revolution.* London, 1930.

New Annual Register of History, Politics and Literature for the Year 1780. London, 1793.

New-York Historical Society Collections.

Palmer, Dave Richard. *The River and the Rock: The History of Fortress West Point, 1775–83.* New York, 1969.

Parritt, B. A. H. *The Intelligencers: The Story of British Military Intelligence up to 1914.* Ashford, England, 1971.

Parton, James. *Life and Times of Benjamin Franklin.* New York, 1864.

Pearson, Hesketh. *Extraordinary People.* London, 1965.

———. *The Swan of Lichfield, A Selection from the Correspondence of Anna Seward.* London, 1936.

Pearson, Michael. *Those Damned Rebels: The American Revolution as Seen Through British Eyes.* New York, 1972.

Peckham, Howard H. *British Secret Writing in the Revolution.* Clements Library, n.d.

Pennypacker, Morton. *General Washington's Spies on Long Island and in New York.* Brooklyn, N.Y., 1939.

Pennsylvania Archives, 1852–56, 1st Series, I–XII.

Pennsylvania Magazine of History and Biography.

Pollock, Thomas C. *The Philadelphia Theater in the Eighteenth Century.* Philadelphia, 1933.

Proceedings of a Board of General Officers Held by Order of His Excellency

Gen. Washington Respecting Major John André, Adjutant General of the British Army. Philadelphia, 1780.

Quarles, Benjamin. *The Negro in the American Revolution.* Chapel Hill, N.C., 1961.

The Remembrancer, or Impartial Repository of Public Events.

Report of Public Archives of Canada for 1914–15. Ottawa.

Riddle, William. *The Story of Lancaster: Old and New.* Lancaster, Pa., 1917.

Riedesel von, Baroness. *Letters and Journals Relating to the War of the American Revolution,* William L. Stone, trans. Albany, 1867.

Robertson, Archibald. *Diaries and Sketches in America.* New York, 1930.

Roe, Charles Harvey. *Major André's Watches.* Tarrytown, N.Y., 1971.

Rogers, H. C. B. *The British Army of the Eighteenth Century.* London, 1977.

Royal Gazette.

Rudé, George. *Hanoverian London, 1714–1808.* Berkeley, Calif., 1971.

Rupp, J. Daniel. *The History and Topography of Dauphin, Cumberland, Franklin, Bedford, Adams, and Perry Counties.* Lancaster, Pa., 1846.

Sargent, Winthrop. *The Life and Career of Major John André.* Boston, 1861.

———. *The Loyal Verses of Joseph Stansbury and Doctor Jonathan Odell Relating to the American Revolution.* New York, 1860.

Scharf, J. Thomas, and Thompson Westcott. *History of Philadelphia.* Philadelphia, 1884.

Scott, Duncan C. *John Graves Simcoe,* in *The Makers of Canada* Series. London and Toronto, 1905.

Scott, S. H. *The Exemplary Mr. Day.* London, 1935.

Seilhamer, George O. *History of the American Theater.* Philadelphia, 1889.

Sener, Samuel M. *The Lancaster Barracks.* Harrisburg, Pa., 1895.

Seward, Anna. *Letters.* London, 1811.

———. *Monody on Major André, to which are added Letters Addressed to her by Major André in the Year 1769.* Lichfield, England, 1781.

Shy, John. *A People Numerous and Armed.* New York, 1976.

———. *Toward Lexington, the Role of the British Army in the Coming of the Revolution.* Princeton, 1965.

Siebert, Wilbur H. "The Loyalists of Pennsylvania," *Ohio State University Bulletin*, XXIV, no. 23, Columbus, 1905.

Simcoe, John Graves. *Military Journal: A History of the Operations of a Partisan Corps Called the Queen's Rangers*. New York, 1844.

Smith, Horace, ed. *Andréana: Containing the Trial, Execution, and Various Matters Connected with the History of Major André*. Philadelphia, 1865.

Smith, John Jay, and John Fanning Watson. *American Historical and Literary Curiosities*. Philadelphia, 1847.

Smith, Joshua Hett. *An Authentic Narrative of the Causes Which Led to the Death of Major André*. London, 1808.

Smith, William. *Historical Memoirs*, with an introduction by William H. W. Sabine. New York, 1958.

Snyder, June Avery, and Martin P. *The Story of the Naomi Wood Collection and Woodford Mansion*. Wayne, Pa., 1981.

Sparks, Jared. *Correspondence of the American Revolution*. Boston, 1853.

———. *The Life and Treason of Benedict Arnold*. Boston, 1835.

———. Papers. Houghton Library, Harvard University.

———. *The Writings of George Washington*. Boston, 1834–37.

Stedman, Charles. *The History of the Origin, Progress and Termination of the American War*. London, 1794.

Stevens, Benjamin, ed. *Facsimiles of Manuscripts in European Archives Relating to America, 1773–1783*. London, 1889–95.

Stiles, Henry R. *History of Ancient Wethersfield, Connecticut*. New York, 1904.

Stillé, Charles J. *Major General Anthony Wayne*. Philadelphia, 1893.

Stokes, Isaac N. P. *The Iconography of Manhattan Island*. New York, 1915–28.

Stone, William L. *History of New York City*. New York, 1872.

Stryker, William S. *The Massacre near Old Tappan*. Trenton, N.J., 1882.

Syrett, Harold C., and Jacob Cook, eds. *The Papers of Alexander Hamilton*. New York, 1961.

Tallmadge, Benjamin. *Memoir*. Edited by Henry P. Johnston. New York, 1904.

———. Papers. At Litchfield (Conn.) Historical Society and included in Jeremiah Wadsworth Correspondence at Connecticut Historical Society.

————. Tallmadge-Arnold letters. At Library of Congress.

Taylor, J. G. *Some New Light on the Later Life and Last Resting Place of Benedict Arnold and His Wife Margaret Shippen.* London, 1931.

Taylor, W. *Historic Survey of German Poetry.* London, 1830.

Thacher, James. *Military Journal of the American Revolution.* Hartford, Conn., 1862.

Thane, Elswyth. *The Fighting Quaker, Nathanael Greene.* New York, 1972.

Tillotson, Harry S. *The Beloved Spy, The Life and Loves of Major John André.* Caldwell, Idaho, 1948.

Tousey, Thomas G. *Military History of Carlisle and Carlisle Barracks.* Richmond, Va., 1939.

Tower, Charlemagne. *Essays Political and Historical.* Philadelphia, 1914.

Treason Papers of Major General Benedict Arnold, Taken from Major John André by His Captors. New York State Library.

Trumbull, Benjamin. "A Concise Journal or Minutes of the Principal Movements Towards St. John's in 1775," *Connecticut Historical Society Collections,* VII, 1899.

Uhlendorf, Bernhard A., ed. *Revolution in America, Confidential Letters and Journals, 1776–1784, of Adjutant General Major Baurmeister of the Hessian Forces.* New Brunswick, N.J., 1957.

————. *The Siege of Charleston, Diaries and Letters of Hessian Officers.* Ann Arbor, Mich., 1938.

Van Doren, Carl. *Secret History of the American Revolution.* New York, 1941.

Van Dyk, John. "Letter to John Pintard," *Historical Magazine,* VII, First Series, 1863, pp. 250–52.

Van Tyne, Claude H. *The Loyalists in the American Revolution.* New York, 1902.

View of the Evidence Relative to the Conduct of the American War Under Sir William Howe, Lord Viscount Howe, and General Burgoyne as Given Before a Committee of the House of Commons. London, 1783.

Vivian, Frances St. Clair. "Capture and Death of Major André," *History Today,* VII, no. 12, December 1957.

————. "John André as a Young Officer," *Journal of the Society for Army Historical Research,* XL, nos. 161 and 162, March and June 1962.

Walker, Lewis B. "The Life of Margaret Shippen, Wife of Benedict Arnold," *Pennsylvania Magazine of History and Biography*, XXIV–XXVI, 1900–1902.

Wallace, Willard M. *Traitorous Hero: The Life and Fortunes of Benedict Arnold.* New York, 1954.

Watson, John F. *Annals of Philadelphia and Pennsylvania in the Olden Time.* Philadelphia, 1877.

Weinhold, Karl. *Heinrich Christian Boie.* Halle, Germany, 1868.

Wertenbaker, Thomas J. *Father Knickerbocker Rebels.* New York, 1948.

Wickwire, Franklin and Mary. *Cornwallis: The American Adventure.* Boston, 1970.

Willcox, William B. *Portrait of a General: Sir Henry Clinton and the War of Independence.* New York, 1964.

Wilson, Lavalette. "André's Landing-Place at Haverstraw: A Mooted Question Settled," *Magazine of American History*, XIII, 1885, pp. 173–76.

Winfield, Charles H. *The Block-House by Bull's Ferry.* New York, 1904.

Woodbridge, Theodore. *Diary.* Library of Congress.

Index